❀ MAYO ❀

The Story of My Family and My Career

:MAYO:

The Story of My Family
and My Career

Dr. Charles W. Mayo

Doubleday & Company, Inc., Garden City, New York

Note received by Dr. Charles W. Mayo from President
Lyndon Johnson. Reprinted by permission.

Excerpt by Dr. Mayo from the December 1956 issue of
American Surgeon Magazine. Reprinted by permission of
J. B. Lippincott Company.

LIBRARY OF CONGRESS CATALOG CARD NUMBER 68–22502

TO MY WIFE ALICE

without whose encouragement and help
this book never would have been written.

EXCERPT FROM LOWELL THOMAS' BROADCAST ON THE DEATH OF DR. CHARLES W. MAYO
July 29, 1968

The world-wide medical fraternity, as well as the fraternity of man, was deeply saddened today by the passing of Dr. Charles Mayo, the son of the founder of the famed Mayo Clinic and an honored surgeon and humanitarian in his own right. He was the victim of an auto accident on the Mayo family estate at Rochester, Minnesota.

The legacy he leaves behind is that of a man who carried his birthright to new heights. Dr. "Chuck" Mayo winning his wings early in his career—when he reassured a frightened woman by telling her: "I'm just starting—I can't afford to lose a patient." Later he earned a reputation as a pioneering surgeon, especially in the treatment of cancer. This led to his eventual appointment as an alternate U.S. delegate to the U.N. General Assembly.

In 1956, President Eisenhower sent him to the coronation of the King of Nepal, Mahendra Bir Bikram Shah Deva. In fact, we were joint ambassadors to that exotic pageant in the Himalayas where both of us rode in the coronation procession in howdahs on painted and handsomely caparisoned elephants. It seemed incongruous to wear a tail coat, striped trousers, seated atop an elephant. Dr. Mayo laughed and laughed about this, as did his lovely wife Alice, who died only a few months ago. Recently, Dr. Mayo had written me a sad letter saying: "Here I am, all alone, rattling around in this big house."

His creed—he once told a patient: "To imagine the kind of doctor I'd like if I were sick, and then to be that kind of doctor." He was.

ONE

I was about nine or ten years old when I performed my first surgical operation, assisted by my brother Joe, who also acted as anesthetist; he was about five or six at the time, but young for his age. Our patient was a puppy which seemed to us to be suffering from a large umbilical hernia.

Joe and I had serene confidence in both the diagnosis and our skill as surgeons. It stemmed, in part, from our medically-saturated upbringing, since almost every adult male in our family was a doctor and all their friends, it seemed, were doctors, and platoons of doctors constantly filled the guest rooms of our house. Dinner conversation rarely wavered from detailed shoptalk about the calamities that can befall the human interior, together with debate on their cause and cure.

Mainly, though, our conviction that we were ready as surgeons derived from our early on-the-job training. From the time each of us reached the age of four, or thereabouts, my brother and I had been allowed to accompany Father and Uncle Will on their rounds of patients in the hospital, watching as they made examinations and listening to their instructions to their young assistants and the nurses. Best of all, we were dressed in masks and gowns, the latter ludicrously pinned up, and permitted to go into surgery and watch them operate. I was mystified one day when a shocked nun hustled me out into the corridor while Father was operating on the lower part of a woman's abdomen. After that, certain operations on women were censored, but otherwise we saw it all—surgery on gallbladders, goiters and colon cancers, surgery on stomachs, bowels and jaws, everything that was being done in the early 1900's. We were never revolted; the tissues under the skin are endlessly interesting.

From all this we were developing some medical expertise, but we were curiously unaware that our lives were somewhat unusual or that Father and Uncle Will were not ordinary small-town doctors. We discovered only gradually that they were famous all over the world as "the Mayo brothers," Dr. Charles Horace Mayo and Dr. William James Mayo, and that their office, the Mayo Clinic, was drawing thousands to our inconveniently located Midwest town of Rochester in Minnesota. And it wasn't until Joe and I were in medical school that we realized that the parade of houseguests had included some of the most distinguished doctors anywhere.

On that summer day when we operated on the puppy, Joe and I were poised and delighted. We fixed up an operating room in the corner of our garage, got one of Father's straight razors, two pairs of tweezers which we found in Mother's cabinet and some needles and thread. We sent the hired man to town to get a can of ether from the drugstore, instructing him to charge it to Father's account.

Then we were ready to begin. We were unprepared for the difficulty we encountered in getting the squirming puppy to sleep. She struggled against our administrations of ether for what seemed an interminable time, but finally succumbed and was still. Next we tied her into the proper position for abdominal surgery, which also turned out to be a more awkward maneuver than we had foreseen. The human physique is much more accommodating. At last she was secured; Joe gave her a bit more ether and we started.

I did the cutting, going very slowly so as not to nick the intestines. When a blood vessel was cut, Joe would catch it with a tweezer and I would tie it off with Mother's cotton thread. Eventually we got through to the fascia and together

2

Joe and I pushed the bulging intestine into the belly where it belonged. Then we sewed the fascia together into overlapping layers with fine professional style, using interrupted double cotton sutures—remembering to begin at the center of the transverse incision as Father and Uncle Will always did. Then we drew the skin together with a flourish of interrupted cotton sutures.

The puppy lived, which we took for granted then but now seems to me a marvel. One of our major oversights had been that, like small boys everywhere, we had neglected to wash. Our equally unsterile instruments were sneaked back to their proper places and we congratulated ourselves on not being caught. We were lucky, but so was the puppy: there was very little ether left in the can.

We later learned some of the Mayo family legends and found that our early feat as surgeons was in keeping with a tradition of child apprenticeship. When Father and Uncle Will were boys, they traveled with their father, my snap-tempered grandfather, Dr. William Worrall Mayo, when he made house calls by horse and buggy. The hospital hadn't been built then so Grandfather would perform operations in country kitchens, hailing in his sons to give him a hand. When they were four and eight, they helped Grandfather treat the gunshot wounds of a stagecoach driver who had been shot by robbers.

Since he was older, Uncle Will was pressed into service more often than Father, who at first was left outside to hold the horse. In his later years, Father suddenly realized that Grandfather told him to stay with the horse not so much to guard the animal as to ensure that Father wouldn't wander.

One day Father was waiting disconsolately outside a farm doorstep when the door behind him opened and a physician who was supposed to be helping Grandfather lurched out and collapsed on the grass with what Father delicately described as "a good exhibition of seasickness." Grandfather's voice roared, "Charlie, come here!" Inside, Father discovered what had upset Grandfather's colleague: a particularly bloody operation was in progress to remove a large ovarian tumor. In those days surgery was so mistrusted, even by many doctors, that such tumors grew to enormous size before the last resort, "being cut open," was accepted by the terrified patient. Uncle Will and Grandfather were busy operating on either side of the woman; the physician who had deserted had been giving the anesthetic. On Grandfather's order, Father found a box to stand on and administered the anesthetic for the rest of the operation, starting and stopping it as Grandfather told him to. He was maybe seven or eight.

There are now four generations of Mayo men who have become doctors, all of them named either William or Charles—which either shows a startling lack of imagination when we name our males or else demonstrates something about our family pride. In 1963, a hundred years of Mayo history in Rochester ended when I reached the compulsory retirement age of sixty-five and left my post in active surgery at the Mayo Clinic. A century before, that strange, ferocious, striving and restless Grandfather of mine had started it all by launching a practice in Rochester.

The Mayo chain seems to have ended with me. The Board of Governors of the Mayo Clinic was reluctant to accept my well-qualified son Charlie into its staff. A portion of his first assistantship as a surgeon was served with me; I know, personally, that he is an exceptionally fine doctor. But I can understand the Board's attitude, a bit; we Mayos have had a long run. We've been a vivid, lusty, independent line of men who could work staggeringly hard and had an equal talent, on occasion, for serenely making fools of ourselves. Time tends to deify my grandfather, my father and Uncle Will until their personalities seem no more human than the heroic bronze statues of them that stand in the park in Rochester. In the public mind, they have solidified into attitudes of permanent nobility.

I have more actual memories of them. I remember how

4

six or eight of us Mayo children would pile all over Father when he stretched out on the sofa for the twenty-minute rest he allowed himself after lunch. He never objected, though he must have been exhausted: he rose at six, made his rounds in the hospital and started to operate around seven thirty every morning, sometimes finishing at eight at night.

I remember Uncle Will gravely sorting through the westerns he read for relaxation. He was a meticulous man in everything he touched, no matter how trivial, and he used to grade his westerns, putting an A, a B or a C on them, right down to F. He gave the lowest-graded ones to Joe and me, keeping the A's, B's and C's for himself for rereading. He also gave us his worn-out ties, come to think of it.

And I won't forget how we hid whenever we decently could from Grandfather, whose good nature in his declining years was in scant supply and did not extend itself to encompass a tumble of hearty grandchildren. Johnny Berkman, my cousin, lived with Grandfather and claims I just didn't know him well enough. Johnny says that he was gruff about things like whistling or chewing gum, but was really kindly and genial. If so, Grandfather certainly fooled Joe and me.

He was a desperately driven man, my grandfather; forever dissatisfied. He grew up in Manchester, England, and his widowed mother saw to it that he got at least fragments of education in medicine and chemistry. His forefathers had been surgeons and sea captains and it seemed Grandfather combined the pride and derring-do of both lines. He was too restless to finish his education or even to stay in England. In 1845, at the age of twenty-six, he set sail for America.

He was a nomad all his life; to put a more sympathetic complexion on it, the family prefers to say that he had a "questing spirit." He started as a chemist in Bellevue Hospital in New York City, at that time a charity institution with an unsavory reputation, then went to Buffalo and from there roamed southwest into the valley of the Wabash. Four years after his arrival in America, he was occupied oddly as a part-

5

ner with two tailors in a clothing business. He soon gave that up, sold his share and resumed his study of medicine, apprenticing himself after the custom of the time to a busy doctor in Lafayette, Indiana. Then he put out one hundred dollars and spent a year at Indiana Medical College, which was sufficient for him to obtain his M.D.

In 1850 he hung out his first shingle. It would be scandalously unethical today, but Grandfather accepted seventy-five dollars a year from a Lafayette druggist in return for establishing his office above the drugstore.

Grandfather had met a girl, Louise Wright, the daughter of a Scot, while studying at the College in La Porte, Indiana. In February, 1851, when he was thirty-two, he went back to La Porte and married her. After that he became the partner of Dr. Elizur Deming, the doctor who had befriended him when he was a tailor's partner.

He was the typical doctor of the period, riding miles through the night, his instruments in his saddlebags and much of his confidence in the efficacy of a good dose of castor oil. They all believed heartily in purges in those days—he must have caused many an acute appendix to rupture.

The income from Grandfather's practice was meager, so when their first baby, a son, died at the age of six weeks Grandmother enterprisingly helped out by opening a millinery shop. She had a great talent for business, that woman. When a daughter was born the following year, Grandmother didn't lose stride—she took in a partner and the business continued to prosper. That winter Dr. Deming was elected to the faculty of medicine at the University of Missouri and he took Grandfather along as assistant to the professor of anatomy. In the spring Grandfather decided to reinforce his Indiana degree: he applied for, and received, a second M.D., which now hangs on the wall of the old Board of Governors' room at the Mayo Clinic. You could get a medical degree in those days with little more effort and learning than a modern Boy Scout puts into acquiring merit badges.

6

In the spring Grandfather announced that he could stay in Lafayette no longer. He set out in a horse and buggy and headed west. In Galena, Illinois, he stabled his horse and put up his buggy and sailed in a packet boat on the Mississippi to St. Paul, Minnesota. I've always envied him that adventure, and the opportunity to know the canny and brave men who were the early pilots on that tricky and beautiful river. Grandfather was delighted with the newness and challenge of all that he saw and he returned home to persuade his wife to transplant her business to St. Paul.

They moved in 1854, four years before the territory of Minnesota became a state and while Indians were still a danger to settlers. Grandmother once again proved her superlative adaptability and soon had such a flourishing millinery business that she was making buying trips to New York for stock. I can't tell you what Grandfather was doing; it was one of his nonmedical periods. He seems to have been the purser on one of the river boats for a while, making a lifelong friend of a fellow employee, J. J. Hill, who was later to build the Great Northern Railroad and earn the title of "Empire Builder."

Next Grandfather became an inspector of copper claims for the Northwest Exploring Company. He staked one copper claim that now belongs to U. S. Steel, so I guess it was a good one. About that time, he also was chairman of the first board of county commissioners in Minnesota Territory; he picked the site of Duluth and made it St. Louis County seat.

He was a small man, but erect and fiercely strong. Three times he walked the wild country between St. Paul and Duluth, a round-trip distance of about three hundred miles. Once his campfire got out of control and burned all his supplies; five days later he had to eat his dog to survive.

He must have been missing medicine, for he returned one day from a solitary, rugged canoe trip and told Grandmother he wanted to move somewhere that he could set up a practice. She loyally agreed and they went up the Minnesota River, pausing to visit some friends from Indiana who had settled along its banks. Grandfather impulsively decided he had found the location he wanted, so he moved Grandmother into an abandoned farmhouse on what then was called the Cronans Precinct. Grandfather applied for the job as coroner, which didn't amount to much, and did a little healing in the neighborhood, but found they would have to rely on farming in order to eat. Two daughters were born to them during the three hard years they lived there, Phoebe in 1856 and Sarah in 1859. Sarah died about a year later.

They gave up the farm and moved next to Le Sueur, a pretty little town about four miles downstream. Grandfather built a diminutive frame house there, with doorways so small that an ordinary-sized man has to stoop to enter them; he made them to his own dimensions, of course. Uncle Will was born in that house in 1861.

The story goes that at this period my grandfather was nailing shingles on his roof when a farmer named J. L. Drake asked him to come and look at a sick horse. "Sure, I'll come," said Grandfather without hesitation. "I'll look at the horse or any other damn thing you've got."

After that Grandfather added veterinary medicine to his other ill-sorted trades, and then a new side line, newspaper publisher. For three months before it folded, he published and wrote the Le Sueur *Courier*. He seems to have been cool and detached in those violent times—one editorial, we're told, advised Mr. Lincoln to seek a compromise between the rights of the Negro and the rights of slaveowners.

His opinions on all subjects were firm and he wasn't a man for keeping them to himself, which steadily enhanced his reputation as Le Sueur's least popular citizen. He certainly handled his rival, the town's only other doctor, undiplomatically. When Grandfather first arrived in Le Sueur this doctor pointed out, reasonably enough I have no doubt, that the town was too small to support two doctors. Said Grandfather coldly, "Well doctor, are you thinking of leaving?"

The Sioux were in war paint at that time and justifiably so, since their lands had been appropriated without proper compensation. To add to their fury, some of the white men dealing with them behaved like fools. During a parley about their food shortage, for instance, one Andrew J. Myrick commented, "As far as I am concerned, if they are hungry let them eat grass." They say the French Revolution started from exactly the same kind of remark; in our country, the consequence was the Sioux uprising.

Every able-bodied man in the district was mobilized to fight the Sioux and Le Sueur was emptied of all but women and children. My resourceful grandmother conceived the brilliant plan of having the women dress in men's clothing and move around the streets with sticks on their shoulders which, from a distance, would resemble rifles. As an added touch, she fastened spoons to the ends of the sticks, to twinkle in the sunlight like bayonets. I don't know if the Sioux ever studied this ingenious charade, but there was no attack.

So-called justice was meted out in Mankato in 1862 when thirty-nine of the defeated Sioux were hanged in one drop, on the day after Christmas. Grandfather took home with him the body of one of them, Cut Nose, an unusual Indian who stood six foot three. He cleaned the skeleton and rearticulated the bones, keeping it for reference in his office. He must have taken a small relish in Cut Nose's bony presence, since the big Indian once had tried to kill Grandfather. Cut Nose and two other braves attacked Grandfather while he was making a call on horseback—Grandfather beat them off with his riding whip and escaped. He was tough, as I said before.

When Fort Sumter fell in April, 1861, Alexander Ramsey, the governor of Minnesota, promised Washington that the state would send a thousand men to fight the Confederates. It was a big order for a new state but the machinery was set up optimistically. To his delight, Grandfather was named examining surgeon for the enrollment board in the First Minnesota District, which comprised the southern half of the

9

state. It meant he would be leaving Le Sueur for the small settlement that had been chosen District headquarters, a county seat called Rochester. He moved there in 1863.

He had little to do, since few settlers were interested in fighting in a distant Civil War. With his spare time, Grandfather set up a medical practice, buying two lots on what was then Franklin Street and later, in 1916, became the site of the Mayo Clinic Building. He built a comfortable house and once again moved his exasperated wife and their small children. My father was born in that house in 1865.

I have a feeling that the main reason Grandfather allowed his family to root in Rochester was that Grandmother finally put her foot down and told him she would wander no more. Certainly his questing spirit didn't fail him; he continued to drift off on his own all his days.

At that time, Grandfather was a Republican and, with his usual lack of forethought, he had placed himself in an untenable position by accepting the post of medical enrollment officer. A Democrat would have been able to seem less partial to what some called Mr. Lincoln's war, but every time father picked a man for the Army it would seem to the drafted man's family that a certain amount of partisan zeal had gone into the selection. When he would pronounce an able-looking man unfit for service, which set tongues wagging, he found it equally uncomfortable. A diplomat might have survived in that job, but never a blunt man like Grandfather. Amazingly, he lasted for two years before the citizens trumped up some charge and managed to have him dismissed. Later, I hasten to add, he was exonerated completely.

Grandfather then built himself an office on a small piece of ground on Third Street in downtown Rochester and began to practice as a full-time doctor. At last, he began to succeed. His popularity grew, a tribute to his medical skill and rough practicality, and he soon was making calls at great distances in his horse and buggy. A Union drummer boy, a veteran of Bull Run named Jay Neville, attached himself to Grandfather and did odd jobs for him, like those of janitor in the office and driving the buggy.

I remember Jay. We fished together and I used to be fascinated by the lump of chewing tobacco in his cheek and the brown stains at the corners of his mouth. He was a crack shot at a spittoon and a marvelous swearer. As the years wore on, Jay's status in our family was sacred—you couldn't fire him, anyway; he just turned up for work the next day as if nothing had happened—but I'm sure his habits annoyed my Uncle Will, who detested all forms of tobacco and never swore.

In 1872, when Grandfather was fifty-three, his talent and good sense were recognized when the Minnesota State Medical Association elected him president, the third in the Association's history. A friend, Dr. Charles Hill, had just moved to St. Paul and he suggested that my newly honored grandfather would do well to go into partnership with him. Grandfather surveyed his well-established office, his prospering family, his comfortable home, his Rochester patients— and left. He returned to Rochester three months later, for reasons we never learned. After that his solitary departures were understood to be trips from which he would return eventually, rather than the ominous prelude to another Mayo move. I see Grandmother's fine, anchoring hand in that.

He reopened a Rochester office over Geisinger and Newton's drugstore and settled down for a life of being the irascible, much-respected "little doctor" who disappeared from time to time. In 1875, he bought thirty-five acres of land southeast of Rochester, not far from the outskirts, and moved his wife and four children to a large, irregular white house. Father was eleven then and Uncle Will fifteen. The house had a square tower attached to it, from which Grandmother, an amateur astronomer, would observe the heavens.

There was a large barn near the house. In later years, when the house and barn were about to be leveled for a housing development, I retrieved four horse-drawn vehicles from that barn. One was the first Clinic ambulance, built by Studebaker Carriage Works; another was a small four-wheeled buggy, closed in, with windows that could be put up or down—it had belonged to Uncle Will; the next was Father's surrey with the fringe on top; the last one was a single-seat four-wheeler with a convertible leather top.

On this farm Father first grew attached to the land. Throughout his lifetime it remained his hobby, an expensive one which made a substantial contribution however to the standard of agriculture in his community. He was a great innovator and most of his best experiments were copied by neighboring farmers. The cost of Father's disasters, however, was staggering. Once Father and his brother-in-law, Dr. Christopher Graham, jointly purchased a Holstein-Friesian bull for twenty thousand dollars. Two weeks later, it died—uninsured.

Father used to say imperturbably that he was an agriculturalist, not a farmer. The difference, he would explain, was that a farmer made his money on the farm and spent it in the city, while the agriculturalist made his money in the city and spent it on the farm. When we had guests for dinner, he would inquire politely, "Which will you have, milk or champagne? They both cost me the same."

Uncle Will, on the other hand, was drawn to the river and relaxed on the Mississippi. He had a steamboat, *The Minnesota*, owned jointly with Father, and then a river boat, *The North Star*, that drew only three feet of water, had a crew of five and in the lean thirties cost him fifty thousand dollars. He wintered it in New Orleans and sailed up the river every spring in that beautiful thing, entertaining doctors and their families at river villages and towns along the way. In the fall, he returned to New Orleans with the same grandeur of hospitality and glory of vista.

From the time Father and Uncle Will were small boys, they were required to perform certain chores, without any latitude for forgetfulness or fatigue or more pressing engagements. As the only sons, it was their responsibility to split the wood for the kitchen stove, clean the barns, feed the horses, tend the vegetable garden and the orchards, as well as helping Grandfather in surgery and attending school. Their sister Phoebe was assigned a few light tasks, as she was becoming weaker all the time because of some sort of splenic malady that never was diagnosed. Aunt Gertrude, the oldest of Grandfather's children, helped her mother with the cleaning and cooking. I remember her as always busy in the house, a woman who was brusque and taciturn, like Grandfather. Later she married a young veterinarian, Dr. David Berkman, who had a livery stable on the side and picked up extra money by meeting the trains.

Grandfather had a passionate interest in politics most of his life, though it wasn't always easy to tell what party he belonged to. He was mayor of Rochester for a stormy year, and then alderman for four years more, and then ran for state legislature. The community respected him and was annoyed by him in about equal measure. He lost two elections in a row, one of them by a margin of one vote. Grandfather refused a recount; that was his style. He eased over from being a Republican to joining the Democrats at that time and in 1889 finally was elected a state senator as a member of a new farmers' party called the Farmers' Alliance.

The family has a sample of his trenchant attitude preserved in one of the many letters he wrote my mother, then his office nurse and favorite person. He informed her that there were "too damned many Republicans and Norwegians" in the legislature to get anything accomplished.

In 1892, when Grandfather was seventy-three and his sons were well established in his office, he developed a master plan. First he taught Edith Graham, his office nurse and later my mother, to administer anesthesia, all about chloroform and the other anesthesia less frequently used then, how to watch blood pressure, pulse, moisture or dryness of the skin, the eyes and other reflexes. She became an expert. Next, he took in a partner, Dr. Augustus W. Stinchfield, a capable and courtly man said to be the best doctor in Rochester, next to the Mayos. Having satisfied his conscience that his patients wouldn't suffer, Grandfather retired. He was free, by God, at last.

From then on he traveled. Even when he was eighty he was still setting off boldly for New York or Mexico or Cuba or Europe. He was almost eighty-nine, still spry and vigorous, when he departed Rochester for Japan and China. His worried sons sent along a tactful acquaintance who pretended to fall in with Grandfather and kept an eye on him throughout the journey. Grandfather would have had their hides if he'd discovered what they'd done.

When he was home, Grandfather lived with Grandmother at the Berkmans'. Grandmother found it too lonely to stay at the farm through his frequent absences, so she moved in with her daughter Gertrude and they left a tenant to run the farm. When Grandfather was in Rochester, he'd check on the farm regularly. In the fall of the year in which he turned ninety, he went out to the farm and found the tenant and a crew shucking corn. While he was standing by the machine, a cob became stuck and he reflexively put his left hand into the machine to push it toward the shuck rollers. His fingers were caught and badly crushed.

The horrified tenant rushed him to the Clinic, where Father and Uncle Will examined the injuries. Uncle Will was as plain-spoken as his father and he said something to the effect that anyone who knew as much about farming as Grandfather did should have better sense than to put his hand in a corn shucker. With that, Grandfather exploded and ordered him out of the room. "Only Charlie will take care of me!" he shouted.

Three fingers had to be amputated and I remember the gray glove he wore after that on his left hand, with the three empty fingers stuffed with some pliable material.

Grandfather was a bull about pain: one time he noticed a growth on his lip that he decided, after a while, was cancerous—he took a jolt of whiskey and instructed an assistant how to cut it off. Father told us once that Grandfather hollered a while, then sat down in front of a mirror and stitched it up himself.

He was not an abstemious man. I learned years after his death that a compassionate policeman used to wait on Saturday nights for Grandfather to emerge from the saloon. When he made his unsteady appearance, the policeman would stroll along beside him all the way to the Berkmans', explaining that he happened to be going in the same direction. He needed to phrase his kind supervision discreetly because Grandfather's pride was something to be reckoned with. When people praised his sons, he would flash, "Why not give me some of the credit? They are mine and I trained them!" Which was true.

Grandfather died on March 6, 1911, just short of his ninety-second birthday, and my somber-faced grandmother followed him four years later. Her death was hastened by a fractured hip that failed to heal. In my opinion, she deserves an honored place in the family history. Her life was a long trial and her patient endurance of my grandfather's moods and disappearances was nothing short of heroic.

But my grandfather's place in medical history is secure: he launched the Mayo Clinic. When I retired from active surgery in 1963, the Clinic was a world model for integrated group practice of medicine, triumphing over the early years of opposition within the profession against group practice in any form. Here 360 doctors were working together on a unique basis, with a fee structure such that all income went into a common fund and paid them salaries. Some six hundred Fellows from all over the world were working on their postgraduate degrees and that year 190,000 patients streamed through our examining rooms. They came from all the world: there were Arab kings, bricklayers, movie stars, housewives wearing white ankle socks with their summer sandals, princes from the Orient, farmers tanned from forehead to throat, wealthy men with worried faces.

They were attracted by the reputation the Mayo Clinic has gained for expert diagnoses and safe surgery—our surgical mortality is remarkably low—and by the knowledge that the Clinic attracts a brilliant crew of doctors, buys the latest and best equipment: the newest cobalt bomb, the costly electron microscopes, a computer center to rival an oil company's, a body scanner to follow radioactive tracers in the blood. In addition, there is the bank of 2,500,000 case histories, the greatest research tool in medicine, and the lively, cerebral cluster of scientists working at Mayo to find new methods of treatment.

The Clinic, I add with pride, was the scene of a discovery that won a Nobel Prize, awarded to Doctors Hench and Kendall for the development of cortisone; their work, of intense value most particularly in the treatment of arthritis, was carried on at Mayo over a period of many frustrating years.

Actually, the up-to-date and exacting Mayo Clinic of today is a reflection of my grandfather's personal style as a doctor. He was a perfectionist who was readily infuriated by sloppy or second-rate work and was always delighted at any opportunity to improve medicine. He was fifty years old, for instance, and a successful doctor in Rochester when he decided he needed to update his surgical technique; he spent several months in the East watching the most gifted surgeons working before he was satisfied that he could perform the same surgery. He was equally impatient with tools that weren't contemporary. In the early days, one family story goes, he kept a primitive microscope and used to show his sons the wonders within a drop of the mother of vinegar. As soon as he heard of better microscopes, he put a mortgage of six hundred dollars on his home without hesitation and sent away for one.

The Mayo Clinic, the extension of that angry little man's implacable integrity, began in a tornado. Tuesday, August 21, 1883, was a stifling hot day in Rochester. At the end of a sweltering afternoon of work in the office, Grandfather was driving with Uncle Will to the slaughterhouse on the north side of town to pick up a sheep or cow head so that Grandfather could give Uncle Will a lesson in the anatomy of an eye that night. Uncle Will had graduated in medicine two months before but he had discovered, as my father did after his graduation, that Grandfather considered an M.D. degree as a good start for a medical education of approximately lifelong duration.

They arrived at the slaughterhouse to find the butchers making a panicky departure. They pointed to some strange clouds moving toward Rochester with eerie, terrifying speed. Father and Uncle Will turned back with them and they had scarcely crossed the Zumbro River bridge when it was hit by the tornado and blown to bits. In an instant, the air was filled with wild debris. Grandfather and Uncle Will managed to scramble into the safety of a blacksmith shop without injury. A clock that was blown down in the few seconds it took the tornado to pass through Rochester established the exact time of the tragedy, 6:35 P.M.

North Rochester, then known as Lower Town, had been hit the hardest. Few houses were left and others were severely damaged. The slaughterhouse had vanished. Rescue work, of course, began as soon as the dazed survivors could get to their feet. In the unnatural darkness that accompanied the storm, lanterns had to be lit. The search for the injured was further hindered by a devastating, heavy rainfall.

All of Rochester's doctors turned out to help. My grandfather, a natural leader in a time of crisis, took charge of the Buck's Hotel on the edge of town and directed stretcher-bearers to bring the victims there. He sent Uncle Will to the office to take care of patients brought there, and dispatched Father to be Will's assistant.

17

It is significant now to note that a convent of the Sisters of Third Order Regular St. Francis, of the Congregation of Our Lady of Lourdes, had been established in Rochester six years earlier. The convent housed nine nuns, all school-teachers. Their building, a brick one on Center Street, suffered some damage to its roof during the storm but the nuns had been unharmed in the cellar. The sisters were inspecting the shambles when a boy came running along the littered street. He said to Mother Alfred, "Doc says come to Buck's Hotel and bring a couple of sisters with you."

Mother Alfred was one of those individuals who are gifts to the human race. She realized instantly, as Grandfather knew she would, that she and the nuns were needed as nurses. She departed with the boy at once, coolheadedly leaving instructions that a few of the sisters should prepare soup, coffee, tea and sandwiches to the limit of the convent's resources.

The nearer they got to Buck's Hotel, the more monstrous the havoc appeared. The tornado had been pulverizing, like a giant's foot. The nuns picked their way over the rubble and found Grandfather in Buck's Hotel, moving from one moaning person to another, splinting broken bones, sterilizing and stitching cuts torn by broken glass and flying metal. He yelled, "More splints!" and the messenger boy went off running to Grandfather's office to get them. Mother Alfred waited until Grandfather glanced up and then notified him crisply that she had room for a hundred of the injured at her convent.

Grandfather nodded in agreement. "That's what I thought," he told her. "Now, tell this hotelkeeper to announce that everyone Dr. Mayo says can be moved should be taken at once to your house. Don't use the word *convent*." He'd been figuring it all out while he worked, including the awareness of the anti-Roman Catholic sentiment prevalent at that time. He told Mother Alfred which path to take, a back road away from the main path of the storm, and advised her to ride in the first wagon leaving Buck's.

He and all the other doctors worked all night. At dawn, Grandfather arrived at the convent, red-eyed and exhausted, to check on all his patients.

The convent was filled beyond capacity and wounded people were scattered all through the town, so Grandfather decided that the most efficient way of caring for them would be to put them all in a central place. He told Mother Alfred that Rommel's Dance Hall on the corner of Broadway and Center was ideal and all the injured should be assembled there. The sisters, he added, would serve as nurses, working in rotation. Mother Alfred was shocked at the notion of her nuns working in a converted dance hall, but she was a practical person and agreed. It was done and it became, of course, a hospital—Rochester's first.

Someone had to be in charge of the arrangement to prevent duplication of effort and unorganized care, so the role fell without dispute to Grandfather. People for miles around, from as far as Chicago, sent donations to the ruined town. With the more than seventy-five thousand dollars received, Rochester started to rebuild without delay.

For a number of years previously, Rochester's citizens had been talking about establishing a hospital, but it somehow never got past the committee stage. Mother Alfred decided that the time had come to go ahead with a hospital, while the town had the example before its eyes. She arrived one day in Grandfather's office and they discussed her plan. It was Mother Alfred's notion that her Order should extend itself beyond teaching school, and should build and supervise the hospital. Grandfather was doubtful. In the first place, as he explained to her, people of that day went to a hospital only as a last, deathbed resort, with the consequence that the community tended to regard hospitals as one stage removed from funeral homes. "You're ahead of your time," he concluded, "and besides, not everyone would favor a Catholic hospital."

Mother Alfred smiled fondly at Grandfather, whose religious views were well known. Nominally an Episcopalian, he was often heard quoting Bismarck: "I never felt the need of any religious faith, and therefore never had any." "Your own life and work, Dr. Mayo," said Mother Alfred, "reassure me that the cause of suffering humanity knows no religion or creed." Grandfather capitulated, as any man would. Mother Alfred's most telling argument, I suspect, was the one she saved for last: a hospital would benefit Dr. Mayo's two young sons, giving them a place to work and develop.

"It's going to cost about forty thousand dollars," Grandfather warned her. In that era, it was a staggering sum. Mother Alfred didn't blanch. "We can get that," she told him smoothly, "and more, if we need it."

She and Grandfather worked together after that in a warm collaboration that surprised those who didn't understand how much courage and common sense they had in common. Within five years, Mother Alfred had built three more floors on her school and had started on the hospital, to be called St. Marys Hospital. It was my grandmother's idea to thwart the religious prejudices of the day by making the hospital as ecumenical as possible. Accordingly, Mother Alfred appointed a jovial Presbyterian, John Willis Baer, as the hospital's first superintendent. Grandfather, naturally, was named chief of staff. The medical community approved of this but opposition, astonishingly, came from local Republicans, since Grandfather was then a Democrat. Mother Alfred handled the difficulty with ingenious ease—she borrowed the money she needed from Republican banks. Her main problem was holding off indignant Catholics, who wanted only Catholics hired as doctors and staff. They complained that the hospital would be filled with unbelievers, but Mother Alfred wasn't impressed.

Despite these colorful difficulties, St. Marys Hospital was finished and opened its doors in July, 1888, with twenty-seven beds and eighteen emergency beds, gaslight fixtures and an empty elevator shaft. Grandfather had insisted on including the shaft in the three-story building. "My son Charlie will build the elevator," he promised Mother Alfred. Father was famous in the family for his ability to repair, invent and build anything. When he was a tot, Grandmother always called him to fix a butter churn or silence a squeaky door. He built St. Marys first operating table and three years after the opening he built a telephone connection between the hospital and Grandfather's clinic—Mother Alfred somehow convinced the city fathers that it was in the public interest to put telephone poles down Zumbro Street for Father's lines.

The hospital charged one dollar a day, or six dollars a week, for ward beds and eight to ten dollars a week for private rooms. The staff worked a seven-day week and was required to be as thrifty as possible. To Mother Alfred's delight, receipts for the first eleven months amounted to a remarkable $1100. She immediately launched a plan to put all profits into improving the hospital and stock-piling a fund for future expansion, which she and Grandfather could see from the beginning would be necessary.

Within five years after its opening, St. Marys Hospital was so crowded that an addition had to be built, followed by more additions. In 1904, the bed capacity had risen to 175. St. Marys was destined to become three blocks long, the largest privately-owned hospital in the United States, to the eternal credit of the Sisters of St. Francis, especially the brilliant Mother Alfred and her superb successors, Sister Mary Joseph, Sister Mary Domatilla and Sister Mary Brigh, the latter the administrator when I retired.

The first operation in St. Marys was performed on September 30, 1889, an emergency procedure for a cancerous eye. It was done by my father, assisted by Uncle Will. For the occasion, my grandfather acted as the anesthetist.

As time went on, the Mayo brothers developed areas of surgical specialization, with Father primarily doing operations on the face, throat, eyes and brain. One time a wealthy and officious man burst into the Clinic and pounded his fist on Uncle Will's desk. "I want to see the head doctor around here!" he roared. Uncle Will looked up calmly. "That'll be my brother Charlie," he said. "He's the head doctor—I'm the belly doctor." Uncle Will used to say, "Charlie drove me down and down until I reached the belly." He was an abdominal surgeon, with a special interest in operations on stomachs.

Uncle Will and Father were gifted as surgeons, as the world knows. Their judgment was remarkable, a blend of sensitivity, experience, technical skill and intuition that led them to be innovators during the years when surgery was in its youth. From the beginning of their careers, goaded by their own energy and curiosity and the harassing of their father, they made self-improvement their daily bread. At the turn of the century, they founded an informal club of some thirty good surgeons who met regularly at one medical center or another to exchange information. In their lifetimes, they made more than eighty medical trips to Europe to study what then were more advanced techniques.

Their hard work and intense preoccupation with perfection paid off almost immediately, both in terms of their patients' well-being and their own reputations. In the early 1900's, for instance, Father was regarded as one of the country's three experts at thyroidectomies, a notable achievement for a man working in the cornfields.

When recognition came for them, it came suddenly. In a few years, the Mayo brothers went from being unknown outside the state to being a magnet for doctors from all over the country, anxious to watch them operate. Wealthy patients heard of them and came from great distances, and paid proportionate fees—Father and Uncle Will became millionaires. Uncle Will was only forty-four when the American Medical Association elected him president; Father became president some years later, when he was fifty-one. Both gave strong leadership, humane and farsighted.

Father and Uncle Will didn't have the only surgical center in Minnesota. There was another in St. Paul–Minneapolis, the twin cities that Rochester people simply call "the cities." But Father and Uncle Will had something extra to offer: group medicine, with total teamwork. The Mayos had been raised to work together, pooling their skills and insights; when it came time to pick partners because of the pressure of the work, they selected men with cooperative natures and a high degree of skill in areas which complemented their own. Sloppiness was intolerable, but so was arrogance.

This concept of interlocking talents and a mood of sharing, evolving as it did from Grandfather's zealous grooming of his sons, is the fundamental reason why the Mayo Clinic is so respected today. It had started with a strong, loyal family working together and it retained that clan spirit. As new staff was added, mainly relatives at first, one or another of the Mayos, usually Father, would undertake to make them welcome by making them guests in his home. Rochester was short of hotel accommodations in those years, so it was natural that visiting doctors would also stay with the Mayos. There was an unmistakable inference: joining the Clinic was inseparable from joining the family.

The Mayo Clinic has grown from this original closeness to be the world's first, largest and most successful practice of group medicine. It is the world's largest private practice, and the world's largest graduate training center for medical specialists. The Mayos have vanished from the Mayo Clinic today, but the Mayo emphasis on sharing is our legacy, and a great one.

TWO

I don't know where you'd find two more disparate brothers than my father and Uncle Will seemed to be. It was as though they calculatingly had divvied up the personalities of their parents, Uncle Will deciding on the cold prickliness of their father while Father adopted the warmth and friendliness of their mother. Certainly their incongruous natures reinforced one another: the more merry and gregarious Father became, the more severe and puritanical Uncle Will would be, assured that Father would smooth ruffled feelings; Father, on his part, had freedom to be agreeable and sympathetic to all, knowing that Uncle Will would be the unswerving enforcer.

Inside, as the family knew, they were exactly the same man: devoted to medicine, tireless in the pursuit of excellence, visionary, wry of humor, courageous, honest and fiercely proud.

Uncle Will was the taller, with an aristocratic face and the bearing of a general. My father's posture inclined toward comfort. Uncle Will's clothes had mannequin neatness and fit, while Father could look disheveled in a freshly-pressed suit. When Father and Uncle Will posed together for photographs, Uncle Will would tweak and straighten Father's jacket and tie despairingly, effecting no discernible improvement. Afterward he would pore gloomily over the picture proofs, trying to find the one in which, as he once said, my father looked least like a groceryman.

I am skeptical of the story that Father's surgical gloves were grotesquely outsized for him, with the result that visiting doctors observed the unnerving spectacle of a man performing delicate surgery with flapping fingers. In the days when Father and Uncle Will were busiest, surgical gloves didn't have the second-skin fit that they do now and, with Father's small hands, it's likely that the fingers were a little long. I can believe that on occasion it would amuse him to exaggerate the effect a bit, however.

Uncle Will would never find his gloves slightly comical. He was terse, austere and demanding of his associates. He could discipline or fire a man coldly and cleanly. My father, on the other hand, was incorrigibly chatty and cheery. His hospital rounds were social occasions. He would sit for half an hour at the bedside of a nervous patient, joking with him until the patient's tenseness eased. Uncle Will thought it a great waste of time. "You should do as I do with some of these mental problems," he once told Father. "I walk in, lay my hands on them like Christ, and walk out."

The two brothers didn't even sound alike. Father mumbled and drawled his words, as I do. People with perfectly good hearing have to ask me to repeat myself, time and again. But Uncle Will articulated distinctly, in a voice that was unexpectedly high and reedy.

It followed, of course, that their styles of living would differ radically. When they became prosperous, for example, both built huge homes, the largest in Rochester. Uncle Will's was close to the Clinic, almost downtown—a formal Kasota stone fortress, complete with a square tower you could imprison princes in. Inside, the walls were paneled darkly and the furniture was heavy, with an immovable look. Father built in the country, a slightly daft, rambling, haphazard arrangement of some fifty or sixty big-windowed, charming rooms that spill around trees and down a hillside.

Uncle Will was always on militant guard against any sign of what he took to be weakness within himself. His sense of

25

guilt was so strong that when he realized one morning that he was looking forward to his regular glass of claret with lunch, he quit drinking the noon claret forever. I think Father's reaction would have been to have two glasses of claret the next time.

We children never saw Father take a drink. Even when we were grown and attended cocktail parties with him, we never saw him with a glass in his hand. We were baffled, since he seemed like a man who was having something to drink. Then we made the discovery that Father was a gulper. He would get a drink and drain it on the spot, in order to put down the incriminating glass.

Yet, incompatible as Uncle Will and my father may have seemed to many people, they loved one another; the verb is used advisedly. "Your great success was not as surgeons," a friend once told them, "it was as brothers. There has never been anything like it." One of the most telling illustrations of their mutual regard and trust is that all their lives they kept a joint bank account. The only checks they ever used were printed "Drs. Mayo." I suspect they may be the only brothers in the country with such faith in one another.

Uncle Will was regarded generally as the more brilliant of the two, the leader. Some thought that his insistence on the phrase "my brother and I" whenever he spoke of the Clinic was in the nature of a tactful consideration. The family knew better, and Uncle Will never missed an opportunity to prove that it was an equal partnership. On one occasion when someone complained to him about a negative ruling my father had made, Uncle Will said flatly, "When Charlie says no, it means no for me."

They had an agreement that they would discuss in private all differences of opinion until they reached a decision that both could accept. One of these joint decisions was that the Clinic could not have two administrative heads; Uncle Will, by seniority and disposition, clearly was better suited for that role. All policy matters and all appointments to the staff, however, were subject to joint approval. It resulted in Uncle Will playing the heavy in many circumstances where severity was required for the good of the Clinic, while Father—though equally responsible—seemed a distressed bystander.

Their reliance on one another for friendship was startling. When my father and mother married, for example, it seemed only natural to the brothers that they would live with Uncle Will and his wife until their own house was built. It was next door, of course. A guest of my father's once asked him when he and his brother found time to confer. Father explained offhandedly, "In the evening I wait around the house for a while and if Will doesn't come over here, I go over there."

Some psychologists believe that marriages succeed best when each partner has superiority in some area, recognized by the other. I think that's part of the reason Father and Uncle Will got along so smoothly: their areas of superiority weren't conflicting and they were certainly recognizable. Uncle Will once said a very revealing thing. He and my mother were watching Father walking along laughing with two friends. "Everybody likes Charlie, don't they," he mused. "They aren't afraid of him. No one ever puts an arm around my shoulder as they do with him." There was a silence as Mother groped for words of consolation and then Uncle Will said brusquely, "But then, I wouldn't like it if they did."

Both men had wit. Uncle Will was dry and acerbic, while Father was droll and puckish. One famed story about Father concerns the dissatisfied patient who had a history which included almost every ailment known to man, with the exception of faulty elimination. Father thought it over and declared, "I think your trouble is constipation." The patient objected. "But doctor, I have a movement every day." Father nodded. "Yes, I know. But the trouble is that each movement is three days late."

Another time the telephone rang while we were at dinner. It was Jay Neville, the Clinic janitor I've mentioned before.

27

He informed Father excitedly that a woman patient had been overlooked in the examining room. She was still waiting for Dr. Mayo, with a speculum in her. Father pondered, and then instructed Jay, "Put on a white coat, go in and take out that speculum and tell the patient to return at ten o'clock tomorrow morning. Tell her, ah, we'll continue her treatment then."

Father's eyes under those bushy Mayo eyebrows would dance when he was involved in something he found comical, but Uncle Will had a poker-faced delivery. One time Uncle Will caught sight of a surgeon friend in the gallery who was watching him remove a stone from a common bile duct. He called up, "Hello there, better come down. You can't possibly see anything from there—I can't see any too well from where I am."

An elderly farmer came into the Clinic during its early days and asked Uncle Will how much he would charge to remove a wen from his scalp. "Ten dollars," said Uncle Will. "Too much," said the man, settling in for bargaining.

"All right, five dollars," said Uncle Will and the man said that was more like it.

Uncle Will squirted a little novocain around and then cut out the wen. Those things really bleed and the blood was pouring down the farmer's face as Uncle Will stepped back and took off his gloves.

"Hey, where are you going?" cried the man in dismay.

"I said I'd cut out the wen for five dollars," explained Uncle Will without expression. "I didn't say anything about sewing it up." The man groaned. "You win. Ten dollars."

Grandfather was fussy about picking the medical schools his sons attended. He selected the University of Michigan for Uncle Will and, to provide variety for the betterment of the Mayo group, sent Father to the Chicago Medical College, which was then associated with, but not part of, Northwestern University. Both schools had three-year courses, a brand new improvement over the previous two-year course. There was still no requirement for internship, which meant that a man in those days was ready to hang out his shingle a few years after leaving high school.

There is a note somewhere in the archives of Northwestern University which Grandfather wrote: "To Whom it May Concern: This is to certify that Chas. H. Mayo is 21 years of age and is of good moral character. W. W. Mayo."

This reminds me of a testimonial which hangs in my office. It is written in Uncle Will's hand on a picture of himself: "To my nephew Charles, hoping for the best but fearing the worst."

Father received his medical degree on March 27, 1888, and started at once to practice with his father and brother. Edith Graham, who was later to be his wife, went to work for the Mayos a year later, upon her graduation from Women's Hospital in Chicago. She was the first nurse in Rochester.

She was a radiant and truly beautiful woman. All her life, the young doctors at the Clinic were falling in love with her, and she was tender and kind as well. Grandfather, uncharacteristically, adored her wholeheartedly and paid tribute to her intelligence and good judgment by training her to be Rochester's first anesthetist. St. Marys Hospital now displays the little brown chloroform bottle that she used for home cases, along with the early instruments and operating table that my father made. By the way, he eventually did build a hydraulic elevator for St. Marys, as my grandfather promised. It worked perfectly for many years; it was slow, but absolutely trustworthy.

Father naturally was attracted to the lovely office nurse. All his life he took it as a sign of moribundity for a man to fail to appreciate a pretty woman. They began to go together on picnics and hay rides with a crowd of young people their age and, after a time, they were married—on April 3, 1893. Father had a practical, unromantic concept of the perfect honeymoon trip: the newlyweds toured eastern hospitals and medical centers.

At the time that Father married, Uncle Will had been married for some nine years. He had married Hattie Damon a year after he graduated as a doctor. She was a pretty, red-cheeked, modest daughter of one of Rochester's leading citizens, a jeweler. They lived in what the family called "the yellow house," on the corner of what was then College and Dakota streets. My parents moved in with them while building their own home next door, an undertaking that required two years to complete, and it thereafter was known as "the red house."

Except for the color of their paint, the homes were similar. They had porte-cocheres, city water, gas heat, and a special feature, a speaking tube connecting the houses to adjoining barns, where the carriages and drivers were.

My father and Uncle Will both made marriages that were enduring triumphs. It must have contributed significantly to their ability to bear the pressure of their profession. Both marriages were supporting to the brothers, both were filled with affection, respect and sweetness. I think my mother and father were passionately and romantically in love all their lives. They always slept in a double bed, which I heartily recommend for the success of all marriages.

Though they were quite different, Mother and her sister-in-law always got along smoothly. Aunt Hattie was very gentle, soft-spoken, retiring; perfectly suited to Uncle Will. She would never have dreamed of disagreeing with him or failing to follow his wishes, or of offering the slightest opinion on affairs at the Clinic, which she considered to be none of her business. My mother was also softly feminine, but she had opinions on every subject under the sun, especially the Clinic, and she was capable of expressing herself with tact, but unmistakably. I suppose that her experience as a nurse in the Mayo office during the early days made her feel more of a participant than did Aunt Hattie.

The two women had dissimilar backgrounds. Aunt Hattie had been raised among the well-to-do and was at home among the teacups. Mother was the twelfth child in a family of thirteen, born to a poor farmer who had settled on a homestead four miles north of Rochester. She told me once how she wept when a heifer was born because it meant another cow for her to milk. On Christmas, the Graham children would pray to find something in their stockings other than potatoes and apples.

Father's long-ailing sister Phoebe had died in 1885, so when Uncle Will and Aunt Hattie had their two daughters they named one of them for her and called the other Carrie. They grieved that two male babies died. Mother and Father had a daughter first, named Dorothy, and then on July 28, 1898, they had me. Since it had been established that Aunt Hattie could not have more children, the family decided to name me for both brothers, hence Charles William Mayo, me.

After this baby, there was Edith, born two years later, then Joe two years after that, then a frail little girl they called Rachel who died very young, and after her Louise and Esther. In all, six surviving children, four girls and two boys.

I wouldn't like to say that Joe was a slow developer, for there is a strong likelihood that he merely was showing early indication of his lifelong aptitude for evading effort, but the truth is that he didn't talk until he was four years old. He got along cheerfully with a language of grunts, using different intonations which we all learned to understand. Mother fretted, as mothers do, but Father was amused. "Why should he use words, when he manages so well with grunts?" he pointed out reasonably.

When he was four, Joe ran into our parents' bedroom in the middle of the night, announcing in a loud, perfectly clear voice, "Charlie fall out of bed. Charlie cry." It was acclaimed as a miracle and while I was a dolt for falling out of bed at the advanced age of eight, still I was the vehicle for Joe's initiation into speech.

At that time Joe and I were sleeping in separate beds, for a rather embarrassing reason: Joe occasionally wet his bed. I have no doubt now that it was another energy-saving device. One night I attempted to solve Joe's problem for him by putting an elastic band around his offending member. With the circulation cut off, he naturally began to suffer swelling and acute pain. My father had to be summoned and it took him nearly three hours to remove the embedded elastic. I was taught a severe lesson that night about the dangers of amateur cures.

I attended Central Public School, a big, three-story building; I was a less than remarkable scholar, much less. Joe, of course, was even worse. He had a wonderful, wild imagination, ill-suited to assimilating rules of grammar and long division. Mother used to utilize his flair for fantasy in ingenious ways. She used to tie a rope around a tree on our front lawn and give the free end of the rope to Joe to hold, informing him that he was a pony tethered to a tree. Joe was enthusiastic about this concept of himself; he would paw the ground and whinny until she released him, however much later, and he never let go the rope.

It was Mother's endearing habit to read to us before she tucked us into bed and one night vivid in my memory I asked her, "Why is it you can kick a football with your right foot, throw a baseball with your right hand and see better out of your right eye than your left?" I think mother stopped breathing. "What did you say?" she asked in a strained voice, and I repeated it.

She got up and ran to tell Father. I was bewildered at all the excitement because it seemed natural to me to have a left eye weaker than my right. They came back together and Mother put her hand over my right eye. I was unable to count the fingers that father held up, and by that time their anxiety was beginning to worry me.

The next day I had my eyes tested at the Clinic and I was fitted with a pair of glasses with an ordinary lens on the right and a thick one on the left, which turned out to be useful for starting fires in dry leaves on sunny days. I was the envy of every boy in the school. I also had to wear a black patch over my good eye, to make the lazy bad one work, they told me. I got around this nuisance by tipping my head back and peeking. After a time I discarded both the patch and the glasses; they had done no good, which didn't surprise me.

I had a marvelous childhood: the horror and hopelessness of piano and ballroom dancing lessons were minor discomforts when compared to the joys of fishing and going to band concerts and making the rounds of all the Graham and Mayo women who could bake cookies. Father and Uncle Will built a cottage on the Zumbro River, near Oronoco, and we summered there, the two families alternating. Sometimes Father and Uncle Will were kept so busy in surgery that they could come only for weekends, but we children had the run of the barn and the boats. I remember sitting on the dock fishing with a cane pole, and I can still smell the water, a good smell, and hear the little waves lapping on the sides of the boats.

The Rochester State Hospital for the Insane had a fairly good-sized piece of property with a dock across from our place. There were long bunkhouses where those patients who could be trusted were rotated for weekly stays during the summer. They had a good wooden pier and boats. I've always admired that kind of therapy for disturbed people, and I understand it's coming into vogue again.

On the State Hospital side of the riverbank some lovely willow trees were growing and their boughs overhung the water. Father, Joe and I were fishing from a rowboat near them one afternoon when Father spotted two water snakes sleeping on one of the willow branches. He stood up in the boat, which he had forbidden us ever to do, took an oar out of the lock and struck at the snakes. The boat almost overturned, the willow branch broke and the snakes landed in our boat, one on Father's lap. In the melee of terrified boys and lurching boat that followed, one snake escaped and Father clubbed the other to death with the oar.

33

We untangled our fishing lines from the willows and each other, and Father then rowed us silently back to the dock. By unspoken agreement, that day's fishing was over.

Mother kept trying to get Father to buy us a baby grand piano, a proposal which certainly received no encouragement from me. Despite all the piano teacher could do, I had learned only one piece, "The Happy Farmer," and I played it doggedly in recital after recital, with decreasing effect. Mother brought up the subject of the baby grand with Father every time she thought of it, but Father always evaded her by saying, "We can't afford it."

One day when we were at the cottage, a motor launch was unloaded into the lake. It was a beautiful boat and mother wondered aloud who owned it. Father said proudly, "We do. What shall we name it?" Mother's eyes glittered. "How about *Baby Grand?*" she suggested icily. She got her piano as soon as we returned to the red house.

I intend to be tactful about this, but it was no secret in our house that Father was entranced rather readily by attractive women. There didn't seem to be any cause for concern, since Mother didn't seem in the least disturbed, so we accepted it as only natural. We children were interested in the ladies he would fancy from time to time and we even had our favorites—and our aversions. One lady who lasted quite a time must have cast a spell over Father; we children found her nasty and fault-finding.

One charmer, however, so dazzled Father that he used to sit her beside him in the front of the carriage, while Mother rode behind with the children. After a few such rides, Mother put a stop to it. Years later, she told my wife about it. "That was too much," she explained. "I just put my foot down."

Whatever Mother felt about her beloved husband's lively, roving eye, she kept to herself. If she ever remonstrated with him, I never heard it; we were never aware of any tension or distress. She was not above using the situation to her advantage, however, when it suited her purposes. For instance, we owned a farm on the outskirts of Rochester which Mother wanted to call Mayowood, a lyrical choice that we all applauded—except for Father, who would have none of it. One day Mother sat down and wrote a gushing letter in some faked handwriting, signing it with the name of a former flame no longer favored. In it she expressed her undying admiration for Charlie and requested his permission to name her home Mayowood. It must have given Father quite a turn when he considered it. That evening he arrived home with the announcement that he had changed his mind—Mother could call the farm Mayowood, beginning at once.

Father acquired Mayowood in 1900. My earliest memories of it are the family picnics we held there whenever it was Uncle Will's turn to use the cottage. Father was turning loose his flair for agricultural invention at the farm. He designed a round barn with a silo in its core which, because of the elevation of the land to the rear, permitted the loading of hay and straw directly to the second floor. I think it proved more economical than barns of a conventional shape and I know that it simplified feeding, since all the animals faced in to the silo and we could drop their rations of hay down the chutes Father had arranged.

The barn had another innovation, a floor of poured reinforced cement. It was a new building material just being developed at the period and father pioneered its use because he accurately foresaw its great possibilities.

I got one of the few spankings Father ever gave me in an incident that happened at the farm. I had been fishing and when I passed the chicken house I noticed that I still had a worm on my hook, which tempted me to experiment with fishing for chickens. I got one too, a Rhode Island Red, and Father happened along as I was struggling to pull in the flapping fowl. We ate chicken for dinner that night, but I didn't enjoy it much.

As I have said, Father and Uncle Will kept their money in a single account at the bank, so it's clear that they must share whatever glory is due them for the sagacity of their business investments, which is almost none. I remember the occasion when they made a purchase which they felt certain would make them lumber barons. That company went into receivership with unflattering speed and, as their share of the liquidated assets, they became joint owners of a stern-wheeler named *The Oronoco,* an honest craft that had served its life poking log rafts down the Mississippi.

The Oronoco had boilers that burned wood, and a crew's quarters, galley, dining room and afterdeck on the second deck. The third deck was bare and black except for a big pilothouse and cables to help hold the two black metal chimney stacks, with their frivolity of filigree ironwork around the outlets. There was a quantity of Victorian gingerbread carpentry around the edges of the deck and the boat had been painted white.

The joint account must have sighed at the cost of turning that big working steamboat into a luxury houseboat, but Father and Uncle Will were as enthusiastic and inventive as schoolboys. For a start, they changed her from wood-burning to coal-burning, which, they pointed out, enabled them to load three automobiles on the lower deck. They hired a crew of captain, mate, first engineer, second engineer, fireman, cook and maid, and it could then go anywhere on the Mississippi in sumptuous style. The captain acted as pilot, which cut down on the overhead minutely.

I'll never forget *The Oronoco.* It seemed so vast to the Mayo children that we were confident it could cross the Atlantic. Sometimes the captain would let us hold the wheel, in safe water; you can't imagine the thrill of it.

Eventually the proud owners decided that *The Oronoco* was past her prime, so they commissioned the Dingle Brothers Boat Works, across the Mississippi from St. Paul, to build them an even bigger boat, a diesel-powered stern-wheeler. It also had space for three cars on its lower deck and even hand-somer fittings; *The Oronoco*'s crew was transferred intact.

That new boat, which they called the *Minnesota,* was 130 feet long and 30 feet wide, and every inch of it opulent. It became Uncle Will's retreat, since Father was more and more enthralled by his farming adventures. Uncle Will turned to the river; the Mississippi has a lure that exerts a strong compulsion for some; I myself feel most at peace when I'm on the river. Uncle Will fitted a study on the *Minnesota* with the maps and geographies that fascinated him, and the best of his westerns, and he used to relax there in uninterrupted peace.

When I was about fourteen I was cruising with Uncle Will one time and I sneaked down to the bow on the lower deck to have a cigarette, believing that my uncle was safely in his study. To my dismay, he emerged suddenly from the engine room. I hastily tossed the half-smoked cigarette overboard, knowing how he loathed tobacco, and he stood at the rail watching without expression as it floated past him. He looked at me piercingly and asked me to come into the study, where he lectured me at length on the evils of all tobacco, but especially cigarettes. I can't recall if I promised him that I would never smoke cigarettes again; it seems likely that he would extract such a pledge from me. I kept it too, about fifty years later.

Father and Mother had decided in 1910 to build their home on the Mayowood farm, and the house caused quite a stir in Rochester. The newspaper reported breathlessly that it cost sixty thousand dollars, had eight bathrooms and more than thirty rooms, including a living room that was 46 feet by 26 feet. There was quarter-sawed oak paneling inside and a sort of stucco outside. Garfield Schwartz, the contractor, hired thirty men to build it and Father's insistence on cement for its construction meant that Mr. Schwartz had to purchase the largest concrete mixer ever seen in Rochester, importing it via a railway flatcar. It marked the first time that cement

37

had ever been mixed in the area without the use of men with wheelbarrows. Father reinforced the concrete with old scythes and plowshares from the local junkyard; we could withstand a siege in Mayowood.

Despite its formidable components, Mayowood had gracious, rambling lines. In time we added a tea house, a long front terrace and a curved drive that was bordered by a low stone wall topped with flat stones standing on their edges, like ragged teeth. It was an extra flourish that father copied from an English fence he had admired.

Father kept on buying adjoining land until he had assembled more than three thousand acres. He had bulldozers and great shovels excavate the land on either side of the Zumbro River that flowed below the house. He used the excavated earth to mound some hills in a meadow near the river and then he built a dam about 150 yards away. He had a time getting a dam that would hold but finally it worked, with logs and rocks and cement buttresses. With this a lake formed over the meadow and the hills became islands. It made for gorgeous scenery, but it had a muddy bottom.

Next Father connected the islands to the shore by means of a swinging bridge, hung on cables on which wild grapes grew. The islands themselves were linked together by high-humped Japanese bridges and there was a bathing house on the largest island with a concealed water tank on top so the sun could warm the water for the dressing room showers. Father and Mother then added fountains and stone lanterns they purchased on their trips abroad. On a summer night, it was breath-taking. It helped that he was building in the days before the tax on income.

Father's practicality showed itself in the construction of the dam. It served a valuable function in flood control, but it also ran the small hydroelectric plant on the property. The first electric lights at Mayowood were operated by our own power plant, and Father even had a backup installation, a large gasoline engine, for the times when the Zumbro River was low or frozen.

Father also built a greenhouse, farther down along the river below the dam. I think he did it mainly to find a use for the thousands of thin glass X-ray plates stored at the Clinic, since he abominated waste. They were too fragile to last long and gradually were replaced with heavier plain glass, but for years one could walk through the greenhouse and see outlines of a stomach here, a gallbladder there, a fractured tibia over the petunias.

There were gateways on the road leading to the greenhouse, flanked with stone pillars bearing huge round stones the size of cannonballs, a find of Father's in Cannon Ball, South Dakota, where a freak glacial flow carved out these curious round stones. Years later, when sight-seeing buses used to drive to Mayowood, the drivers would pause in front of those pillars and announce, "These are the largest gallstones ever removed by the Mayo brothers."

Father was far from being retired while he was planning and executing all these improvements. He was using spare bits of his prodigious energy and I can't imagine where he found the time, since he sometimes operated twelve hours at a stretch. A guest at Mayowood commented one evening that he had just seen Father remove a cataract, tonsils and a goiter, resect ribs for empyema, perform a gastroenterostomy, which is an operation joining the stomach and intestine, shorten the round ligaments for prolapse of the uterus, correct bowlegs and finish off with his operation for bunions —*before lunch.*

It was about this time that Mother and Father made what seemed to me a ghastly decision. They decided that I should go east to a good preparatory school to continue my education. Uncle Will had made himself responsible for the education of my good-natured cousin, Johnny Berkman, the son of his sister Gertrude, so it was agreed that Johnny and I would go off together. They chose the exclusive Hill School in Pottstown, Pennsylvania, which still enjoys a reputation for turning out some of the country's most distinguished citizens. Johnny and I arrived there in the autumn of 1911, unimpressed, awkward and already homesick. It didn't help matters that Hill School instantly set us both back a grade, apparently having a low opinion of the academic standard of Central Public School in the middle of Minnesota somewhere. This made no hit with us.

Hill School, in fact, never became less awful as time went on; if anything, my original poor impression of the place sank. I spent the five loneliest years of my life there, hating it all the time and performing so wretchedly in such subjects as Latin, French, German and mathematics that I invariably had to spend my summer vacations studying in order to be promoted in the fall. My only consolation was that it was the same for Johnny. The only tangible achievement of those miserable years is a green and white wastebasket that I wove in manual training. It isn't half bad, and I made some bookends as well.

My depression must have activated some latent longing for spiritual comfort because I remember teaching Sunday school for a while in a ragged little slum known as Chicken Hill. The language used by the children in my class proved more interesting and memorable than anything I picked up at Hill School but I quit finally when we got to the lesson of the virgin birth. Try teaching *that* to a wise and bitter eight-year-old who has seen everything.

Not long ago I came across a diary that I kept sporadically while in Hill School. On January 7, 1916, I wrote: "I am darned shure now that I would rather be a surgeon than any other profession that I can think of. It has more chance in it for advancement, altho one has to work like the devil to do anything in it. Still one has to work like the devil to amount to anything in any line of work."

1. Residence on Dr. W. W. Mayo's farm, Rochester, Minnesota

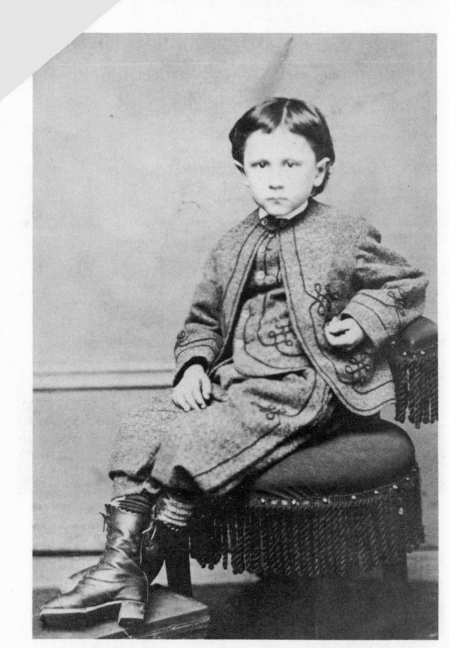

2. Dr. C. H. Mayo

3. Dr. W. J. Mayo

4. Phoebe Mayo, sister of Dr. C. H. Mayo and Dr. W. J. Mayo

I can't admire my spelling—I was, after all, seventeen years old. But you can't beat the philosophy for opening up the West, or discovering a better fuel, or anything else you care to name. And it's just as well that Joe and I picked medicine— it certainly was taken for granted by Father and Uncle Will that we would be the next Mayo brothers. No other career ever interested us anyway.

In my fifth-form year, I was elected president of the YMCA, my crowning accomplishment at Hill School, along with the wastebasket. I was required to give a speech in the study hall, and I was terrified at the prospect. I spent hours preparing some flowery words of acceptance and then, to make it seem extemporaneous, I printed it in tiny letters with a fine-point pen on the backs of two calling cards I could cup in my hand.

As I sat on the platform, listening to my introduction by the immediate past president, my terror gradually eased into paralytic panic. I rose numbly to my feet and faced the audience but my hand was shaking so violently that I couldn't read the small print on the cards. Things began to get hazy, so I simply recited the Lord's Prayer and sat down. I think this first speech was better than any I have made since.

In the summertime, when Johnny Berkman and I could escape the annual misery with our schoolbooks, we would slip away to St. Marys Hospital and help a surgical orderly named Mike. His duties included wheeling patients to the operating room, returning them after the operation and lifting their sleeping, inert bodies onto their beds. He also prepared the patients for surgery, shaving the area where the incision was to be made—except for the pubic hair of women, which the Sisters did themselves.

I think Johnny and I were about seventeen when Mike told us one day that he was planning to be away for about three weeks, visiting relatives. We offered ourselves as substitutes for the interval and we were accepted. We discovered instantly that we had been underestimating the role of orderly.

We were required to start work at five in the morning by shaving the patients—with a straight razor. Neither of us had ever used such a wicked-looking thing. Our first few patients appeared on the operating tables looking as though they required stitches rather than an incision, but we improved with experience.

When I was in the fourth form at Hill School, my brother Joe joined us there. He was only eleven and was even more homesick than I was, which I had thought was impossible. He also got into more trouble, because of two factors: his carefree, whimsical nature and his ill-starred fate to be caught in every wrongdoing he attempted. Hill School expelled him in his second year, to our parents' distress, and he then was sent to Gilman School in Baltimore where, mysteriously, he remained until graduation.

Joe was a lovable person, sunny and witty and without a shred of meanness. His good humor was infectious: you could lose a game of poker to him and enjoy it.

Around this time I showed my inherent good judgment by refusing to wrestle with Joe any more. Joe and I never wrote to one another during the months we were separated at school but we communicated by wrestling all over Mayowood as soon as summer united us. As the years passed, I was finding my four-year advantage in years was counting for less and less. One day it took a titan effort to pin Joe down; I rose exhausted and panting and promptly retired, undefeated. I explained that wrestling was a childish pastime.

My father came to my rescue after my fifth year at Hill School. That summer he hired an excellent tutor, Edward Pulling, a Princeton honor student, and I was given the opportunity of missing the last year at Hill if I could prepare myself for the Princeton entrance examinations during the summer. It was the most attractive goal of my life and I was inspired to work myself mercilessly. Pulling was a truly gifted teacher and between the two of us I somehow managed to be accepted by Princeton that fall. It remains the greatest scholastic achievement of my life.

Pulling later established Millbrook Preparatory School near Poughkeepsie, New York, and I gratefully sent three of our sons there.

The United States had entered World War I in April, 1917, while I was still at Hill. We older students patriotically bought Lee Enfield rifles discarded by the British, at fifteen dollars apiece, and organized three companies, who drilled spiritedly. I felt it gave me some slight prior experience when I joined Princeton's S.A.T.C., the Student Army Training Corps. The initials generally were interpreted to mean Safe At The College.

I rose splendidly to the rank of corporal. In the spring of 1918, the country faced a difficult situation with an untimely railway strike. College boys, largely unsympathetic with the strikers' point of view, volunteered to save the war effort by manning the railways themselves and the colleges obligingly set final examinations early that year. To my relief, I passed in everything but Greek and set off immediately for the Pittsburgh rail yards.

I was given a boring but simple task; I went around with a calibrator and a notebook, keeping record of the wear on the wheels of freight cars. I lived with the other college students in Pullmans in the railroads, so we could avoid facing the understandably outraged strikers outside. I think I must have even enjoyed myself. I remember that I felt the part of a railroader called for a plug of chewing tobacco in my cheek. I was chewing on my first plug, sitting loosely on a boxcar, when the train suddenly lurched a few feet and I swallowed the entire wad. That ended experiments with chewing tobacco forever.

Six weeks later the strike ended. I went home and pleaded with my parents to allow me to enlist, but they refused. In the fall of 1917, I went back to Princeton for my second year.

43

THREE

Father and Uncle Will had been commissioned as colonels in the Surgeon General's Office in Washington just after the United States went into World War I. They took an apartment there and alternated in it for six-week periods at a turn. Before long, both were promoted to the rank of brigadier general, which greatly facilitated such urgent matters as securing permission for me to visit them from Princeton.

I must say that being a brigadier general suited Uncle Will perfectly; he could look as though he were in full parade dress while wearing pajamas. My father suffered in comparison. If he couldn't find his overcoat with the general's brassy epaulets, he'd appear in a black civilian coat instead. The uniform somehow appealed to his sense of humor; he used to salute hotel doormen. And he griped like any buck private about army regulations, such as the one disqualifying men for active service if they wore dentures. "What do they want?" he'd snort. "Soldiers who can bite the Germans to death?"

I was still hoping to get my parents' permission to enlist, my strategy now being directed toward becoming a medical corpsman, which I reasoned would appeal to the Mayo brothers. They said, flatly, no. Instead I picked up some rugged training at an officers' training camp at Plattsburg, New York, where my good right eye won me a sharpshooter's badge. I was promoted to the rank of sergeant, which isn't easy to do if you're attending a camp to train officers.

The goal of the training, I was advised, was to turn me into a killer, with guts. It did succeed in making me courageous. With some other Princeton men similarly encouraged to heroism, I would steal pass slips, sign them myself and sneak out after taps to taste the giddy delights of New York night life. Our maneuvers were as brilliantly planned as military genius could ask: we would coordinate our watches, a vital factor, then hire a cab but defer paying the driver, instructing him to meet us at an agreed time and place so that we could return to camp before reveille.

Over and over, it was a faultless operation in the highest tradition of the service. We outdid ourselves on November 7, 1918, the day of the false armistice. That time, we hired two taxis to accommodate all the celebrants. The crowds in the streets of New York were so tumultuous that we had to hide one of our taxis in an alley to save it from being tipped over. I went into Delmonico's sometime during that night and saw women standing on the tables, drinking champagne.

Four days later, when the real armistice was announced, we had to do it all over again. This time we were issued genuine passes and we spent the entire night in the crowds that surged up and down Broadway, in and out of restaurants, over to Fifth Avenue, down to Greenwich Village. We sang "Tipperary" and screamed until we were hoarse.

In the melee, drunks who passed out were propped humanely against buildings so they wouldn't be trampled to death. Somehow, we made it back to Princeton and spent the next two days assigned to the task of cleaning up the astonishing amount of debris left from the celebration there. I still don't know how they cleaned up New York in time for World War II.

That year, Christmas at Mayowood was the usual joyful, impetuous family gathering, as far as I was concerned. To my parents' annoyance, I refused to interest myself in the crisis that was occurring at the Clinic, the greatest in its his-

45

tory to date. It smoldered all through that vacation, however, and I couldn't avoid knowing about it.

The background was this: As the group practice of medicine started to prove itself in the early 1900's, Father and Uncle Will began to be concerned about the structure of the partnerships. They realized that any deaths among the practicing members of the Clinic would cause a lawyers' feast, as the heirs and surviving members tried to estimate the worth of a Mayo Clinic partnership. They decided on a prudent and practical solution: papers should be drawn up establishing the agreement that heirs of any deceased partner would receive the equivalent of one year's income and have no further claim; also, while they were at it, that a partner who wanted to resign would be given a year's income as the value of his share. That way, the Mayo Clinic could not be depleted in perpetuity by gaps in its founding fathers.

It meant an expensive sacrifice for the families of all the doctors concerned. Dr. Stinchfield, the partner Grandfather obtained when he wanted to retire, signed it first, but reluctantly. My mother's brother, Dr. Christopher Graham, hesitated a long time but eventually signed it too. All the other partners were demoted, in a sense, and made members of the Mayo Clinic staff, with a satisfactory compensation.

I've realized many times since what a masterful piece of forethought is represented by that agreement. It means that I and my children don't own the Clinic, or any part of it, so as a principal victim I am in a good position to say how much I admire it. Without it, the Mayo Clinic would have been in fragments generations ago, pulled apart by the descendants of doctors.

Mother's brother Christopher was her favorite among the Grahams, which made her feel torn by his anguished indecision over signing that 1919 agreement. He was a remarkable man. He had attended the University of Minnesota, playing on the first football team there and getting a bachelor of science degree in 1887. Then he taught for two years before deciding to enroll at the University of Pennsylvania, where he obtained a degree in veterinary medicine in 1892. After a stint as a teacher in veterinary school, he was still dissatisfied so he put himself in medical school on the same campus and got his M.D. a year later, at the age of thirty-nine. In 1895, Father and Uncle Will made him a full partner in the Clinic.

The next partner arrived six years later. He was Dr. Henry Plummer, from nearby Racine, Minnesota, who filled a need in the partnership by being an authority on blood as well as skilled in microscopic examination of tissue, a developing science. The firm then became *Drs. Mayo, Stinchfield, Graham and Plummer.* The following year, a promising young surgeon named Dr. E. Starr Judd was assisting Father. Since he had married Father's and Uncle Will's niece Helen Berkman, it wasn't exactly astonishing that he would be the first surgeon ever to be admitted to the partnership. Father and Uncle Will liked to do all the surgery themselves, but the demand for operations had grown beyond their capacity to meet it. In 1903, the group added the name Judd to the list.

Although the partnership didn't resemble any existing clinic arrangement, the group in Rochester was known everywhere as the "Mayo Clinic." In 1909, the partners made it official and dropped their unwieldy title. With that, they sealed off expansion by partnership and hired new doctors on a salary basis.

It was a period of rapid development, in several directions. As young doctors turned up at the Clinic for postgraduate training in medicine, they were welcomed and designated as fellows of the Clinic. Uncle Will was on the Board of Regents of the University of Minnesota when he conceived the notion of making the Clinic a graduate school for the University's College of Medicine, something that was well on the way to happening on an informal basis.

He started the move by forming the Clinic into a corporate organization, in 1915, to simplify the paper work to come. Then Father and Uncle Will established what was

47

called the Mayo Foundation for Medical Education and Research, which they launched with a no-strings grant of $1,500,-000 out of their fraternal account. It was arranged that trustees would hold that fortune for a trial year, while the Clinic and the university tested the affiliation.

They were engulfed at once with an uproar of complaint from doctors all over the state. Some of them may have been motivated by the irritations of living side by side with doctors as mortal as they but well on their way to immortality. For whatever cause, they were protesting against the Mayo postgraduate school because they were certain that the Mayo brothers, somehow, would be gaining by it. The advantage to the Mayos was by no means clear, but bafflement only increased the fury of the opposition.

It *was* an unusual venture, unique to this day: the association of a university medical school with a private enterprise, the latter unsupported by a single tax dollar and therefore not susceptible to government influence. Luckily, the good name of the Mayo brothers withstood all the antagonism and the bill passed through the Minnesota legislature. The Board of Regents promptly demonstrated its support by extending the trial period from one to six years.

The following year, however, in 1917, the enemies of the graduate school had gained sufficient strength to have a new bill introduced to the legislature to have the affiliation dissolved. Uncle Will was asked to appear before the legislative body. He was an impressive man in any circumstances, but his dignity and composure that day were compelling. "I can't understand why all this opposition should be aroused at the affiliation with the university," he said quietly. "It seems to be the idea of some persons that no one can want to do anything for anybody without having some sinister or selfish motive back of it.

"If we wanted money, we have it. That can't be the reason for our offer. We want the money to go back to the people

48

from whom it came and we think we can best give it back to them by medical education."

It was clearly stated, and true. He closed with a quotation from Lincoln's Gettysburg Address: " 'That these dead shall not have died in vain.' That line explains why we want to do this thing. What better could we do than help young men become proficient in the profession so as to prevent needless deaths?" It was an emotional speech from that flint-faced man. Twenty-five years later, men who heard it were still talking about it. The bill of opposition to the graduate school was defeated.

Father and Uncle Will wiped out their savings with their endowment to the graduate school. They were left with their hugely profitable partnership in the material assets of the Clinic, such as the buildings, real estate, cash and securities, all of which amounted to about ten million dollars. Their next move was to protect these valuable assets, and at the same time the good name of the Clinic, by moving them out of reach of any partner, themselves included.

It was this final reorganization of the Clinic that caused the family disaster that lasted through Christmas of 1918 and well into the following year. Father and Uncle Will set up a new board of trustees to hold all the Mayo Clinic assets, calling it the Mayo Properties Association (it now is known simply as the Mayo Foundation). They asked the other principal partners to go along with them in forfeiting this fortune but, to their consternation, my beloved Uncle Christopher flatly refused. He had endured stripping his descendants of most of their legacy, but this final disinheritance was too much.

The storm at Mayowood shook the family profoundly. Mother kept pleading with Father to stop Uncle Will from continuing with the scheme, or to find a solution acceptable to her brother. Father kept quiet; he deemed it inadvisable to admit to Mother that every detail of the plan was as much his as Uncle Will's and that he was in total agreement. Angry and bitter, Uncle Kit resigned. Father and Uncle Will were

49

desolated by his decision, but they didn't hesitate to accept his resignation. Mother was in tears for days.

Today, an independent Board of Governors operates the Mayo Clinic. No one "owns" it, or ever will, which is its guarantee of survival. Proof of this was demonstrated beyond dispute in 1939, when my father and Uncle Will died, only two months apart. People speculated on what would happen to the Clinic—nothing happened to the Clinic. It continued without a ripple, thanks to the unselfish arrangements Father and Uncle Will had battled through twenty years before.

The final reorganization was completed in 1923. The partners then became known as "voluntary associates," an awkward term, and Father and Uncle Will went on salary. They went so far in their altruistic devotion to the Clinic that they pegged their salaries legally, along with those of others on the staff. Uncle Will said he didn't want any doctor getting an income large enough "to keep his children on the beach in Miami when they ought to be working."

The rift in the family healed slowly. Father and Uncle Christopher had been close warm friends for too long to remain hostile forever. Gradually, their mutual interest in farming drew them together again and their relationship seemed as before. But it was more than two years before Uncle Will and Uncle Christopher were over the bitterness. Mother wrote me at Princeton in May, 1921: "You will be glad to know that Uncle Will and Uncle Kit have become reconciled. I'll tell you about it when I see you. Uncle Will made the first advances in a very fine way."

My mother was slow to forgive Uncle Will too. Over the years, she often was furious with him over something he did or said, usually because she felt he was slighting Father in some way. She fumed for years over a casual remark Uncle Will made shortly after she and Father were married. "Now Charlie," Uncle Will announced, "you will have to be the work horse and I'll be the show horse." Mother quoted that whenever she was indignant at Uncle Will even years later, while I was growing up. Her nature basically was forgiving, however, and her attitude to him always eased back to genuine friendliness.

She was a truly loving person, unstinting of her strength and compassion. She would take off in the middle of the night to nurse a sick neighbor or friend. She was always adopting people; I remember one aged man I used to encounter on the terrace, napping in the sunshine—he spent his last years with us, tended by her.

And she was unflappable, even in the face of Father's impulsive tendency to invite visiting doctors and their entire families to stay at Mayowood for as long as they liked. Once he telephoned Mother to say that a hundred librarians, members of the American Medical Library Association, were on their way to Mayowood at his invitation. Would she show them around? She did, and served them tea as well.

She was an extraordinary hostess. She could, and did, effortlessly entertain the President of the United States or exotic royalty but she had a flair for the big parties she gave for Rochester friends and relatives. I can give an example of one that she wrote me about in 1925, when I was in medical school. She wrote that she was giving a dinner party for seventy-five that evening, "a la country dress in clothes of the 1870's." She was putting tables in the gallery and two dining rooms, red tablecloths in the first two rooms and old-fashioned blue in the children's dining room "and some marvellous colored artificial flowers for decorations."

There was to be a fiddler, she continued gaily, with Uncle Kit, Aunt Blanche and some others accompanying him. "They were out to practice last night and we made out a program and selected pieces. It's upstairs, but we begin dancing with a Grand March, then have a few old-fashioned waltzes scattered through the evening, the old Sour Kraut, Virginia Reel, three-step, polkas, heel and toe, two Schottisches, two quadrilles and end up with Home Sweet Home, early.

"Have marvellous prizes for the best performers (from the ten cents store). Will have tables for cards for any tiring of dancing.

"I will give you my menu: peanuts (salted, prepared at home), boiled ham (hot), escalloped potatoes, root-a-bagas (?), cucumber pickles, cabbage salad (with vinegar sugar), baking powder biscuits (hot) with honey and butter (both on tables, butter in old prints with butter dish and knife to be passed), coffee (soft sugar and cream on tables). For dessert, pumpkin pie, cheese and big soft cookies with a raisin in the center of each. One change of plates for pie, but same fork used."

The attention to detail was characteristic of her, and so was the energy and zest. She took time to write me on the morning of the party, I gathered, for she concluded, "I'm a little short of help so must go and help set tables. I'm going to the Congregational Church for lunch and International Study class afterwards. Very interesting."

Another time that prodigious woman wrote me, "Had dinner for fifty-three last night, and had the Magazine Club out today, one hundred strong, and had a good time. Have Auntie Trude's club tomorrow."

She rarely mentioned the pain she was enduring in those years from an arthritic hand, so swollen and distorted that she detested the look of it. She referred to it only when it made it difficult for her to write her weekly letters to her brood.

In addition to all these activities, she found the time and heart to take in two children who needed homes and raise and educate them along with the troublesome six of us. One was John Nelson, who came to Mayowood as a small boy and remained until he graduated with a degree in engineering. We're out of touch but the last I heard he was in California with a wife and some five or six children.

The other was an infant girl when Mother brought her home. "The baby came a week ago," mother wrote me, "and we have her all settled in her new home and diet. She needed us and I do wish I felt young enough to keep her. . . . She should have a young mother and father I think, but just now she needs food and love and good care and she is getting it." She certainly was; Mother mentioned in passing that she was feeding the baby herself, starting at five-thirty in the morning.

The next note about the baby made the matter of finding her young parents recede somewhat. Mother said she intended to "give her a good start and perhaps find a dear home for her." After that her letters were giddy with fondness whenever she reported on the baby. Her eyes were such a beautiful blue, she told me, that she was calling her "Eyes of the Sky." She asked for suggestions for a name, and I sent "Marilyn," which was accepted.

It was a clear improvement over Eyes of the Sky but it led to later difficulties. I was seeing Marilyn Miller at the time, which is why I liked the name, but mother's adored little infant grew into a teen-ager who was convinced—in the absence of her own natural parents—that she was Marilyn Miller's illegitimate daughter, fathered by me. The family was more than a little flustered when she first began spreading news of this interesting parentage, but no proof to the contrary could dissuade her. Eventually she married and left Rochester and I haven't heard from her in years. Come to think of it, we never did call her Marilyn; she was always Sally to the family. *Sally* was one of Ziegfeld's fine plays.

I fell in love with Marilyn Miller, the Ziegfeld Follies star, while I was at Princeton. One reviewer of the period described her as "a sunbeam who sings like a skylark on a spring morning and dances divinely." I would subscribe to that. We met in 1920, when father took Joe, me and a roommate of mine, Robert Bruce Young of Fort Worth, on a trip to England. Marilyn was on the boat going over, traveling with her sister Claire. She was only nineteen at the time but

53

she already had been married twice: her second husband had died recently.

We were all infatuated with her, including Father, of course. Her nickname, incongruously, was "Lumpy"; she had been called "Sugar Lump" as a baby. I don't think she ever took me too seriously, but she always welcomed me backstage with flattering warmth and I was able to cut an impressive figure with my friends with my ability to get tickets through her for her sold-out Broadway shows.

It was on the boat trip that Father gave Joe and me his first and last lecture on the subject of drinking. He was below in his cabin with a bout of seasickness and Joe and I took advantage of the situation to order a bottle of wine each with our dinner that night. We were sipping it grandly when Father made a surprise appearance. He looked at us stonily for a long moment and then said, "I'll see you in the cabin when you finish."

When we joined him nervously, he was very grave. "Your mother doesn't drink at all," he began, "and I don't drink very much. Your grandfather drank some, but then your grandmother didn't drink at all." He paused to consider. "I guess it comes out even," he decided, "so just be careful about the future." He wasn't much inclined, as you can see, to playing the heavy father.

Mother had no taste for severity either. Once she wrote me, after a visit together, "It was nice to see you kiddies and to feel you are getting *the best*. . . . We do so want that you dear children should have all that we missed and still regret. No doubt you'll have your regrets—and some day may criticize us for misdirecting you, but you will be very sure that it was lack of *light* on our part and not intentional."

We disembarked at Edinburgh and Father had a mysterious trip of his own to make, about which we were tactful enough not to inquire, so he arranged to have us driven to London in a chauffeured Daimler. The massive car had a luggage rack on its roof, which inspired us to the decision to ride all the way to London on top of the car. Which we did, putting the luggage inside with the mortified chauffeur.

My next year at Princeton was made memorable by my visits to Broadway and Marilyn Miller. When we went out, I had no compunction about allowing her to pick up the check; after all, I was a college student and she was making $3500 a week. She would scoop me up into whatever she was doing at the time of my visit and I went along, dazzled and delighted. Once when I went backstage on a Saturday night, she announced that she had been invited to a house party on some Long Island estate and that I must come along.

I demurred, having nothing with me but a comb and toothbrush, but she paid no attention. When we arrived at the lavish mansion where the party was in gaudy progress, I found that I was assigned to share a bedroom with an elegant and famous actor, the lead in *The Cradle Snatchers*, I believe, who had brought with him the most costly and abundant wardrobe I'd ever seen. One item that struck me as particularly splendid was his pajamas, silk and striped like a zebra. When breakfast was brought to us in bed the next morning, I skulked down under the sheets to conceal the fact that I had slept in my shorts.

Later a chauffeur drove me to the station so I could get a train. Just as it was pulling away, he slung a big pigskin bag up beside my feet. There was no time to rectify the error—some helpful maid had packed the actor's clothes, thinking they were mine. He had been so haughty with me I must admit I took a wicked relish in envisioning his apoplexy at the loss of his garments. Through Marilyn, the suitcase eventually was returned to him.

That same winter I was at a particularly gay party at Marilyn's home when I decided to demonstrate my skill as a surgeon. Marilyn's mother had a wen on her scalp and I suggested that I could remove it for her, on the spot. She was as reckless as I, for she agreed and I got a razor blade and some eyebrow tweezers and sterilized them in gin, which happened to be in good supply.

I had seen the operation performed dozens of times and I was airily confident. I cut out the wen with some dexterity and then it began to bleed. Lord! how it bled. The people around me were laughing and drinking, confident that this was part of the performance, but I was terrified. Never in my life have I sobered up as quickly. I finally did get the bleeding stopped, but I never again volunteered surgery as a party trick.

My letters home were full of Marilyn, of course, and I think I told Mother once that I planned to marry her, after I became a doctor. She wrote me a gentle caution, "Look for the genuine, the wearing qualities in both men and women. When we are young, they all seem sincere and fine, but as we get older we get disillusioned sometimes. Use your head, Sonny dear, and go slow."

My ardor took little note of such subtlety so later she had a talk with me. Speaking very carefully, she said, "You know, if you marry Marilyn Miller, you will always be known as Mr. Miller. And her career will be so distracting that you won't be able to concentrate on your own—you could never develop to be a good doctor." That sunk home at once. I decided she was right, and my relationship with Marilyn remained where it was, a warm friendship and nothing more.

The following year, Marilyn put me into an exceedingly awkward position. I had graduated from Princeton, though narrowly, and was a first year student at the University of Pennsylvania Medical School. She was in Philadelphia trying out a new show, *Peter Pan*, and I was called out of a classroom to take a telephone call from her.

"I have something wrong with my nose," she explained. "What should I do?"

My professor of ear, nose and throat ailments was a Dr. Fetteroff and, since I knew no one else in Philadelphia in

56

that specialty, I recommended him. Marilyn thanked me and made an appointment with Dr. Fetteroff for the next day. Around the time she informed me that the appointment was taking place, I was called from class a second time for a telephone call. It was my professor, Dr. Fetteroff. He informed me, in a level, expressionless voice, that Miss Miller would not permit him to treat her without my approval.

Horrified, I hurried to his office. With all the respectful manners he would have accorded a distinguished colleague, he told me that Miss Miller had polyps in her nose and they should be removed. He then went through the charade of showing me the polyps, although he must have known I'd never examined a nose before in my life, and then he stepped back and waited for my opinion. Marilyn was watching me expectantly, so I assured her that I agreed that Dr. Fetteroff should remove the polyps. I avoided looking at him, and got out of the office as quickly as possible.

My most serious escapade in medical school was the time I got arrested and put into jail. It was during prohibition and we medical students were having a beer party. When supplies ran low, we tossed a coin to see who would go out for more and, as inevitably happens when I'm involved in a coin toss, I lost. I took the two gallon jugs to the speak-easy we patronized, Schick's, on Woodland Avenue near 38th Street, and rapped on the door in the approved code. I was just getting the jugs filled when the police broke in. They lined everyone in the place up against a wall and then herded us all into a police wagon. We called them Black Marias then.

During the bumpy ride to the West Philadelphia police station, I considered my ruined medical career. When my disgrace was discovered, I was certain to be expelled. When we arrived at the station, all the prisoners were required to sign their names on the police register, a chore that put quite a strain on some of my more inebriated associates. We then were locked in a cell, packed in so tightly that we were obliged to stand.

I waited in dread and despair, but sure that my friends eventually would find me. A few hours passed before John Henry, a fellow medical student, arrived. He whispered that he couldn't find my name on the register. "What name did you sign?" he asked. I remembered only that I'd had the presence of mind not to write Charles W. Mayo, but I couldn't remember what I had substituted.

John Henry somehow obtained the register and held it up to the bars so I could read it. I went down the list of scrawls and finally found my own handwriting. I had signed John Alden, an interesting choice. My friends paid my fine and I was free a few minutes later and, by a miracle, was never reported.

In medical school, my best subject was dermatology. It was the direct result of the professor of dermatology being a man who disliked the Mayos, having left the Clinic under circumstances not of his choosing. When he found a Mayo registered in his class, he saw his opportunity for revenge. I think it was the only name he bothered to learn all year. He always started his classes with a question period and he always asked me the toughest questions he could devise. In self-protection, I took pains to be prepared, with the result that I got my highest marks in his subject.

My marks in other subjects fluctuated. I think first year chemistry was my poorest. We were only six weeks into the course when the professor set a small test. Afterward, he called me aside. I can see him still. An explosion in the laboratory had left him with a droop at one corner of his mouth, due to a cut facial nerve, and it gave him a permanent sneer under the best of circumstances, which this wasn't. "Mr. Mayo," he said coldly, "if I am to judge what you know by what you wrote, you don't know anything."

It was not a very heartening remark, but contained some truth. As a matter of fact, this same tough professor later flunked my jolly cousin, Johnny Berkman, who had accompanied me to Pennsylvania. Johnny enrolled at the University of Iowa after that, and got his medical degree there.

In my sophomore year one afternoon, I found myself feeling desperately ill. I was writing a midterm examination and Dean Gallagher happened to notice me. "Dean" Gallagher, as she was known affectionately by undergraduates who came to her with their troubles, was really Miss Lillian Gallagher, secretary to Dr. William Pepper, dean of the medical school. She arranged to have me excused from the examination and taken to a doctor, where my temperature was found to be 104. I had a prostatic abscess, for which an operation was done, and then rheumatic fever.

Dean Gallagher realized that I needed months of quiet in bed so she arranged with a friend of Father's, a Dr. Edward Martin, that I would be taken to the spare room in his home near Marion, which is just outside Philadelphia. I knew the Martins slightly; he had been a professor of surgery and invited me to visit him some weeks previous to my illness. Father and Mother were consulted by telephone and agreed gratefully to the arrangement; they were about to leave on an extended trip, to Europe I think.

I stayed with the Martins for five months and it was the most momentous period of my life. I emerged fully restored to health, without the slightest damage to my heart, thanks to Dr. Martin's masterfully simple treatment, but this was the smallest benefit of all that I gained at his home.

For one thing, I learned about pain: it is a lesson every young doctor should have as part of his formal training. It must be learned firsthand, I regret to say; no one can describe adequately how livid pain feels, how it turns all your thoughts to the selfish ones of endurance and survival and robs you of your concern for others. The agony I endured was such that I couldn't bear the slightest jarring, not even the vibration of a person walking across my bedroom floor. I spent weeks in that kind of pain and I have had no trouble since putting myself into the place of a person who is suffering. During those months of illness, I became a much better doctor than I would have been. Medical school gave me my professional training, but pain gave me compassion.

I recovered slowly. The Martin home was a quiet one in the country, surrounded by the most beautiful garden I have ever seen. I felt a sense of peacefulness and was content to lie alone and still in bed for hours, watching with interest as my wrists or knees ballooned with swelling. When it came time for me to leave my bed I was so weak that I came downstairs the first time by sitting on the steps and going in this position from one to the other.

During my convalescence, I discovered that the great gift the Martins had for me was more than my health, and the wisdom I gained from pain; it was the gift of myself. At their home, I learned to have confidence and pride in myself for the first time in my life.

It wasn't surprising that as a young man I should have felt a wretched sense of my own inferiority. Joe and I eventually had discovered that our father and uncle were world-famous men, not only respected in countries we scarcely could spell, but revered. If one of them was ill halfway across the continent, tracks were cleared so the other could rush to his side and the newspapers would chronicle the trip on their front pages. As a small child, I had an adoring relationship with my genial father but saw little of him; as a teen-ager I was intimidated by his importance.

He felt it, I gather, and it made him lonely. His letters to me were brusque: "My dear Charles: I have a minute to write and will send $200 in this," a rare note from him, received at Princeton, said, "which will be needed anyway, without waiting to hear. Love, Father." He was generous with me, in this offhanded way; on my sixteenth birthday, he gave me a four-cylinder Saxon, a single-seater convertible with wire wheels. I was delighted, but what I wanted more was his admiration.

Mother used to tell me that Father felt that Joe and I weren't close to him. In her letters, she pleaded with me to confide in my father, assuring me that he had a high regard for me. And I had a high regard for him, but we couldn't get through to one another. I understand it is not uncommon in sons of famous men; it has happened, in some degree, to me and my sons.

It was Dr. and Mrs. Martin who healed the sense of aching inadequacy that I had been feeling ever since my boyhood. They loved me, and they showed it without reservation; to them I wasn't the less-than-brilliant son of a Mayo, I was a fine young man, valuable, unique. They were thee-and-thou Quakers, simple and wise, and they accomplished the miracle of my growth to self-respect with gentleness and gaiety. As the months of my recovery passed, I gained a sense of my own worth and the courage to believe in it.

I cannot measure my gratitude to the Martins. When I met the woman I wanted to marry, they were the first people I wanted her to meet. She fell under their spell at once, as I expected, and adopted some of their tastes, such as their Quaker preference for all-white flowers. And when our first son was born, I wanted to name him Edward Martin. Mother was dismayed at the suggestion of disloyalty, so we agreed to name that boy Charles Horace, after my father. Fourteen months later we had another son and this time there was no objection to calling him Edward Martin Mayo.

If I can digress for a moment, I'd like to mention Dr. Martin's surpassing tenderness with his namesake and godchild. When Ned was born, he sent him a gold cup engraved with a rare gift, a motto of Ned's own. It is *Inter Primos*, which means *Among the First*. A man can live by that with dignity and achievement, and avoid breaking his heart in the brutal quest for solitary glory; it demonstrates Dr. Martin's compassion and sensitivity.

After that, Dr. Martin regularly wrote chatty man-to-man

61

letters to Ned, even when he was an infant. He was one year old when Dr. Martin wrote, "I am keen to see you that we may talk over matters of mutual interest." A few years later, when he had word that I was overworking and had been instructed to get more sleep, Dr. Martin sent Ned a police club, with instructions to "brandish it and yell scram at guests who stay late."

On one occasion, Ned sent him a gold spoon. "It is not a soup spoon," Dr. Martin wrote, in thanking him, "nor a tea spoon, nor a salt spoon, nor a gravy spoon, nor a mincemeat spoon, nor a scrapple spoon, nor a sausage spoon. It is designed only for sweet things, candy and sugar. It shall never be used by me for purposes other than these."

He added, "Should you see your parents, give them our love."

When he was invited to the christening, he sent Ned a telegram of comfort and instruction: "USUALLY SAFE AND PAINLESS. SHALL YOU BE HOME WEEK BEGINNING JUNE NINE-TEENTH PLAN TO COME ABOUT THEN. ADVISE INVITING PARENTS TO CEREMONY. MAKE IT INFORMAL BUT CORDIAL. THEY WILL BE PLEASED AND MAY COME. LOVE TO YOUR WHOLE FAMILY. EDWARD MARTIN."

We sent him a picture of Ned at the age of two. He wrote Ned immediately, congratulating him on the expression of "revolt at past, present and future tyrannies and grim determination to even things up some day."

He died in 1938, at the age of seventy-nine, of a painful and disfiguring cancer of the nose. Swarthmore College named a biological lab building in his honor. Two weeks before his death, we happened to visit him at Orchard Farm, where the Martins had cared for me during that long illness, and Ned, then six, gave Dr. Martin an all-day sucker. Despite the fact that he was near his death, and knew it perfectly well, Dr. Martin wrote Ned a gravely courteous thank-you: "I still have the all-day sucker, and each time I take a lick at it, I think what a fine guest you were and how nice it was to have you."

As can be seen, he was a man of outstanding kindness and tenderness, and knew how to make vulnerable people feel mighty. I came to the Martins feeling lost, frightened and inferior; I left with inner strength and a degree of conviction that I would succeed. More than forty years later, I was asked which year of my life I would repeat, if I could, and I answered unhesitatingly, "The year I spent with the Martins." I would take it again anytime, pain and all.

In the fall following my bout of rheumatic fever, I was able to return to medical school. I shared an apartment with two other medical students, Mark Nesbitt and Huston St. Clair. Huston and I were not neat—let's put it that way—and it fell to Mark to keep control of the debris from time to time. One morning when things were particularly disheveled, Mark having fallen behind in his duties, we were appalled to notice out of the window that a limousine had just arrived and Father and Mother were emerging from it, accompanied by several distinguished-looking people.

We performed a miracle of instant housekeeping by hurling bottles, dirty dishes and discarded clothing into the closet. By the time Father knocked on the door, the place looked reasonably presentable. He ushered in Lord and Lady Dawson of Penn, and their daughter, the Honorable Sybille. Lord Dawson was physician to the king of England and was in Philadelphia with his family to attend a medical convention. Father thought the Hon. Sybille would appreciate meeting people her own age, so he invited them to visit us.

Just as he finished the introductions, Mother happened to open a closet door. A cascade of empty bottles flowed around her feet and there was a frozen moment when we were a tableau. Then Mother laughed, followed by Father and the British. When it seemed safe, we joined in.

In my junior and senior year of medicine, I served a regular tour of duty in one of Philadelphia's poorest quarters, where the population was mostly Italian. It gave me a good supply of wine and also my only experience at delivering babies. I discovered at once that babies have a strong inclination to be born in the middle of the night, rather than in normal working hours. We medical students took turns going out on night calls and I was exceedingly nervous when I encountered my first delivery.

The woman was having a slow and difficult labor, which added to my alarm. The bed on which she lay didn't have a footboard, so I stood at the end of it with a sheet in a tight grip, gave her the other end of the sheet and begged her to pull. She cooperated at once, with which her membrane ruptured and I was drenched in her water. With practice I improved, at least so far as positioning myself. I think I delivered about thirty babies, and quite a few of them, Italian, Negro, all kinds, were named for me by their kindly grateful mothers.

Since then the closest I have come to delivering babies is when I encountered an extrauterine pregnancy, the so-called "tube" pregnancy, which requires the surgical removal of the fetus. Early in my career I joined my father in writing a paper for the *Southern Surgical Journal* on a method of performing hysterectomies chemically, rather than surgically. He advocated packing zinc chloride into the uterus; in seven days it comes out, leaving the uterus intact but destroying its mucous membrane.

Dr. B. C. Hurst was professor of obstetrics while I was in medical school. He was a relaxed man. "The best obstetrical instruments," he used to say, "are a long black cigar and patience." Caesarians were just becoming popular at that time and he felt that they were performed more often than they should be. He advised us, "There are three requirements for doing a Caesarian: one, that the patient must be a woman; two, that she must be pregnant; and three, that she can't speak any English."

My roommate Huston kept a horse while he was a medical student. He had paid $350 for the animal and another $75 for the saddle and bridle. As graduation approached, he was anxious to sell. Ed Ryan, our bartender and mentor, suggested that we take it to the horse auction conveniently located across from Schick's, the speak-easy.

On the day appointed for the auction, I rounded up some of our friends to ensure that the sale would go well. The bidding started at sixty dollars, which was outrageously low, so I said, "One hundred and fifty!" to give it a boost. After that, there was silence. The auctioneer began counting, "Going . . . going . . ." and in my agitation I heard myself cry, "One hundred and *sixty!*"

We were glum when we realized that we had bought the horse, bridle, saddle and all. We trudged back to Ed Ryan and told him about it. He seemed to find it vastly amusing, which pained us, but he calmed down and went to the auctioneer and explained what had happened, convulsing himself with laughter again, and got our money back for us. Huston eventually gave the horse away to the woman from whom we rented the apartment. She had been most kind to him all winter.

It was in the fall of my final year at medical school that I happened to attend a fraternity dance in the Sylvania Hotel. I was stag, and looking over the attractive women in the room when I happened to see a stunning, small blonde. I had come with someone who said he knew her—Nicholson, it was, who became an orthopedist and practiced outside of Philadelphia—so I persuaded him to introduce us the next time she danced by and then I cut in.

Her name was Alice Plank and I was impressed with her from the first moment I saw her. There was a grace to her, and a lot of femininity, and she was ravishingly pretty, with dark blue eyes and a gamin grin. I tried to think of some-

65

thing debonair to say, but what came out was, "Do you ride horseback?" She said she did and I was encouraged, thinking I could learn her telephone number if she agreed to go riding with me. I put it to her with that subtlety for which I'm famous up and down the Mississippi: "We must go riding sometime. What's your telephone number?"

She glared at me. "I'm not in the habit of giving my telephone number to people I've just met," she informed me loftily. "Particularly not when they've been drinking."

I retired defeated but some months later, in the spring, toward the end of my senior year, I saw her again. This time it was at the university's annual dance, known as the Ivy Ball. I was stag again and this time she was with Karl Robinson, who played on the Pennsylvania football team. Nothing daunted, I cut in again and offered to drive them both home if they required a ride. It was cunningly planned so that I could obtain her address.

It turned out that several of her friends wanted lifts, so I stuffed them all into the four-door Packard convertible that had been my Pennsylvania graduation gift from my parents. My scheme was dashed again, however: that night, Alice was staying with a girl friend.

Somehow I finally did get her telephone number and, just to make sure that she didn't think I was indifferent about her, I called her every hour all day.

My courtship of Alice meant that I lost the title "One-a-Week Mayo" that had been bestowed upon me by friends. Until she arrived, there had been a brisk turnover in the girls I dated, mainly because I had the sensible plan to delay marriage until I was established as a doctor and could afford to support a wife. This plan no longer seemed sensible, or even feasible, after I met Alice.

Alice lived in Upper Darby, which is outside Philadelphia, and her father was in the butter and egg business. He was a quiet man, which I found unnerving. When I would call for Alice, he would sometimes come out just as I was

66

getting out of the car and survey me silently. Once, when I feared that he might smell alcohol on my breath, I declined to accompany him back to the house, but pretended instead to be examining the tires. I'd look at one closely and then kick it a bit, repeating the farce with the next tire. I circled the car three times before Alice came out; I don't know what he was thinking about my performance.

Alice wanted to be a painter and she was studying at the School of Design for Women. I used to refer to it, in my jocular fashion, as "the School of Designing Women" and I had a gag for a time, which she never appreciated much, in which I'd complain that I had been misunderstood—I hadn't been proposing marriage, I'd been asking her to go to the movies. Despite these portents, she agreed to marry me. I asked her father's permission in the traditional way, and he gave it. He added proudly, "You're getting a filly with not a pimple on her." You don't often hear eulogies like that.

When my sister Esther heard of the engagement, she thoughtfully sent Alice an early picture of me. In it, I was wearing round spectacles, a high hard collar and the expression of a sick simp. Alice must have had second thoughts, but she stuck by me. That Esther is a card.

Mother invited Alice to visit Mayowood, "so you can see what you're getting into," as she graciously put it, and my parents welcomed her warmly. Alice was only nineteen and naturally was tremulous but Mother endeared herself forever with Alice by saying, "Look us over carefully, Alice. I want you to like us—we're so hoping you will like us."

Mother had some forthright advice for Alice. "You're going to do just as I did, exactly," she cautioned her. "You'll find you haven't married a Mayo, you've married the Mayo Clinic. Remember, the Clinic will always come first, then you, then your children." I think Alice discovered that Mother hadn't been exaggerating.

Mother was as consecrated to medicine as any Mayo. She wrote me when I first started medical school: "Medicine, the

67

greatest profession in the world, not excepting the ministry, when not undertaken lightly or for commercial reasons entirely. A doctor's calling is a sacred calling and only high-minded men should enter the ranks. It is our earnest prayer that you and Joseph may meet this requirement."

I may have given the impression that I was a frivolous student, but this attitude was confined strictly to my spare time. In the classroom I did my level best, worried all the time at the cost to my own self-respect and the Mayo name if I failed. Where my education was concerned, I was earnest and humorless.

But I did cavort afterward. Perhaps the best example of the capering side of my nature was my membership in the West Philadelphia Athletic Association, a barmy group of four medical students, none of whom was athletic. The WPAA once awarded me a small cup, which I still treasure, engraved "To the Club's Best Singer." This is pretty comical in itself. Other members were Ralph Lynch, our founder, John Barnwell, his roommate, Charles Killen and Henry Smith (hard-boiled and the only non-medic).

It amused us at dances where there was an orchestra to request what we claimed was our favorite piece of music, a ghastly gem titled "Love Sends a Little Gift of Roses." During the rendition of this, Lynch would recite the Club Poem, which all of us could recall accurately for the rest of our lives:

> Ah, girls who never can be mine!
> On every lane and street
> I hear the rustle of their gowns
> The whisper of their feet.
> Their glances shy as wine
> Provoke the unpossessive sigh.
> Ah, girls who never can be mine!

I've been told there seems to be a line missing, but I refuse to believe it.

68

The most illustrious organization I ever joined, by contrast, was the Princeton Quadrangle Club, which later included Adlai Stevenson. I knew him quite well but had a slighter acquaintance with another illustrious Princeton undergraduate of the same period, F. Scott Fitzgerald. Our paths seldom crossed, even though he came from St. Paul, Minnesota, which is my part of the country.

The Quadrangle Club, as I recall, used to gather in what we called "bicker sessions," those wordy, idealistic and philosophic debates that are a valuable part of campus experience. In those years the sessions invariably got around to the subject of sex, which interested us all profoundly. I'm told this custom endures, wherever college students collect for any length of time.

As someone who was a youth in the Roaring Twenties, I affirm my conviction that while the do-gooders will always be with us, and are not without influence, they will never be able to interfere substantially with man's appetite for three things: alcohol, tobacco and sex.

In retrospect, considering the tumultuous years of my formal education, I am more and more persuaded that education doesn't come entirely from books, lectures and laboratories. An inestimable part of a man's knowledge is derived from the friendships he makes in his lifetime. These have much variety, of course, and some seem very slight. But it's my theory that every human relationship can be an asset for personal development, if put in its right perspective.

My father hung a quotation from John Ruskin on his office wall and I now keep it near me. It is: "The entire object of true education is to make people not merely do the right thing but enjoy the right things—not merely industrious, but to love industry—not merely learned, but to love knowledge —not merely pure, but to love purity—not merely just, but to hunger and thirst after justice."

He tried to live by that, and so have I.

69

FOUR

I began my required year of internship in 1926, in Robert Packer Hospital in Sayre, Pennsylvania. It's about eighteen miles southeast of Elmira, New York, and was founded by a Mayo alumnus, Dr. Donald Guthrie, who had been one of Father's first assistants. Quite a few Robert Packer interns seem to turn up at Mayo Clinic later for their postgraduate study.

In my day, interns were paid one hundred dollars a year. Salaries have improved considerably since then. When my son Charlie took the same route from the University of Pennsylvania Medical School to Robert Packer Hospital a generation later, he was paid $175 a month. I couldn't refrain from protesting at the injustice of my stipend compared to his, but Charlie said he could explain it.

"Did you ever stop to think, Father," he suggested kindly, "that was all you were worth?"

In any case, I didn't even get the hundred dollars. I had a casual habit while at Sayre of picking up the hospital telephone whenever the spirit moved me and putting in a call to Alice. As I was leaving in June, counting on that hundred dollars to help with the cost of the honeymoon, I was presented instead with a telephone bill: I had not only spent my entire year's income phoning Philadelphia, but I owed the hospital an additional hundred dollars.

Alex Steward, a great friend of mine from medical school, also interned at Robert Packer. He had been in the LaFayette Esquadrille during the war and cut quite a dashing figure. Our youngest son is named for him.

Alex and I shared in all the really cerebral undertakings which are part of an intern's life, such as using the ambulances to transport bootlegged stimulants and smuggling alcohol from the hospital stores to further a serious research project we were conducting, our attempt to determine the exact proportion of raw alcohol which, when mixed with soda pop, will render an exhausted intern intoxicated without actually causing paralysis or blindness. I understand interns all over the world are still at work on this intriguing medical problem.

Whenever we were short of funds, we had a quick and easy source: we would sell our blood to the hospital. I think the blood bank got gallons from Alex and me that year, a pint at a time.

Alex was from Virginia and had plenty of southern pride. One night when we were returning unsteadily to the hospital, I was indiscreet enough to call him a sonofabitch. I forget why.

He stopped. "Do you know what we do in the South when someone calls us a sonofabitch?" he inquired softly.

"No," I said, interested. "What?"

For an answer, he knocked me down. As I sat there on the sidewalk, I remembered that I had been carrying a pint of whiskey in my back pocket. Alex helped me up, apologizing profusely, and I felt the trickle of liquid running down my leg, hoping desperately that it was blood. Unhappily, it was not.

One night I was returning to the hospital from a supply mission at the speak-easy. As it was after hours, it seemed a prudent maneuver to escape detection by crawling through a dark ward on my way to my room, rather than using the lighted corridor. I was halfway across the sleeping ward when the light switch suddenly clicked on and I beheld the figure of the outraged night supervisor.

71

A friend was with me in this venture so we were both called up on the carpet, in quaking fear that we would be thrown out. We were fortunate; our punishment was the relatively minor one of losing our Christmas leaves.

For my Christmas dinner that year I therefore went along with Alex, who admired the beautiful daughter of a local Episcopalian minister and had been invited to her home for the day. We attended the church service, of course, under the circumstances. Alex had a ten-dollar bill in one pocket and a one-dollar bill in another and when the collection plate was passed, he accidentally put the ten-dollar bill on it. We could hardly stand the rest of the service. As soon as it ended, we rushed to the rear of the church and retrieved his ten-dollar bill.

As an intern I was now "Dr. Mayo" for the first time. I found it created a number of problems. Most people asked if I was a relative of the famous Mayo doctors, and my affirmative reply usually led to lengthy inquiries about Father and Uncle Will and the Clinic, or anecdotes about someone's great-aunt who had gone to the Mayo Clinic with some fascinating symptoms, which the narrator could recall in detail. In self-protection, I learned to mumble my name so indistinctly that the patient never caught it.

I suppose there may have been deeper reasons for mumbling the name Mayo. Certainly, it was an intimidating name for a young doctor to carry, particularly one who was displaying only moderate ability. I was conscious of the older doctors assessing this young Mayo. It was to be expected, but I was plunged into despair whenever I intercepted an exchange of significant glances between them, particularly if I was doing something in an uninspired manner.

To protect myself as much as possible from the disdain or disappointment of the older doctors, I determined to be the best damned intern I could. I performed my medical assignments with care and concentration, at the pace of a painstaking man, and I was hard on myself when my inexperience

72

caused me to make a mistake. Whenever there was an opportunity to watch a treatment or technique new to me, I paid attention. I even formed the habit, and it became lifelong, of getting to the hospital just a little earlier than anyone else and staying just a little later.

I didn't think it was a good idea to let the Mayo name down any more than I could help. By pushing myself to the limit, and then a bit more, I could perhaps make a decent showing. But I felt inadequate, so often.

I finished my internship in June, getting off a week early so Alice and I could have time for a honeymoon before I was due in Rochester. The wedding was on June 25, 1927. I was twenty-eight, almost twenty-nine, and Alice was only twenty.

My brother Joe was best man, arriving in time for the wedding somewhat bleary-eyed from what apparently had been a highly successful honeymoon of his own. Two weeks previously, he had married a startling beauty named Ruth Rakowsky, a diabetic girl whom he met while she was at the Clinic as a patient.

I have a poignant letter from him, written just before his wedding, complaining that our parents and Uncle Will were asking him to wait until after he finished interning, as I had. I was always more amenable to suggestions that made sense than was Joe, who had decided that delay would be intolerable. He wanted me to be his best man, which was impossible —I couldn't get away. He concluded with the anguished sentence, "Jesus Christ, Chuck, what shall we do!"

I knew what he meant: we two young Mayo doctors would be working at the Mayo Clinic, where constant comparison with our father and Uncle Will could not be avoided. My heart also sank when I thought about it. Uncle Will had sent me some money as a graduation gift just before I left Princeton and with it a note:

"Dear Charles, I happened to find the enclosed in my pocket; I have no immediate use for it and thought perhaps you might find a place for it, considering that you are graduating this spring and may need a new necktie or something.

"Work is keeping up and going very well, especially since we are getting some extra men on the staff. Your father and I are anxious to have you boys with us. Affectionately yours, W. J. Mayo."

The letter was charming and the check appreciated but the last sentence tightened my nerves. I had the same reaction when Mother wrote me, after my sister Edith became engaged to a surgeon, Dr. Fred Rankin. "There's a good many of the family in the Clinic already," she wrote. "You've got to have judgment, education, executive ability and *force* to get and keep your place when you come into your own, Charles. But I want you and Joe to be just as fine and square as they make them. . . ."

As the time drew nearer for both of us to join the Clinic, Joe and I had to fight panic. Somehow, unconsciously, we had both decided how we would handle the challenge. I had opted for working at the ultimate of my strength and ability; Joe had concluded that he wasn't going to be tested so cruelly—life was too short, and should be not only sweet but enjoyable. He would be a jester and work when he had to, but not unreasonably hard.

I still don't know which was the better choice.

Joe's progress through school was a saga, punctuated by Mother pleading with deans to give him another chance while they appalled her with tales of his drinking or poker games or falling asleep in morning class. As I have said, Joe had no luck in getting away with anything. He was expelled from Princeton and eventually finished at the University of Iowa.

During those hectic years, Mother's letters to me were filled with news of Joe's escapades, and occasionally she would be furious at him. Usually, though, they had their funny side. Joe was a poor correspondent and Mother frequently would inquire sarcastically of me, "Is Joe alive and well?" One year, I think, she heard from him only via the bills that arrived at Mayowood and complaints from his dean.

So when he finally was to receive his medical diploma from the University of Iowa, Mother said she wasn't going to miss the ceremony, having never had the opportunity before to see Joe graduate. She settled herself in the audience and started looking for Joe's face among the young doctors waiting to get their diplomas. He wasn't there. She looked again, sure that she must have missed him, but there was no Joe.

They began calling the names of the graduates and the presentations had begun, but still Joe wasn't there. At the last possible moment, he arrived. He was puffing from a run, wearing an ill-fitting gown that didn't conceal his plus fours and Argyle socks. He had been playing golf.

When Alice and I were married, Father gave me some money to finance a honeymoon trip, which could last only a week because I was due to begin my four-year fellowship at the Mayo Clinic on the first of July. In a burst of lightheaded generosity, I loaned most of the money to a friend who was being married at the same time.

Alice and I went to Atlantic City and stayed in the pokiest little room. You could lie in bed and reach out with your feet to put up the window shade. We decided to visit the friend to whom I had loaned the money, since he also was honeymooning at Atlantic City. We found him at the Ritz, in a lavish suite, drinking wine on a balcony which overlooked the ocean. Alice was a little tense about that for a while.

Later, we were eating dinner at Childs' when she took a bite of something that broke a piece off her tooth. I felt I had a grievance to compensate for the doleful room: the least she could have done before marrying me, I told her, was to make sure her teeth were sound.

We went back to Philadelphia to pick up a little Boston bulldog, Mitzie, that I had purchased at Sayre. Alice's father had been taking care of the dog while we were in Atlantic City. We planned to travel to Rochester by way of the Great

Lakes, putting our car on the boat at Buffalo and sailing to Duluth. It's a pity you can't do that any more. I wired ahead to Buffalo for accommodation for me, "my dog and my wife." Alice didn't think that was very funny.

We moved into what the family called the Ivy Cottage, one of the small homes on the Mayowood property, and I went to work as a Mayo fellow at $66.67 a month. It meant I still had to be dependent on my father, which bothered me. I don't think he was too entranced when I asked him for money either: sometimes he would refuse. It helped that the cottage was rent-free.

To find an outside source of income, I hit upon the notion of raising English bull terriers, a courageous dog that betting men used as pit fighters years back. I kept them in the basement of Ivy Cottage and my stock was up to eighteen before Alice complained and ordered them out. I found another building for them, but no market. Despite my frantic efforts, I couldn't sell one of them. Father dryly suggested that I give them away, and I tried. I gave the first one to a friend, shipping it to him in a crate. A week later my friend asked me to take the dog back—he had killed a neighbor's valuable cow and my friend was being sued. Father's comment was, "Next time put two in the crate."

You'd have thought the dogs were catastrophe enough for any young husband but my next venture was even worse. Alice and I happened to be visiting a wealthy man who dropped the remark that he had made a quarter of a million dollars the day before on the stock market and another hundred and fifty thousand that afternoon. I couldn't wait to get home and cash in my only asset, a ten-thousand-dollar insurance policy. I invested it all, with impeccable timing: it was just two weeks later that the stock market crashed. I was wiped out.

That was when I developed an ulcer. I was packed off to the hospital and for two weeks I was subjected to that bland Sippy diet which was in vogue then as the medical treatment

76

for ulcers of the stomach. I became so heartily bored with it and so ravenous for roughage that when they brought me a baked potato one day, instructing me to eat only the pulp, I scraped out the pulp all right but set it aside and ate the skin. It did no discernible harm.

It was a period of chronic hospital bed shortage in Rochester, as the Mayo Clinic demand for space kept ahead of existing facilities. To meet the emergency, we resorted to converting hotels into hospitals. John Kahler, a hotel man who was a close friend of Uncle Will's, turned his new Colonial Hotel into a two-hundred-bed hospital, which was a great help.

Kahler, an experienced innkeeper who had been born in Canada, came to Rochester by invitation in order to straighten out the other serious shortage, that of places for the relatives of patients to stay. He built the Kahler Hotel and, out of deference to Uncle Will's abstemiousness, refused to sell liquor in it for many years. For a while, the Clinic even used part of the Kahler Hotel as a hospital, taking over the top three floors for operating rooms and surgical beds. It was an excellent arrangement—I wish we still had it—because the patients and their families were under one roof, to the improved morale of all.

The Colonial Hospital and all the other temporary hospitals operated at a financial disadvantage because they were obliged to pay taxes as stock corporations. St. Marys Hospital, being run by a religious organization, naturally was exempt from such taxation. It was an unfair arrangement for the patients, who had to be charged increased rates in the Colonial or Kahler if those hospitals were to survive.

For a long time, it seemed to the impatient staff at the Clinic that St. Marys was overly cautious about expanding. As early as 1905, Father and Uncle Will complained about this to Sister Joseph, who was Mother Alfred's able successor and a surgeon herself who had trained with Uncle Will. They begged her to use her influence to have St. Marys build a new wing, and she said she would include the matter in her prayers that night.

The following morning, she informed Uncle Will that God didn't seem to approve of expanding St. Marys just then.

"That's odd," said Uncle Will coolly. "Charlie and I consulted God too, and He told us to go ahead and build." They locked eyes, but Sister Joseph felt her contact was more authoritative. Certainly no one can charge St. Marys with being timid any more: at the time I retired, it had more than a thousand beds.

Eventually the problem about the tax inequality was solved, by having the Methodist Church in Rochester take over the old Colonial Hospital and all the other emergency arrangements. In 1967 the church expanded its Rochester Methodist Hospital to 650 beds by building a new hospital having some remarkable and ingenious facilities that have been a delight to staff and patients.

As the bed shortages eased, we were able to move the surgery and hospital beds out of the Kahler Hotel. They put a luxurious rooftop dining room right where the surgery used to be. I can order a delicious meal on the exact spot where I once removed gallstones, a circumstance which doesn't affect my appetite in the least.

The postgraduate training as a surgeon that I commenced at the Mayo Clinic in 1927 included a year of medical diagnosis at the start; it is intended to give young surgeons a broader base of experience for the surgical diagnoses they'll be making all their working lives. I was permitted to live at home with Alice, but I wasn't overwhelming my bride with attention. I was distracted and anxious because the information I was being asked to assimilate seemed mountainous, and I was determined to succeed.

She had a distraction of her own, an eccentric actor wished on us by Marilyn Miller. He arrived with the most unusual symptoms in the Clinic's history: "nausea of the feet and tightening of the teeth." The Clinic used all the ingenuity and resourcefulness at its command, but was unable to relieve these extraordinary afflictions. We thought he would be staying only a few days, but he remained for three or four months, accompanying us on all social occasions despite the inconvenience of the nauseated feet.

If we left town for a few days, hoping he would get the hint, we would find him graciously at the station to welcome us on our return. He was a constant threat to our young maid, chasing her all over the house. Alice was pregnant at the time so she used her condition to solve our dilemma—she fluttered helplessly and asked her guest if he would help with the spring cleaning.

He was trapped, of course, and had to make a show of being glad to be of assistance. Under her supervision, he washed walls and windows for four days. When he finished, she announced pertly that evening that she had obtained some bricks and he could begin the next morning to build a walk around the house. Unfortunately, he said, he was leaving the next morning.

My real training as a surgeon began in the second year of the fellowship, and I was required to live in St. Marys Hospital. I was a second assistant in surgery and sometimes was assigned to operations done by my father and Uncle Will, which were heady experiences for me. I wasn't doing much, sometimes only trivial duties such as holding a hemostat, but I was part of the team cupped in the drama around the incision and I found it profoundly moving, beyond anything I had imagined in all the years I had watched surgeons.

I watched, carefully and steadily performing the minor chores of my role, and tried to learn my trade. I played a game in my head during the evenings when it was my responsibility to make the rounds of patients scheduled for surgery the following morning. I'd imagine how I would do their operations, plotting every move in detail. I was shocked, at first, at how many times I would watch the surgeon the next morning do the operation entirely differently from the

79

way I planned it. Sometimes I couldn't accept the possibility that a patient could even survive an operation that departed so radically from the one I thought was right, so I'd keep checking on his condition, expecting his collapse. Instead, he would thrive. My confidence in my judgment sank to a new low for a time, until I made the discovery that there can be several ways of doing the same operation, and all of them can be successful.

That year, my second in postgraduate training at the Clinic, Uncle Will retired. He was sixty-seven and his powers were undiminished, but he said he wanted to quit "while I'm still good." He was developing an increasing tremor, which made him dread to perform operations in front of visiting surgeons who might go home and report that he had hung on too long.

There was a quality of good timing in his stepping down then, to which he would not have been insensitive. The Clinic had reached a peak in 1928 with the opening of a three-million-dollar, fifteen-story building to house examining rooms, research facilities, X-ray equipment and labs. It is a beautiful building, built of peach-toned Siena stone, richly carved and ornamented with vivid blue tile design and a graceful four-story bell tower. The latter was Uncle Will's touch; he enjoyed carillons. The building later was named for Dr. Henry Plummer, whose brilliance and farsightedness in the organization of the Clinic's system for handling patients contributed enormously to the Mayo success story. Uncle Will always said he was "the best brain the Clinic ever had."

Father's retirement from surgery came abruptly, a year and a half after Uncle Will left. For the first time, I was acting as his first assistant and he had a long surgical list that day. We were working together, with me quite successfully concealing the equal parts of exultation and terror I was experiencing, and it was growing late in the morning when Father suddenly had a dizzy spell. Following his examination at the Clinic, it was diagnosed as a retinal hemorrhage.

He recovered, but he never operated again. It seemed to me somewhat ironical: I had been dreaming for years, Walter Mitty-wise, of being his first assistant, amazing and impressing him with my skill. I thought, I suppose, that it would draw us together. But fate gave me only that one morning to prove myself.

Soon after that, Mother phoned me to come to the Big House because Father had collapsed. I found that he had suffered a stroke, a mild one, as it turned out. He was paralyzed on his right side for a time, just partially. He got over that with only slight impairment to speech and his extraordinary mental agility.

Father and Uncle Will had offices in the new Plummer Building and they came to work every day, going to meetings and dealing with the vast amount of correspondence, the same as before, and sallying out just as frequently to attend medical conventions. When they were in Rochester they continued to make rounds in the hospitals too. When you've been a surgeon for a long time, there are always friends who come to the Clinic and want to see you again, and friends of friends who have asked you to look them up, and former patients who want the comfort of a visit and assurance that the new surgeon is a first-rate man, and friends of former patients who are appreciative of a call. In addition to these demands, hospital rounds gave Father and Uncle Will a better excuse for dropping in to watch surgery. Nothing can replace the drama and fascination of an operating room for a surgeon who has retired, as I well know. It's natural to be drawn to return and observe others operate, imagining how you would handle the unexpected things that develop. Father and Uncle Will turned up frequently, two or three times a week.

Some people have asked if it used to upset me when Father or Uncle Will came into the surgery to watch me work.

I'm amazed at the question, really; being upsettable is not a very good trait in a surgeon.

The tension of performing an operation, in fact, exerts its own kind of analgesia. I found that I not only was indifferent to the arrival and departure of visitors but also to my own personal fatigue or hunger. I could operate from seven thirty in the morning until two or three in the afternoon without stopping to rest or eat, and then I'd make rounds to see those patients on whom I'd operated. When I was finished, the feeling of being fresh and alert would vanish and I'd realize I was a desperately exhausted and hungry man.

Patients who find themselves scheduled for the last operation of a surgeon's list sometimes take this to be an extra hazard, assuming that the doctor will be tired by the time he comes to them and might display clumsiness or dullness. It wasn't true for me; I felt as stimulated and ready for the last operation as I had for the first.

My main problem in those early years was that I looked only slightly older than a high-school boy, which didn't particularly inspire patients with confidence. One of my first unsettling encounters with a patient occurred only a few weeks after I arrived at the Clinic, during the year when I was learning medical diagnosis. The patient was an old man from Missouri or Oklahoma or someplace—I forget where—and he said he followed the race tracks.

I'd been taught to get a thorough medical history, starting with the top of the head and working down to the feet. The questioning of the patient always began by finding out the chief complaint and then launched into every detail of his health. This patient answered the first question all right: he said he had a sore at the bottom of his tongue. I made a note of that and then started on my other questions.

He shook his head impatiently. "None of that," he told me. "I didn't come here to see anyone but Charlie or Will Mayo, and I didn't come for an operation. I just want a little salve for this sore on the bottom of my tongue."

I persisted, explaining that I needed his entire medical history. He refused to answer anything I asked, repeating only that he had a sore on the bottom of his tongue. After forty-five minutes of fruitless pleas for his cooperation, I used my last card—I told him I was Dr. Charles Mayo, the son of Dr. Charlie.

The old man glowered. "That doesn't make a damned bit of difference," he snapped. "I've known plenty of dumb sons of smart fathers."

During my third year of postgraduate training, I was first assistant to my brother-in-law, Dr. Fred Rankin, the one who had married my sister Edith. He was an impressive bowel surgeon and later became president of the American Medical Association, but I cannot be numbered among his fans.

I can illustrate why. Once, just after I was taken on the surgical staff at the Clinic, a patient asked to have me perform his operation and I was greatly encouraged by this show of confidence. Fred heard about it and, for some reason of his own, asked that the patient be switched to *his* list. I was able to make the switch back in time, but it was the kind of officious thing Fred would do.

Eventually his temperament was found unsuited to the cooperative mood of group practice and he left the Clinic, with the customary severance gift of a year's pay. Mother was upset at this treatment of her son-in-law and she railed against the Board of Governors, and against Uncle Will, of course, who then was chairman. The Board refused to change its decision about Fred, so Mother turned to me and urged me to demonstrate family loyalty by resigning from the Board. I, however, had learned Father's strategy in such emergencies, and I kept quiet and waited out the storm. The Rankins left town and Uncle Will once again was designated a villain, a role he bore with equanimity until Mother got over her indignation.

I was Fred Rankin's first assistant for a time, as I have said, and then was assigned to be first assistant to Dr.

E. Starr Judd, a master surgeon who became head of the surgical staff when Father and Uncle Will retired. He had been Father's first assistant and then one of the early partners; later he also was a president of the American Medical Association.

All residents go through what I did; it is about the hardest work in the world. I got up at five every morning, seven days a week, to make the rounds of all patients so I could have a report ready when the chief arrived. Except on weekends, I would assist in the operating room most of the day and then make the rounds again to check on the postoperative condition of all the patients. During the night, I'd be on call for emergencies, such as cases of acute appendicitis, ruptured ulcer or some accident victim.

I was living in a tacky little room on the second floor of a decrepit boarding house during my fourth and final year as a fellow. I then was chief resident at the Kahler Hospital as well as Dr. Judd's first assistant so I decided the prestige entitled me to something better. I asked for permission to move across the street from the Kahler, to the Damon Hotel. It wasn't a very impressive room either, but it was a vast improvement.

At the end of my first month there, I was handed a bill for seventy-five dollars. That was all I was making at that time, seventy-five dollars a month. I was so furious I considered quitting, but Mother and Alice calmed me down and I went back to my rent-free hovel, the boarding house.

Alice was alone a good deal and she complained about it from time to time, but not inordinately. She was always a very good wife for a doctor, which is the highest praise I can give any woman. I'd never advise any girl to marry a doctor, if he is a good one. She will be in for a lot of loneliness. Mother understandingly filled in during my absences by including Alice in everything she did. Alice reported to me that Mother would consult her as if Alice was the senior person and Mother was hoping to learn from her. "She makes me feel that I'm indispensable!" Alice would say, in wonder. It was a demonstration of tact typical of my mother, not too common anywhere, but maybe especially rare, I've been told, in mothers-in-law.

Alice was being kept fairly busy having babies. It seemed to me that for years she was always having a baby, or about to have a baby, or just recovering from having a baby. We had a daughter first, born three weeks before due and a bit blue from cyanosis. Alice had eaten blueberry muffins at a dinner dance we attended the night before and she was convinced, in the first dazed moments of seeing her baby, that this was responsible for the blue tinge. We named the child Mildred, after Alice's only sister, but nicknamed her "Muffin," and she has been known as "Muff" all her life.

After that, we had Charles Horace II, named for my father; Edward Martin, called Ned and named for my great benefactor Dr. Edward Martin of Philadelphia; then Joseph Graham, named for both my brother and my maternal grandfather; then a most welcome little girl, Edith Maria, named for Mother, and then a few years later, Alex Steward, named for my good friend during my student and interning years. Six children in all: two girls and four boys.

I couldn't pay much attention to the babies, having my hands full with the twenty-hour day I was working. Father believed that writing medical papers was important discipline for a doctor, teaching him to marshal research and conclusions informatively, and he kept urging me to prepare papers. In his lifetime, he authored 413 papers; my Uncle Will, 575. I broke into print at an early age, as the result of Father's insistence. As early as 1929, only two years after my interning year, I had a paper on surgery in the *Annals of Surgery* and another in the *American Journal of Physiology*. Sometimes my papers were written in collaboration with my father and sometimes with Fred Rankin. It gradually dawned on me that every time Fred invited me over for dinner, it meant that I was going to be asked to do the digging for another paper.

One early paper I did was on appendicitis. It seems appalling now but during the early thirties about twenty-five thousand people a year were dying of appendicitis in the United States. Most of the deaths occurred because uninformed doctors were still prescribing cathartics casually for every patient with a bellyache. It is about the fastest way known to medical science to rupture an appendix. My paper suggested that all bottles containing cathartics should bear a printed red label warning people of this danger. It wasn't a bad idea; many years later it was accepted.

Another of my papers around the same time dealt with hysterectomies and suggested that in cases of women who hadn't reached menopausal age, such procedures should include the cervix, which is one of the areas in women most vulnerable to cancer. Many doctors had the same idea and that procedure now is followed whenever possible.

I really was proud of the paper I did on hiccups; it's a rather unusual subject in serious medical journals. I noted, "Perhaps one is justified in saying that there is no disease which has had more forms of treatment and fewer results from treatment than the persistent hiccup." That was certainly true: more than two thousand years earlier, Pliny had suggested some fifteen or sixteen cures, and none of them worked any better than the standard non-cure, which is to drink water while standing on your head. My interest in hiccups was aroused when my father had a devastating bout of them; over a long period of time, hiccups are exhausting.

At the same time, I was working on the thesis required to obtain my master's degree in surgery from the University of Minnesota. The subject was chosen with great deliberation, although some associates suggested uncivilly that I was attempting to push the frontiers of medicine well into the seventeenth century. I undertook to study leeches, and the

86

advantages of using those loathed worms to obtain blood samples.

My interest in this antique medical device was aroused while I was interning at Sayre, and learned that leeches were still being used in some of the more isolated mining towns in the vicinity. I was intrigued—at that time, I was having the great difficulty young doctors usually experience in getting blood samples from the buried veins of very fat people or from the thread-fine veins of infants. I began to wonder, idly at first, if the blood sucked by leeches would be as dependable in tests as blood obtained in a hypodermic syringe.

In my curiosity, I began to experiment with leeches. I soon found that a healthy leech takes in about an ounce and a half to two ounces of blood. The next problem, getting the blood out of the leech without bashing him, was solved when I discovered that the leech will vomit up the blood at once if a pinch of salt is put on his head. The next step was to analyze this regurgitated blood and compare it with blood that had been drawn by needle.

I encountered some adversity, of course; it is the common lot of pioneers. For one thing, people objected strenuously to having leeches put on them. I overcame this obstacle by concealing the leech and applying it, out of sight, on the patient's back. Another difficulty then arose: the leeches extrude a substance which causes blood to flow freely and I had a devil of a time stopping the seeping of blood after the leech was removed. In haste, I read all the ancient medical texts I could find and was relieved to come across the information that spider webs stopped bleeding.

A doctor who conscientiously applies leeches cannot flinch from spider webs, so I visited some nearby barns and collected a fine supply of spider webs. They certainly were effective in stanching blood, but I hastily abandoned their use—they also caused a dandy infection.

Eventually, despite such adversities, I was able to establish conclusively that the blood obtained by leeches tests exactly the same as blood drawn by needle for every diagnostic purpose, excepting only Wassermann tests. The men who received this information at the University of Minnesota may have been somewhat startled, but they accepted it as a valid thesis. One thing about it, it was original.

Father and I wrote an interesting paper in 1935 that covered one of the Clinic's most distinguished contributions to medical history. The reputation of the Clinic, it would not stretch a point to say, began with Father's goiter operations at the turn of the century. The ailment was common in the Midwest at that time; people with grossly swollen necks were a common sight. Around 1908, surgery had advanced so that competent surgeons were removing simple goiters with a good measure of safety, but Father was one of few who dared to touch exophthalmic goiters. Most surgeons avoided the operation because even when the surgery was flawless, patients with exophthalmic goiters often became violently ill afterward and slipped into a coma or death. Father, however, had done about five hundred of them, with only 5 per cent mortality; other surgeons in the United States had performed the operation no more than a score or two times, with mortality around 25 per cent.

Doctors came from everywhere to learn how father was accomplishing his miracle, but he couldn't tell them himself. He and Dr. Plummer had worked out a multiple-stage procedure, gauging from the look of the patient when he was ready for the next operation. Their judgment was based on instinct and followed no rule; the visiting doctors decided it was safer for them to simply send their patients to Rochester rather than attempt to try to duplicate something so subtle. In a four-year period, the Clinic did five thousand goiter operations and it became the one performed most frequently, replacing even appendectomies.

Dr. Plummer was in the habit of conducting what were called "goiter lunches," at which everyone especially interested in goiter pooled their ideas and discussed the problem.

a wonderful woman

The founder

5. Back row: Grandmother, Dr. W. W. Mayo
Front row: W. J. Mayo, Phoebe, Gertrude

6. Mother and Father

7. Me, Mother, Dorothy

8. Me, age three, wearing what my mother called my "candy suit"

Iodine had been accepted as a prevention for simple goiter but was believed to be dangerous as a treatment for exophthalmic goiter. Dr. Plummer, in reviewing the wealth of goiter histories at the Clinic, came to the conclusion in 1922 that iodine would be effective and he began using it for his patients, with spectacularly beneficial results.

The paper that Father and I wrote in 1935 established conclusively to the remnants of doubters that he was right. It was inescapable: we were able to cite 37,228 cases, all of them treated at the Clinic between 1892 and 1934. We compared the pre-iodine treatment statistics with the post-iodine ones and reported that deaths from exophthalmic goiter had been reduced 75 per cent by the use of iodine.

I'm proud of my contribution to that paper; in fact, I soon learned that Father had been right about how much a doctor could develop if he frequently put himself to the task of researching and preparing papers, and I didn't mind the tedious work involved. But I came to dread the requests for speeches. Father and Uncle Will were getting into the habit of having me substitute for them, sometimes at the last moment, whenever they were too hard pressed to keep a speaking engagement. Both were magnets on the platform, Father's style being to wander hilariously off the subject and back again, Uncle Will to deliver a weight of information crisply and vividly. I filled in for them with a heavy heart, realizing the enormity of the disappointment my presence would cause the sponsors and audience.

I remember one time over in Wisconsin, I've forgotten the name of the county, when I was obliged to stand in for Father at a large medical meeting. After I had finished my nervous speech, an older doctor came up to me and said, "I drove 150 miles to this meeting because I thought your father was going to be here. I just want you to know that you did a good job." I never forgot those kind words and they supported me through the succeeding ordeals when I represented the Mayo brothers.

My brother Joe arrived at the Clinic the year after I did. He avoided surgery, for his own good reasons—the hard work, I suspect, and also a prudent disinclination to be compared with legendary Mayo surgeons—and chose to get his fellowship training on the medical side. The routine was such that he could play golf regularly, and poker with his friends, and go hunting with his retrievers. He and Ruth were having a stormy marriage, full of love and quarrels; being a young Dr. Mayo did not dominate his life, as it did mine.

Alice used to say I was the plodder. I wasn't a "natural," as some are, and I could see no alternative to hard, steady plugging along. Joe had more potential, I always thought, but he was a freer spirit and he lived joyfully, escaping the irksome and dutiful whenever he could. He had style.

Uncle Will favored Joe over me, which I never resented—I did too; Joe was such a laughing man. But Uncle Will could never figure him out. He'd say, "Joe, I want you to make rounds with me. I'll meet you over at the Colonial Hospital at ten o'clock." Joe would forget all about it until ten o'clock had passed, and then it would hit him like a bolt. He would run over to Uncle Will's office and spread himself out over a chair, with his feet on Uncle Will's desk. When Uncle Will came in, indignantly demanding to know where Joe had been while he was making rounds, Joe would pretend amazement. "Uncle Will," he would say convincingly, "don't you remember you told me to meet you here in your office? I've been waiting for more than an hour!" Uncle Will knew that he didn't usually make a mistake like that, but Joe confused him.

Another time, Joe got wind of the fact that Harry Harwick, the Clinic's efficient executive head, was on the warpath because Joe was parking his car every day directly in front of the entrance to the Clinic—it saved steps, of course. Rumor had it that he was going to give Joe a tongue-lashing and order him to park elsewhere. Joe was equal to the situation. He went in to see Harry in his office and, before Harry could say anything, reminded him that there was a heat wave going on in Rochester. "My car is on the street," Joe told Harry, "and it gets unbearably hot standing in the sun. I wonder if you could construct an awning for it. I'd appreciate it greatly, awfully good of you." Harry stared, and then burst into laughter. They were grinning at one another as Joe withdrew.

Joe's wife Ruth was a diabetic, as I have said, and therefore wasn't expected to be able to bear children. Nevertheless, with her warm nature she was anxious to try, despite the hopelessness of it. They were heartbroken as she gave birth to three dead babies in succession, all boys. Then they adopted a baby, naming him David. Father had been musing about her medical problem and he speculated that she could give birth to a live baby if she were to be delivered early by Caesarian section.

Ruth gamely agreed and went into the hospital during the fourth month of pregnancy and remained in bed there under observation until the seventh month, when a Caesarian section successfully delivered her of a son, whom they called William James, after Uncle Will. It was a medical first, and it was widely imitated for totally diabetic women who want to be delivered safely.

Joe and Father often went hunting together, to North Dakota, South Dakota and other places where pheasants and ducks were plentiful and to northern Minnesota for prairie chickens. I didn't have time to go along and I wasn't much interested anyway. My life was filled with surgery, which tends to shrink the real world until it consists only of hospitals and patients and shoptalk. The harder a surgeon works, the smaller his world becomes.

Joe, Ruth and their two small sons lived at Mayowood, in a house the family called "the chicken house." It was the site of one of Father's most dismal failures as an agriculturalist. Father had purchased a flock of four thousand chickens one time, which failed to make a profit. He then converted the house to a duck house and bought four thousand ducks, but this was an equal disaster. After that, the house was changed extensively and became a charming home for Joe.

Although we were living on the same property and both spent our working days at the Clinic, Joe and I rarely saw one another. Our friends weren't the same, and I had little spare time for social life anyway. In addition to my work, the medical papers and speeches, I was also getting some administrative jobs at the Clinic, such as being on the Board of Governors. Joe didn't care for that sort of thing; I can't say I cared for it too much, but I did it because I thought I should.

Because of Father's interest, I was also keeping myself informed on health matters at a civic and state level. Father had served as head of the Public Health Association of Rochester for a time, at a dollar a year. He paid a doctor who was a public health specialist to act in his place, under his supervision, and instigated a number of imaginative projects.

He referred to this one time in 1928 during a speech in Galveston, Texas. "I have a good deputy who looks after all the real public health work," he explained, "but I am kept busy supporting the real public health officer before the public and city officials, just trying to fix things so he can carry on his work without interference."

On that occasion, he offered some canny advice: "When you start to educate the people, you should start with the women because they will fight for the health of their children. If they haven't any children of their own, they will fight for their neighbor's children."

Father launched a series of weekly public health lectures at the Clinic, to which the public was invited. They were a resounding success in Rochester. He also initiated an ingenious system for disposing of Rochester's garbage profitably: he bought a farm southwest of Rochester, put pigs on it and fed the city's garbage to the pigs. The pigs thrived, since garbage contains much nutritive food, and the project not only paid for itself but made enough profit to pay the salary of the public health officer, as well as the additional costs to the city of this unusual disposal service.

Except for the loss of a few pigs when thoughtless people included broken glass in the waste, it was a complete triumph of garbage disposal. I believe it could be applied in certain areas today with equal success, unless some bureaucracy trying to justify itself should intervene.

Father also was one of the active supporters of state legislation to prohibit tuberculous cattle from being brought across the state line. It was a wise move and supported the policy of the state's veterinary association, but Father's interest in tuberculosis-free cattle was not entirely detached. He had the bad luck, before the bill was passed, to buy a herd of thirty-six Guernsey cattle in New York State, only to discover that all of them but one had tuberculosis when tested in Minnesota.

FIVE

I finished my fellowship in June, 1931, picked up my degree in surgery from the University of Minnesota and then went east to Princeton to attend a reunion. I was jolted to discover that all my former classmates were settled and prospering in their chosen fields while I was still dependent on my father. Ten years after my graduation from college, I was only *beginning* my career.

The progress of medical education can be seen with a glance at the training of three generations of Mayos. My grandfather received his M.D. after a year in a medical school;

my father and Uncle Will were doctors in practice three years after they finished high school; my training after high school lasted for twelve years, thirteen if you count the year I lost through illness.

I returned to Rochester from the reunion with just enough time to report for duty as Dr. Judd's first assistant. I hurried from the train directly to the hospital, dashed to the surgical floor, undressed and got into my surgical outfit. When I arrived huffing in the operating room, Dr. Howard Gray, a friend and colleague, seemed surprised to see me. "Haven't you looked at the lists?" he asked. I said I hadn't taken the time. "Better look," he advised, with a wide grin.

So that was how I got the news of my appointment to the surgical staff of the Mayo Clinic, the goal to which I had been aimed from birth. One of the lists was headed by my name, followed by the names of thirteen patients on whom I was to operate that morning. My throat dried and my stomach was a knot as I made the rounds of those thirteen, my first patients. I think I consulted an anatomy book, in a hysterical burst of nervousness.

I thought, "Well, I guess I have to go through with it." My emotions were a jumble, with a fair amount of pride and jubilation, laced with panic. I knew I was capable of performing the operations, but the shock of finding out so abruptly that I was a staff surgeon caught me unprepared.

I calmed down and did the thirteen operations successfully—none of the patients died. When I consider all the people involved in that day of initiation, it was the fourteenth, Chuck Mayo, who was closest to expiring.

Uncle Will, in congratulating me later, added a dry warning: "Charles, now that you're the new member of the staff, you know what you're going to be? The garbage pail. You'll get the things that no one else wants to do."

I found he was right—it fell to me to do the tedious operations, the fiddly operations, the trivial operations. And I had a further problem in the immaturity of my face which, de-

94

spite the fact that I was thirty-three years old and the father of many children, still looked almost adolescent. I would have a patient on my list and when I would make my rounds and introduce myself, the patient would take one alarmed look at me and ask for another surgeon. The turnover of names on my list was discouraging. At times, I fought back. One woman required an operation to remove a stone from her gallbladder and she asked me who should do it.

"Dr. Judd has done thousands of operations on the gall-bladder," I told her earnestly. "You may have him, or you may have me. I'm just starting and I can't afford to lose a patient." She grinned and decided to have me do the operation.

Surgery in the thirties had advanced a long way from Grandfather's time, when it was considered daring to cut someone open to remove an ovarian tumor. The textbooks of his youth had been full of false concepts, microscopes showed only very obvious things and it was before the germ theory of disease had been put forward. In his mature years, Grandfather thought himself fortunate to be a doctor in such a time of medical discovery and he pitied the men of the previous generation. Father once said, astutely, that "we cannot always be sure that a century from now somebody will not be saying the same sort of thing about us."

It has come to pass already. In Father's day there was no surgery on the heart, for instance, brain and eye surgery were undeveloped, comparatively, plastic surgery was only beginning and the transplanting of organs was a subject envisioned by mad doctors in horror movies. One of the greatest handicaps surgery faced was the relative crudeness of anesthetics available to us. When a patient died, surgeons frequently blamed the anesthetic; it was a face-saving convenience, but not always justified.

Father had made a study of anesthesia and could be wry on the subject. He once informed a medical gathering that Hippocrates used opium, mandrake and Indian hemp as

95

anesthetics, adding that later "the lack of good anesthesia induced rapid operating. Surgeons like Paré could amputate a leg or could take off an arm at the shoulder joint in the twinkling of an eye, because the bulk of the anesthesia was provided by strong men and ropes."

Pathology, however, had been refined in the thirties so that it was possible to diagnose cancer with accuracy, using Broders' system of grading it. Father and Uncle Will didn't have a reliable means of identifying cancer during their careers. I was reminded of this in 1966 when I received a check for $150 from a woman in Texas, who wrote me crisply that I had operated on her in 1912 for cancer of the colon and she wanted to pay her bill. I think fifty-four years constitutes something of a record for nonpayment of an account.

I looked up her record, knowing that it was impossible that I could have done the operating, being only fourteen at the time, and found that Uncle Will had performed a resection of a portion of her large bowel. We keep all specimens of removed tissue at the Clinic, so I was interested to check on hers. It had been misdiagnosed, I found; she had tuberculosis of the colon, rather than cancer. But Uncle Will must have done superlative work on her, judging from the more than a half century of health she had enjoyed.

I'm wary of patronizing the work done by early surgeons because I keep coming across evidence of inspired surgery that triumphed over the prevailing limitations. For example, I was in England after World War II observing the world of Clifford Naunton Morgan, now Sir Clifford, and some of the other great surgeons at St. Mark's Hospital. I watched them do a two-surgeon operation, what we call a synchronous combined abdominoperineal resection. It is performed on patients suffering from cancer of the rectum and it is done by two surgeons working simultaneously, one of them performing the abdominal part of the operation while the other does the rectal part.

The British surgeons were understandably pleased with

what they believed was an advance in surgery, so I refrained from telling them that my father had described exactly the same operation in a paper entitled *Cancer of the Large Bowel,* which he wrote in 1904 and published in the *Medical Sentinel* of Portland, Oregon.

For those who are interested, the following is a partial quotation from that paper:

> The distal bowel is now separated and pushed below the uterus and bladder or the bladder and prostate. A gauze pack is placed over this, and the peritoneum nearly closed, forming a pelvic floor, and the abdominal wound is closed, the remainder of the operation being completed from below.
>
> A gauze pack is placed in the rectum, to render it palpable, and the anus closed by a purse-string suture. An incision is made around the anus, and separation of the rectum is made until the point is reached where it is loosened from above. All the glands and fascia in front of the coccyx and sacrum are removed at the same time. A portion of the pack previously placed in the pelvis is now withdrawn through the perineal wound for drainage, the remainder of the incision being closed. *If the surgeon has a good assistant, the perineal operation, with the removal of the rectum, can be performed by him during the time the abdominal work is advancing above.*
>
> If the median incision discloses an inoperable condition, that is, inoperable from a curative standpoint by reason of extensive metastasis in glands or neighboring organ involvement [this means, in layman language, that the cancer has spread and the patient cannot survive] an inguinal colostomy is made and the median wound is closed.

It is the measure of Father's genius that this identical operation was being demonstrated forty years later as the latest word in surgery. Sixty years after he described it, in fact, I was doing operations that were almost exactly the same.

Early in the history of medicine, hospitals were used almost exclusively for surgery. People whose illness wasn't to be treated surgically generally remained at home, nursed there by their families and visited as the need arose by a doctor. But medical care developed rapidly after the turn of the century and treatment became too sophisticated to be administered at home. Uncle Will, with his customary gift for recognizing trends at their beginnings, realized that one day medical beds would greatly outnumber surgical ones in hospitals, which is now the case. He therefore encouraged young doctors who wanted to do their graduate work in medicine rather than surgery and made certain of their place in Rochester's hospitals by reserving beds for them, to the discomfiture of some of the bed-hungry surgeons.

Surgery was still dominating Rochester's hospitals when I began on the staff of the Clinic. I was finding that my obsession to succeed didn't leave me after I finished my training; on the contrary, I was working even harder than before. I couldn't shake my awareness that I was a surgeon named Mayo, the only one active in the Clinic. The name seemed heavy, which meant I would have to grow stronger. There wasn't an alternative that I could see.

There is a situation among surgeons in this country that is unique in medicine: each man is a lone wolf, and no surgeon who has completed his training ever works under another surgeon. It is regarded as an individual craft, practiced by individualists; once a surgeon is on his own, he is really on his own. He can call for help and get it quickly, but the operating room is his personal kingdom. It corresponds to the unquestioned authority of a ship's captain and is accepted for the same reason—emergencies requiring quick decisions cannot be entrusted to debating teams.

But it helps to explain why some people regard surgeons as prima donnas, tyrannical and vain. It may be true of a few—there are people like that in every profession—but it's unusual to find such a surgeon despite the heady working conditions, the awareness every working morning that you are ruler over a realm whose preoccupation is life and death.

The catch is that surgeons must accept Shakespeare's concomitant of the privilege of wearing a crown, which is an uneasy head. Surgeons at a social gathering are a study; it's as though they are made up of layers, with the outer one appearing to relax and joke while the inner ones continue to grapple with that morning's operation, if it could have been done better another way, or tomorrow's, how to handle that tricky thing that showed on the X ray. No man can predict what will be found under the skin of a human being. The clinician who made the original diagnosis may have been skillful in drawing inferences from the tests he has done, but nature is whimsical and sometimes sets organs in peculiar places, or omits them entirely. Not infrequently, she makes some organ insanely large or another astonishingly small.

This presents great adventure and fascination for a surgeon, who accustoms himself to facing the unknown regularly. In the face of the infinite surprises the human body holds, it is essential that surgeons keep a cool and alert brain. Emergencies, when they occur, will likely be sudden and they can be as violent as a geyser of blood.

Like others involved in high-tension occupations, such as professional golfers or actors, I used to lie awake for hours every night going over every move I had made in a difficult operation and, in my mind, doing it ten other ways. If the patient had died, I put myself on a rack of agony, reviewing every detail. It made no difference that there was no possible way to save the patient.

Some operations are a delight. I remember the anticipation with which I opened the abdomen of a woman with an enormous swelling and removed, without rupturing it, an ovarian cyst so large that it overflowed a dishpan. I can still see the yawning cavity it left. The woman had been carrying the steadily increasing weight of it for many years and, the next day, was ecstatic at how light and free she felt. It must have been like the feeling one has when driving through a countryside that has no telephone poles. The view seems marvelous and then the realization strikes that the glory is the absence of telephone poles.

When Father and Uncle Will started their practices, they operated seven days a week, which seems awesome to modern surgeons—much like football's old sixty-minute men. In my early days, surgeons operated only four days a week and I think the schedule has been reduced to three days now. When a surgeon is not operating, he sees patients, consults with other doctors, answers correspondence and attends staff meetings. Besides such duties, I took my regular turn at being on call for night emergencies.

One time when I was called out at two in the morning, Alice sleepily insisted on going along. She had never watched me operate as head of the team before, so she took the opportunity to sit in the gallery, a solitary spectator at that hour. I was absorbed in removing a patient's innards, setting them aside to reach the point of difficulty somewhere deeper in the abdomen, when I heard her wail, "You've got it all out. Can you get it back in?"

I silenced her with an imperious gesture, but I must admit that getting all the abdominal contents back into a patient sometimes presented some strained moments. When operating for abdominal conditions, a surgeon often has to probe around blindly with his hands, lifting out the movable contents in what amounts to a minor evisceration in order to get a better view. A substantial amount of the contents of a human abdomen are movable—there are twenty-three feet of small intestine in there, and some six feet of large intestine; packed out, it makes quite a mound.

My two forefingers are slightly clubbed at the first joints as a result of thirty-two years of abdominal surgery, with its requisite exploring against the heavy bones of the lower part of the body.

The year after I became a staff surgeon, I was made an instructor in surgery in the Mayo Foundation Graduate School, which meant I was on the first step of being part of the University of Minnesota's academic staff. Three years later, in the summer of 1935, I was advanced to the rank of assistant professor. After the prescribed intervals, I was made associate professor and, lastly, was honored to be professor of surgery in the Mayo Foundation.

As a staff surgeon, I had two second assistants assigned to me and two first assistants whom I chose myself, all four of them fellows in surgery. Their training was primarily my responsibility. I had a rule I followed: I would never let my first assistant do any operating that I wouldn't want him to do if the patient were Alice or me. That was one rule, and the other was that I would never select for a first assistant any man or woman who did not demonstrate a feeling for people.

The assistants, along with the anesthetist and surgical nurses, were my surgical team. They were assigned to two adjoining operating rooms, with one first assistant and one second assistant in each. The patients on my list were scheduled for one room or the other, at overlapping intervals. The first assistant, guided by careful instructions I gave him in advance, would make the preliminary incision and usually would have the damaged organ requiring repair exposed by the time I arrived in the operating room. From then on, he would actively assist me on the opposite side of the table, while the second assistant held retractors where we needed them.

As a former second assistant myself, I had found this chore more awkward than I thought necessary. I gave it some thought and was able to design a simpler, easier-to-hold retractor which was received gratefully by second assistants everywhere. It is called the Mayo retractor and I've been told that it is still being sold.

I have digressed from describing how the double operating rooms and surgical teams are coordinated. To return to it: while I was operating on the first patient of the day, the second patient would be wheeled into the adjoining operating room. The second team of first and second assistants would wait for a message from me, which I sent when I judged that I was a few minutes from finishing with the first operation. They would then begin the incision on the second patient and have it ready for me as soon as I left the first patient. The first team of first and second assistant remained behind to make the routine closure of the first patient's wound and await the arrival of the third patient.

It was an arrangement that was superlatively economical of the surgeon's time and skill, but clearly it depended on a high degree of harmonious cooperation. I remember that when I was first assistant to Dr. Judd, he would often be held up because I closed the incisions so slowly. One morning he complained testily about this, but I was able to respond disarmingly, "I admit I am slow, Dr. Judd, but there have been five wounds which broke open after operation in the last quarter, and none of them has come from my room." There was no further criticism of my deliberateness.

My second assistants spent most of the day in the hospital to which they had been assigned, either the Colonial or St. Marys, but the two first assistants usually accompanied me in all my routine duties in the Clinic and in both hospitals.

Some students were better than others, naturally, and I developed a means of being able to assess a new man quickly. In that kind of apprenticeship, it is vital to discover at once which man can be relied upon to do the right thing and which one is not ready for too much responsibility. By watching them and listening, I could generally make an accurate appraisal of their abilities.

One of my tests for determining which second assistant was a good candidate for the desired promotion to first assistant was less subtle. It might take place after midnight, sometimes long after, when there had been a particularly rough operation during the day. In such cases, I wasn't able to sleep well and after a few hours of tossing and turning, wondering how the patient was progressing, I'd finally get up and dress and drive to the hospital.

If I found my first assistant beside the patient because he was equally concerned for his well-being, I would make a mental note that he was a first-rate doctor, worthy of top grades when the time came. If my second assistant was also there, without having been summoned, I would remember him when selecting my next first assistant; sometimes I promoted him on the spot. I figured a surgeon was not worth a damn if he could leave his sense of obligation when he left the operating room.

The qualifications I looked for did not include color, religion or sex, which seemed to me irrelevant considerations. I had several first assistants who were women and I let them do everything a male colon surgeon would do, catheterize men, everything. It might be expected that an overly modest male patient would complain that he didn't want a woman doing these things to him, but we never had a single protest. And I was the first surgeon to take on a Filipino as a first assistant. No one seemed to want them around the Clinic when they first started coming to us, but I found that they were very good. Father, I recall, had a Jewish first assistant one time, the first in the Clinic's history. This young doctor happened to be unusually confident; Father used to complain that he was tired of being *his* first assistant, and being instructed what to do.

Commitment to the patient's welfare was the principal quality I sought in my assistants, and after that, of course, expertise. I put surgical judgment at the top of the list in this area, and it isn't easy to learn because some of it is intuitive. It develops after medical school, the combined result of studying what is happening everywhere and of experience. It is also necessary to have a thorough knowledge of anatomy and physiology, obviously, but real genius in surgery lies in knowing when to operate and when not to operate, with the latter more important than the former, and when there has been enough done within the patient and the time has come to stop and get out.

The surgeon I would select to tend my family or me must first know when not to cut, then when and where to cut, and how to cut, and when to stop cutting. That's what surgical judgment is.

Besides that, he must have the sort of nerves that can bear the strain of being responsible for a human life. I don't know how to describe surgical nerve—you recognize it when you see it but, like jazz, if you don't know what it is no one can tell you. I suppose good training is part of it, together with the courage that goes with faith in your own ability. Great surgeons have it in abundance; their teams worship them as heroes, and with good reason.

I would place technique next, although many of my colleagues would rate it first. I would much prefer that a man who operates on me have a high degree of surgical judgment and adequate technique, rather than a high degree of technique and adequate judgment.

Most important is the surgeon's attitude toward his patients. At the Mayo Clinic, we used to find that doctors who had been trained in charity hospitals rarely showed the kind of warmth and thoughtfulness toward patients that we value in a doctor. They would tend rather to be brusque and inconsiderate. I used to speculate wickedly on the advisability of arranging, if it were possible, for a few weeks of pain to be part of their curriculum. I can guarantee that it makes a person more compassionate.

I worked hard, as I have said, but I found time to enjoy one hobby, namely riding and showing horses. Alice and I loved to ride and shortly after our arrival in Rochester I had asked Uncle Christopher to let me buy two of his fine horses. He raised standardbreds which his brother, Tom Graham, would drive in county and state fair races all around the Middle West.

Uncle Kit sold me two handsome two-year-old trotters. Aware of my lean purse, and considering that I was his nephew, he reduced the price to a shameless hundred dollars for the pair. As I recall, I had to borrow the money from Father. Alice and I named the horses Tom and Jerry and we held them in genuine esteem and affection. Don't ever believe that horses are stupid and ungrateful animals. Shortly after we first put Tom and Jerry in our barn, which was about four miles south of Rochester, they broke out and found their way back to the man who had raised them, a kindly person whose place was four miles north of Rochester. It was extraordinary navigation on their part and I felt guilty about fetching them, but I went and brought them back to Mayowood.

Tom and Jerry were easily trained to be saddle horses, but their conversion was a blow to my uncle Tom Graham, who had the typical harness-horseman's passion for racing and thought any other use of a good standardbred was a sacrilege. One time while attending the Minnesota State Fair, I was watching the harness races. Two sulkies locked wheels and one of the drivers got caught in the reins and was dragged for some distance. The public address system reported that the injured driver was Tom Graham, so I hurried to the first-aid tent in alarm. Uncle Tom was then seventy-six years old. I found him shaken, bloody, bruised, burned and agitated about the welfare of his horse. But most of all, he was angry. It seemed the repairs to his person were making him late for the next race.

Alice and I entered our horses in every class possible in every horse show in Rochester and surrounding towns in Olmsted County, and even vanned them to shows in distant counties. She really was irritated with me the time I entered her in the Parent and Child Class, by herself. I thought it was appropriate, since she was pregnant at the time and hiding the bulge neatly under the long skirt of her riding jacket, but she wasn't in the least amused. I've kept the program with the entry: "Mrs. Alice Mayo and child." I am disappointed that I didn't go further and enter her as "Mrs. Alice Mayo *with* child."

One time I arrived at the Clinic still wearing my breeks and riding boots and encountered an outraged Uncle Will. "Who the hell do you think you are!" he snapped at me. For once I didn't flinch. "A surgeon," I told him hotly, "and a damned good one."

I somehow found time to serve a year, in 1934, as president of the Rotary Club of Rochester. It happened that I didn't operate on Thursdays and this was the day of the Club's luncheon meetings. Later Thursday became a surgical day for me and I rarely finished in time to attend meetings. I was embarrassed about this because Rotarians attach importance to their attendance record, and rightly so. I offered to resign but they offered a flattering alternative: they made me an honorary member.

I like the Rotary Club. Rotarians have a fine motto: *Service Above Self*. That's what life is all about, in my opinion.

Father and Uncle Will used those years of retirement for well-deserved travel, much of it to commencements for honorary degrees. Uncle Will was becoming mellow as he aged, more tolerant and sympathetic with the people around him. He and father seemed more and more alike as time went on. It confirms my theory that they were identical all along, with different poses for the world.

Uncle Will had a sensitivity to cottonseed oil. I cannot count the times I have seen him with his face swollen and his eyes almost shut because inadvertently he had eaten something cooked in cottonseed oil. To avoid this danger when he traveled, he hit upon the idea of buying a sumptuous trailer and equipping it with an elaborate kitchen and cook.

As always happened with the brothers, Father then bought himself a trailer much like Uncle Will's. He and Mother traveled with a chauffeur and a Filipino who was both valet and cook, and they were so eager to try out the new vehicle that they set off on their first trip in it before it was entirely ready. Among other minor shortcomings, the trailer lacked window screens.

Like many other travelers, Father always figured that the spot he was passing now was slightly inferior to the one that would materialize about ten miles further. Accordingly, one night it was almost eleven o'clock and they were still on the road. Mother was tired and exasperated.

"Charlie, we're going to stop at the next possible place," she told Father.

He therefore gave the order to stop at the next likely spot and they then spent a hideous night, beset by hundreds of flies which came in through the open windows and by a heavy, filthy odor in the air. With dawn, they discovered that they had parked beside a sewage disposal plant.

Not long after that, Father gave the order to stop during a drive along the scenic Mohawk Trail in northern New York State. Mother stepped out of the trailer to admire the view and just disappeared. They had parked by a sharp incline and she rolled down the hill until fortunately caught in a small tree. She called to Father for help and he put his head out of the window, saw her predicament and gravely put on his topcoat and a muffler before descending to help her. She was amused by this, which illustrates something about Mother's sense of humor.

Their travels abroad were turning Mayowood's Big House into a collector's dream. Both Mother and Father loved to shop and they had discerning taste. Because taxes on personal income were negligible at that time, they could afford some genuine treasures, museum pieces, and they installed in their home such beautiful objects as thirteen immense mirrors from Mexico with scroll-carved frames coated with gold leaf. The largest, more than nine feet high and five feet across, hangs at the top of the stairs leading from the entrance to the house.

They also found an Irish Waterford chandelier for the main dining room, Georgian silver hollow ware, Sheffield trays, Chippendale chairs and sideboard and a French porcelain dinner service. Father was so delighted with a unique brass fireplace fender seat he found in England that he couldn't bear to have it travel separately and insisted that it come on the ship with him.

Father and Mother filled hanging shelves and table tops with exquisite things that were a joy to touch and see. My favorite, from the age of eleven, was a bronze sun goddess which Father purchased from an exhibition in Edinburgh. From the outside, the Big House resembles a friendly Mediterranean villa—the sloping gardens are hung with stone lanterns from Venice and filled with Italian marble statues.

Mother cherished the superb objects that she and Father were collecting but she maintained a sense of proportion about them. Alice discovered this one day when she accidentally broke an irreplaceable porcelain cup. She was horrified and on the verge of tears but Mother comforted her. "Don't worry, my dear," she said. "It is only material."

On her desk, Mother kept a quotation from the Hindu poet Tagore: "Give me the strength to raise my mind high above daily trifles." She truly lived that way and I think Alice succeeded in instilling in all of our children some of that capacity to rise above trivia. *High* above trivia, Mother would have reminded me; the elevation can't be skimpy, of course.

Father failed to make one addition to Mayowood that he strongly fancied—a chimpanzee. The chimp was Bertha, an experimental animal which contributed to the pioneer research that laid the groundwork for the development of the vaccine for polio. Bertha adored my father and would embrace him enthusiastically when she saw him, and Father felt affection for her. She was kept in the tower of the Clinic's Plummer Building and most Sunday afternoons Father would slip away from Mayowood and visit Bertha.

Between visits, he would try to persuade Mother that Bertha should live at Mayowood, where he thought she would be happier. He even planned the alterations he could make to a large downstairs bathroom off his study, where he felt Bertha would be comfortable. Mother kept saying no, and never budged. Father finally dropped the scheme when Mother flatly declared, "If the chimpanzee comes, I go!"

Mother accompanied Father one day on a visit to Bertha. The chimp must have sensed Mother's rejection of her and, in a surge of jealousy, she grabbed Mother's purse from her hand and threw it over the Clinic parapet. Mother had some difficulty in retrieving the purse, I recall. Not long afterward, it was decided that Bertha had served her noble purpose in the program that Dr. Rosenow had been conducting to discover the cause of infantile paralysis, as poliomyelitis was called then. She was donated to the Bronx Zoo in New York and ended her days there, giving pleasure to thousands of visitors.

In 1933, I was made a fellow of the American College of Surgeons, which wasn't too remarkable an accomplishment in those days. If one had a good medical education, all that was needed were a few commendations from doctor associates. Nonetheless, my mother was intensely proud of this modest honor and when my portrait was painted a few years later, she insisted that I sit for it in my American College of Surgeons' gown.

My brother Joe was added to the staff of the Clinic in 1934 and received his master's degree in medicine two years later. This sequence is exactly backwards to the usual custom, and illustrates how Joe's charm tended to cause people to make uncommon adjustments in the normal order of things. His arrival on staff meant that once again there were Mayo brothers active in the Clinic, a situation which many people thought rich in historical significance and symbolism. Much of these lofty observations were lost on Joe. He thought unctuous talk about our Mayo heritage was so much poppycock and he could be quite voluble and hilarious on the subject.

The Mayo Clinic was no longer charging the rather spectacular fees of its early years, when Father and Uncle Will thought it seemly that a millionaire should be prepared to pay the equivalent of a summer's vacation in Europe in return for an operation that saved his life. Some tales of those fees are greatly exaggerated, but it is true that Uncle Will once discovered that a wealthy man had been charged ten thousand dollars for an operation on his wife. Uncle Will sent back four thousand dollars of it, apologizing for the excessive fee, but the man gallantly returned it, saying his wife was worth the full ten thousand.

The Clinic fees have always been adjusted to the individual's financial circumstances, and I think fairly so. Uncle Will once operated on a boy just out of high school, charging him one hundred dollars and agreeing to accept payment of ten dollars a month until the account was settled. When ten months had passed, Uncle Will handed the money back to the boy, along with generous interest, and advised him to open a bank account with it. There are similar stories about Father and his more impoverished patients.

The financial arrangement at the Clinic is that all fees are established by the Clinic business office, but are subject to adaptation by staff doctors if the circumstances are unusual. Sometimes I raised the fee charged for my operations, usually because the patients were demanding special hospital rooms and unnecessary nursing care. More often, I requested the office to reduce the surgical fee.

The most I ever charged, and this in rare circumstances, was a thousand dollars.

Sometimes patients inquired anxiously how much the operation was going to cost. "Well," I would assure them, "this Clinic wouldn't have lasted very long if the fee structure were exorbitant, so you can be sure the fee won't be too high.

"However," I would continue, "we have a special arrangement: if the fee charged you seems too low, you have the privilege of adding to it." This usually concluded the discussion.

Some grateful patients have left a donation with the Clinic, to be used to pay the bills of those who can't meet the medical costs. Such donations usually were made with the condition that they be anonymous; there are always good people who will do this sort of thing.

Father and Uncle Will insisted from the beginning that whenever bills were paid in installments the hospitals would receive their money first and the Clinic would be paid only when the hospital account was settled. This rule is still followed.

On November 9, 1936, Alice and I were in Temple, Texas, where I had been asked to give an address at the Scott and White Clinic, which happened to be where my brother Joe had served his internship. I gave the talk and spent a happy evening with friends of Joe's, laughing at their recollections of Joe's eventful year there. At an early morning hour, someone came to me, white-faced, and said Joe was dead. There had been an accident, he said; I didn't get any details.

There wasn't a satisfactory plane schedule at that time, so Alice and I boarded the train for the dazed journey home. Our good friend, Robert Bruce Young, the one who had been with Joe and me on that crazy trip to Europe in 1920, got on the train at Fort Worth and rode to Rochester with us. All along the journey, other friends joined the train and rode with us a stop or two. Like me, they were stunned that so much mirth and jubilation could die.

It was a front-page story in all the newspapers, so we were able to learn the circumstances of the accident before we reached Rochester. A brand new magazine, *Life*, published a story about Joe's death in its first issue and included several heartbreaking pictures.

Joe had been duck-hunting around Alma, Wisconsin, on

the day that the season was closing. In the evening he ate dinner at a small local hotel and then drove off in his car with Foosie, a golden retriever he took everywhere with him. When he got to a railway crossing, he turned his car and drove along the tracks. It was a risky thing to do but it was a fairly common practice for hunters and farmers in that area. There's a good possibility that Joe misjudged the turn —a new highway, parallel to the railway tracks, was just a bit down the road.

In any case, a light snow made greasy traction for his wheels and the rails were high along that stretch of track. I think that he tried several times to wrench his car off the tracks, but the two wheels remained trapped between the rails. So Joe drove along, probably looking for a crossing where he might get clear.

The train from Chicago came up behind him in the darkness; the engineer later stated that he didn't see the car until he was on top of it, with no chance to stop in time. The car was cut in two and Joe was killed instantly. I walked along the tracks afterward, and as I reconstruct the accident, Joe must have been worried that his heavy car would derail the train, possibly killing some passengers, so he stayed with it until it was too late, in the hope that he could get it out of the way.

It was such a strange accident that there was talk for a long time that it must have been a suicide. It is hard to conceive that any man would kill himself in such a bizarre manner, but in Joe's case suicide is out of the question. He enjoyed life more than any man I ever knew. His style was to savor, his existence rollicking. He would never even consider killing himself.

The funeral arrangements had been made by the time my train arrived in Rochester, but one detail was still unsettled. Joe's dog Foosie died in the car with him, and Father, Mother and Ruth agreed that Joe would want her buried with him. The minister was reluctant to officiate over a casket that contained a dog, but I knew they were right and so, without saying anything further on the matter, we slipped Foosie into the coffin beside Joe. The service at Mayowood was simple and then we buried Joe. He was only thirty-four.

Alice maintained, all these long years since Joe's death, that half of me died with him. I don't dispute it. When he died, I lost the only person who really knew what I am and what I faced. I was left alone with the whole weight of being a Mayo successor. Until then, it had been easier to keep up my courage because Joe's irreverence cut through my gloomy self-consciousness and made me chuckle. With him gone, I felt utterly lonely and vulnerable.

For a long time my grief was raw; it would come in spasms, unexpectedly, and mostly when I was alone. It is duller now, but it hasn't gone away.

My own experience with the washes of black sorrow that come in the night has influenced the way I feel about that continuing medical debate over whether or not a patient should be informed that he is going to die. Many doctors count it virtuous to "always level with the patient," but I have no great admiration for truthfulness that isn't also kind.

My reasoning is this: there is always a time, no matter how ill a person is, when he is left alone. It may be only for moments, but it happens. For a person aware of dying, those solitary times are a horror; if it is at night, the desolation is worse, since everything is worse at night. I therefore would rather that a patient with little time left to live be kept in ignorance of it. Naturally, though, I had to be guided by the family's wishes. If they preferred that he be told, I somehow managed to do it.

I note that people with strong religious faith take such tragic news best, because of the convictions about God's will and life after death. By and large, it is Roman Catholics who display the greatest acceptance of death. But even they are second to those patients who have been in pain for a long time, regardless of whether they have a great faith to support them or none at all. After a long period of pain, people are relieved to be told that they will die soon.

The worst moment doctors face, as any of them will tell you, is when they must enter a room where relatives are waiting and tell them that the patient has died. Some surgeons cannot do it; they delegate the terrible task to their assistants. I always felt the obligation to do it myself. I'd begin by suggesting that we all sit down, and then I would say that the patient was dead as simply and quickly as possible, and offer any help I could. Most people are numbed by what they hear; they stare in shock and don't seem to comprehend. Later on they cry, and it is a safety valve for which I have profound respect.

Almost always in my experience, there was no possible way in which the patient could have been saved. All surgical procedures carry a risk, even such minor operations as removal of a tooth after an injection of novocain have been known to be fatal. I could never accustom myself to death, however. I always kept track of my patients who recovered and, as the consecutive number of them grew, I would feel better and better about being a surgeon. I rejoiced once when I had a streak of one hundred and three cases of a certain kind of major operation without a postoperative death. Then, in only a week, three patients died of that same operation; I know I wasn't easy to live with for a long time after that.

I always warned my assistants to beware of any patient who showed no interest in living. I've seen patients who pulled themselves through a surgical ordeal which gave them little expected chance to survive, using gritty will power to work a near miracle, and I also came to realize that when a person wants to die, he *will* die—and no amount of good surgical treatment and postoperative nursing care can stop him.

Often such patients are frank with their doctor, and declare that they don't want to live. They are getting old, they

say, or they are fed up and tired. I would promptly ask them
to have another surgeon consult with them. "Find someone
who won't worry about you," I would recommend. "I'm not
your man."

I was so sickened by Joe's death that it was hard for me to
take any interest in what I was doing, but I fought my feeling
of lethargy by working even harder. Hard work is good
therapy for grief, I think. I filled my time almost frantically,
preparing and writing papers for medical journals at a whirl-
wind clip, which had the added advantage of keeping me on
my toes as a doctor. And on other doctors' toes too, I discovered.

For instance, I was interested in following up surgical repair of inguinal hernia for a five-year period after the operation, to determine the rate of recurrence. I made a survey of
some of the Mayo surgeons who performed a lot of these
operations and asked them to guess at their recurrence rate.
The answers varied. One said, "Well, I think about two per
cent"; another said, "Maybe six per cent." No one estimated
a recurrence rate of more than 10 per cent.

I already knew the correct answer, which was 19 per cent as
a Clinic average. I acquainted the surgeons of my observation, which naturally didn't produce too much applause for
my efforts, but I had no cause to be pleased with my individual average either. I therefore changed my method of repair-
ing inguinal hernias slightly, using underlying tissue sheath
from the belly wall instead of catgut to mend the tear and
making other minor changes. I waited eagerly for another
five-year period to pass and then made another follow-up
study. I found that I had reduced my recurrence rate
sharply, but it still wasn't good enough.

I pondered this for some time before hitting on a conclusion that I think was important: that a surgeon should never
adhere to a single method of performing a certain operation,
that he should always individualize. After that, I tried being
more flexible in my technique. Five more years passed, and

I made the satisfying discovery that my recurrence rate was one of the lowest.

The necessity to wait for five years, or even ten, before it can be established that the technique being used today is proper, is one of the built-in frustrations about surgery. We are interested, quite properly, in the long-term health of a patient after an operation; simply sending him home alive after an operation is not in itself proof of good surgery.

This explains why the medical profession doesn't become giddy with delight every time a magazine article proclaims that a new wonder cure or treatment has been discovered. The public gets very excited about such accounts, and puts considerable pressure on family doctors and surgeons to try the great "breakthrough" at once. Doctors prefer to wait a few years, until case histories can be evaluated, before they make up their minds. It is not a good idea to forget that human beings are not experimental animals. In surgery, in every aspect of mental and physical health, carefully and honestly evaluated clinical research is the only measure of excellence.

It's astonishing how optimistic some surgeons can be about the results of their operations, so long as they are careful never to review the records. One of my surgical colleagues, a man who had left the Clinic and was highly regarded, used to declare that his mortality for a certain type of procedure that he used at the Clinic was only 6 per cent. He decided to write a paper about his success and he wrote me, asking that I check the records and make sure that the 6 per cent was an accurate figure.

I did as he requested, and found the rate was 36.7 per cent. He was outraged, and asked me to check again, this time more carefully. I was meticulous, but the answer was the same. He said he didn't believe it and subsequently published a paper claiming a mortality of 6 per cent. I still get annoyed when I think about it.

SIX

As I learned for myself, one of the most serious failings a surgeon can have is rigidity. I've seen older surgeons using a thirty-year-old technique that they learned as surgical assistants, unaware or indifferent that it had been greatly changed and improved. It seems that the older a surgeon becomes, in many cases, the more difficult it is for him to accept an innovation. I had some experiences in my career with developing a surgical procedure, proving beyond doubt that it was safe and effective, and then finding that some colleagues were ignoring it, or even attacking it.

I will describe the more important of these later, but a minor example is my one-inch appendix incision, which isn't widely imitated. Some of my colleagues dubbed me "Buttonhole Mayo" because of it and I'm rather proud of its neatness. Danny Kaye, the comedian, has one and I'm told he is so delighted with it that he has displayed it to interested friends.

I wasn't able to make this minute incision in all appendectomies, of course; in many cases, I was obliged to enlarge the opening because of some condition that required greater exposure. Uncle Will, I know, wouldn't have approved of it at all—he was a surgeon who liked plenty of exposure when he operated and he always advised young surgeons to make an adequately long incision. He explained that, since incisions healed from side to side rather than from end to end, a long incision would heal as quickly as a short one. With all respect to my distinguished uncle, I still maintain that there is equal logic in making a small incision in *selected* cases of appendectomy.

Most of the criticism of my buttonhole incision centered on the difficulty it presents in getting a look around the patient's interior; commonly, in appendectomies, surgeons make use of the opportunity to check other organs, looking out in particular for the presence of cancer. I prepared a defense of my technique, assembling and studying case histories of Mayo Clinic patients who had been operated on for cancer of the colon or rectum.

I collected 154 cases of patients aged eighty years or older and 126 cases of patients younger than thirty years of age—all of whom had undergone resections more than ten years before. I found that the younger patients in almost every case had cancer that had confined itself to the rectum and to the rectosigmoid (the junction of the rectum and the abdominal portion of the colon). This discovery, that colon cancer in older people is deeper into the abdomen than such cancer in younger people, indicated to me that X-ray and proctoscopic examinations are dependable methods of detecting cancer in young people, without the necessity to make an internal exploration during their appendectomies.

Besides, I had discovered that a surprising amount of exploring can be done through a one-inch incision, providing the patient is not too obese and the surgeon has special instruments and a sensitive index finger. In children, the surgeon can put his finger in the appendectomy incision and explore the pelvis. In women, it is possible to reach and palpate at least the right tube and ovary. With instruments we call "long fingers," the cecum and terminal portion of the ileum can be located gently. I was able to pull out about two feet of the terminal portion of ileum—which is the last eleven feet of the small intestine. I could examine it in two-foot sections, replacing each bit and withdrawing the next, in order to check for a condition known as Meckel's diverticulum, a hollow and blind appendage attached to the small intestine, which can cause trouble if it becomes inflamed. Sometimes it happened that the appendix was affixed or there was some other difficulty, in which case I lengthened the incision and proceeded in the traditional method. Incisions can always be made larger, of course, but nothing can make them smaller.

The result of my procedure is a startlingly small surgical scar, almost a dimple. I took secret relish in performing that operation before visiting surgeons who had never seen it. I could feel their skepticism when they saw the size of the incision, though nothing was said. In those circumstances, it was gratifying to complete the operation smoothly and without a hitch, appearing casual and unconcerned all the while.

One of the most important services a surgeon can offer, when you come right down to it, is a proper appendectomy. Perhaps the proper repair of a hernia should be included as well. Both operations can be lifesaving, but for the most part they are done to add to the comfort of human existence. It is a great pleasure for a surgeon to renew in his patients their sense of well-being.

In 1934, I delivered a paper on appendicitis which dealt with some of the peculiarities of that strange, fickle structure, the appendix. At that time, some twenty-five thousand persons were dying of appendicitis every year in North America, a mortality that I found exceeded that of ectopic pregnancy, infected Fallopian tubes, gallstones, pancreatitis and splenic and thyroid disease *combined*. Doctors then, as now, were of different opinions as to certain phases of treatment. I maintained that no other subject was of more vital importance to public health than the appendix. I'm still of that mind; with our increasing population, deaths from appendicitis naturally are again climbing and we still need research in that field.

Oddly, doctors in many other parts of the world rarely encounter appendicitis. Dr. Walter Judd, a former fellow in the Mayo Clinic, spent seven years in China as a medical missionary before he came to Rochester and he told us that he had never seen a case of appendicitis among the Chinese there. It occurs, however, among Chinese who emigrate to the United States. A British army doctor who served in the Himalayan Mountains in India for fifteen years never saw or heard of a case of appendicitis there. Dr. Paul Harrison, a medical missionary in Arabia, saw only one case of appendicitis during his twenty years in that country.

Appendicitis, it might then be reasoned, might be related to our diet. There is good cause to suspect this, but it can also be traced to foreign bodies, such as worms, hairs or nails, which become lodged in the appendix. I have studied the history of appendectomies and I found that the first modern operation for abscess of the appendix was performed in 1759 by a French surgeon. He found a pin perforating the appendix, which had caused the abscess. Rupture of the appendix, which all patients dread without exactly understanding what it is, usually occurs as a result of obstruction at the base of the appendix. The infection, blocked off, explodes the walls of the appendix and seeps out, creating a hazard.

Physicians mainly are agreed about the treatment of the early stages of appendicitis. It is the treatment of the latter stages, especially after the appendix has ruptured, that is still in dispute. In order to avoid the serious complication of peritonitis, some surgeons are prone to operate on an appendix rather readily, in the presence of only scant symptoms of inflammation. Others delay, waiting until the signs are certain, and this delay is sometimes unfortunate.

I tend to side with the former group and with the witty Dr. Bastianelli of Rome, a contemporary of my father and Uncle Will, who once observed, "When physicians are discussing whether a case is appendicitis or not, it is; when they are inclined to admit the possibility of appendicitis without being sure of it, it not only is, but it is about to perforate; when the diagnosis is sure, there is already perforation with more or less circumscribed peritonitis."

A few years after I became a staff surgeon at the Mayo Clinic, I collected some data to present a paper at the forty-third annual meeting of the Western Surgical Association, held that year in Cincinnati, Ohio. My subject was that most familiar of all doctors' perplexities, the patient with the vague abdominal pain that appears to have no cause, even after laboratory tests and roentgenologic examination of the stomach, gallbladder and colon.

Some physicians label this malady "chronic nervous exhaustion" and dispose of the patients by urging them to "take it easy," whatever that means. Others pass the patient along to a surgeon who will perform an exploratory operation, and perhaps halfheartedly remove a normal-appearing appendix just because it is handy and "it might as well come out."

I was intrigued by this latter group of patients when I was a young surgeon. I wondered how they turned out: was the patient better off or was the operation the waste of time and effort and money that it seemed? Accordingly, I reviewed the records of all patients at the Mayo Clinic who had undergone such exploratory operations at least five years previously. I sent out questionnaires to 146 of them and received 92 replies.

For a while I was so irritated at the poor response that I considered launching a separate research project to determine why 54 persons would not answer a simple, seriously-intended questionnaire, particularly one which included a stamped, addressed envelope for the reply. I eventually dropped this line of investigation, figuring it was more suited to a sociologist or psychiatrist than a surgeon. With the 92 replies that I did receive by mail, I was able to add 8 more cases because these patients returned to the Clinic for various reasons and were available for personal interview. So I had a nice round total of 100 cases.

Of this number, 69 reported that they had been unqualifiedly cured. Seven patients said the operation had produced very good results; 14 reported fair results. Only 9 said they had not obtained any benefit whatsoever. One patient, I discovered, had died of peritonitis seven days after the operation. Interestingly, the operations had not been an indulgence after all—in all cases, the pathologist reported that the removed appendices showed moderate to definite signs of chronic infection.

I concluded therefore that in 90 of the cases, or 90 per cent, the appendix must have been the focus of the sense of ill health the patient was experiencing, since its removal gave him relief. I cannot account to what degree the relief was psychosomatic; certainly most people expect to feel better as the result of submitting to an operation and I cannot quarrel with those who say that the power of suggestion is a very good doctor. Nevertheless, the evidence tends to dispute that medical wag who once classified appendicitis as falling into two categories, "the acute and the remunerative." The so-called remunerative appendix, it seems, might well be removed to the benefit of the patient.

I took the view in that paper of long ago, and I still hold it, that there are some patients who have atypical intra-abdominal symptoms, whose tests will show negative results by all available methods, but who may be advised to submit to an exploratory operation and appendectomy with a great deal of safety. The prognosis justifies the procedure.

This may seem a contradiction of my tendency throughout my surgical career to avoid operating as much as was possible, consistent with the health of the patient. I once wrote a handbook of operative surgery—the only book I have written other than this one—it is called *Surgery of the Small and Large Intestine*. It was by no means a runaway best-seller, but it is still consulted by surgeons. In it, I expressed the fundamental principle that guided my conscience as a surgeon: "It is as important to know when not to operate as to know when to operate. The ideal surgical approach is not, 'Can I operate on the patient?' but is, 'Should I?'"

This is a dictum that I wish medical schools and training hospitals would emphasize until it is imprinted into the subconscious of every surgeon in the land. It can be extended to apply to those surgeons who remove far more tissue than is necessary when they operate. In my opinion, there is altogether too much play in the interpretation of "radical." I have noted that some surgeons perform what can be only described as superradical operations, while others show humane imagination and skill in order to avoid sacrificing more function than is necessary for the patient's recovery.

I'm speaking particularly of my own field, abdominal surgery, where, for instance, some surgeons operating in cases of cancer of the lower portion of the colon and upper portion of the rectum will unhesitatingly remove the rectum, leaving the patient with a colonic opening. In many of these cases, as I will describe later, the rectum and that muscle which controls elimination, the wondrous sphincter, might have been preserved.

I think it happens because the surgeon was trained to remove the rectum and he does so whenever he encounters the condition, without a qualm of conscience. He doesn't pause to reconsider what he is doing and try for an effective result using a less distressing technique. In the surgery that I did, I strove to do as little as possible that would intervene in normal functioning, without jeopardizing the patient's health. Really radical operations are a depressing business.

I must admit that it takes raw nerve for a surgeon to change his technique and then hold to the new method for five years, or until he can assemble at least one hundred carefully analyzed case histories. It is much more comfortable to stay with the familiar method, the one most colleagues also use. But without surgeons who have the courage and compassion to dare, there would be no surgical progress.

My fastidiousness about wasting a patient's organs was part of my general attitude toward squandering. I detested

123

putting the hospital laundry to unnecessary expense, so I flinched from the usual way that surgeons piled several layers of towels around an incision. I thought it sufficient to use what we at the Mayo Clinic call "salts," which are small damp cloths. I put two of them around the incision and considered that enough.

This kind of frugal housekeeping is a Mayo trait, I have been told. We spend a fortune buying the best equipment on the market but we protect our investment by giving it the kind of care which will ensure a long life for it. A medical museum once inquired if the Clinic still had any antique anesthetic apparatus. We not only had kept two of them but when they were removed from storage they were found to be still in excellent working condition.

I'm reminded that Father used to be concerned at the extremes of cleanliness that hospital procedure requires. He felt that scrubbing the skin excessively, as usually is done before an operation, can sometimes do more damage than good. He once made the suggestion, facetiously, that old-time farmers who had been sewn into their winter underwear by their wives should be operated on in the underwear, the surgeon cutting through flannel and skin with one stroke. He judged that the farmer would have immunized himself within the winter skin of the underwear. I think there was sound reasoning behind Father's joke, if only to register a protest that some things are overdone.

Similarly, I used to be aghast at the excessive examinations and palpations of such tissue as suspected cancer of the breast, which is still not uncommon today. It has been documented that such over-manipulation can cause cells to break off and drift away into the bloodstream, where they settle in vital organs. Some doctors seem insensitive to this genuine, mortal risk in their concentration on making a far too thorough examination.

I am inclined toward what I call "masterful inactivity."

I've noticed all too frequently that meddlesome kindness has been the straw that put the balance on the side of death. How much to do and when to stop are all-important in the treatment of patients. It usually falls on the surgeon to make the decision, since the patient on the operating table is inaccessible for a chat and the relatives may not be convenient.

Often, a moment comes in the operation when one or two minor repairs remain to be done but the surgeon senses the patient's exhaustion. I always felt it best to ease out of the abdomen at that point, if the safety of the patient was ensured. After the operation, I was loathe to disturb a patient's restful recovery with more tubes and needles than were absolutely required. It is terrifying to patient and relatives alike to have a science-fiction assortment of bubbling bottles and mysterious machinery arranged around the bed. It can be demoralizing, which is no way to encourage recovery.

But even the most brilliantly conceived and executed operation may fail to achieve the slightest improvement in the patient. In cases in which death occurs, the autopsy may fail to disclose an adequate reason for it. I was disturbed by this strange phenomenon from the beginning of my medical career and frequently made it the subject of a report, whenever I thought I had any light to shed on it.

My first paper on this enigma was written as early as 1931, my first year on staff at Mayo. I read it at a meeting of the Iowa County Medical Society and opened my remarks with the observation, "There is not one of us who, as referring physician or surgeon, has not had the alarming and unfortunate experience of seeing death follow a comparatively mild surgical procedure such as opening a boil, performing a tonsillectomy or removing a mildly infected appendix." After such an experience, I added, "it is impossible to avoid being aware that *all* surgery is major surgery, a lesson readily forgotten when years pass by with uneventful simple operations."

I then traced the postoperative complications of that period, many of them mercifully rare today, such as pneumonia, phlebitis, embolus, hemorrhage, inflammation of the salivary gland, streptococcus infection, and even hiccups, gas pains and vomiting. Last, but of equal significance, were the mental complications, ranging from severe postoperative psychosis to a general inertness and lack of desire to get well.

I proposed that excessive fear was the fundamental cause of the inexplicable collapses that doctors encounter. The fear would be associated with a generally unstable nervous system, or from the patient's conviction that his situation was hopeless. It used to anger me if I discovered that a nurse or resident had made some thoughtless remark in the presence of a patient, one which might have stimulated his concern for himself. I drilled my assistants to remember that patients can hear, even those who seem to be dozing, and they are easily confused and upset by a half-understood fragment of medical discussion. I would insist that they go down the corridor—well down the corridor—before reviewing the condition of any of my patients.

Six years later I published another paper on the same subject in the *Surgical Clinics of North America*, reporting on those few but terrifying cases of patients who become mentally ill after an operation. I discovered that in many cases a carefully-taken mental health history would have provided clues that the patient was a fearful, tense person and such a disaster was possible. At that time, we rarely took histories of mental health, and the patient and his family didn't usually volunteer information about emotional instability. Mental health is discussed much more openly now.

In my experience, fear kills. I have had patients who died of pure fear. Before their operations, they would appear to be in the grip of utter horror, weeping that they knew they could not live through the surgery. Very occasionally, such a patient died on the operating table; a few others died shortly after the operation. In both instances, the necropsy failed to disclose any obvious cause for death.

I have known good surgeons to become so upset by this brush with voodoo that they were ready to believe in occult powers. I saw no mystery in it: it was plain, stark fear. After a few experiences with it, I learned to postpone the operation or even cancel it, if the patient appeared excessively alarmed. I believe there is a relationship between people that we might call chemical compatibility, for want of a better term. With another surgeon, the patient might be calmer.

Surgery is an eternally alluring profession. I know now how cut off and lonely Father and Uncle Will must have felt after they retired. For one thing, there is the camaraderie. Much surgery can be carried out with two levels of concentration, one deeply focused on what is happening within the incision and the other free to answer questions from the gallery, to joke with doctors and nurses in the room and chat about the crops and weather. The operating room is friendly and, to the uninitiated, relaxed.

Quite often the camaraderie was of a different kind, akin to the closeness men feel in combat. The operation would be difficult and we worked in a tense silence, broken only by clipped instructions. With my curious indefatigability while I was operating, I'm told that I acquired the reputation around the Clinic of being an iron man. As the hours passed by in my adjoining surgeries and I still showed no signs of fatigue or hunger, some of my young assistants would sigh gently, by way of a hint. I'd send them off for rest and something to eat with a solicitous "Getting tired, doc?" which my friends tell me became identified with me. I recognized that it was gaining some kind of immortality one morning when I was leaving the operating room for some purpose and an assistant convulsed the team, and me, by calling out cheerily, "Getting tired, doc?"

The most dramatic mishap that can occur in an operation is when an artery is in the wrong place and the surgeon accidentally cuts it. Instantly a pulsing spout of blood floods the wound, making it impossible for suction to drain it away fast enough to uncover its source. Father gave me excellent advice for coping with this emergency. It sounds difficult to do, but it works. He told me to put my forefinger in the strong stream of the blood, judging by the feel of the current where it was coming from, and then to jam my forefinger firmly against the artery and hold it there until suction could clear away the blood and make the artery visible. After that it is a simple matter to clamp the artery and ligate or repair it.

This gory crisis is often too much for inexperienced student nurses and even for some interns who happen to be in the gallery at the time. Early in their careers, some young doctors are still sensitive to the sight of a volume of blood. Even the mature surgeon may experience a thudding sensation when it is over, but it is unthinkable that he should panic at the time. It is a similar situation to that of a jet test pilot, for instance, whose preconditioned reflexes enable him to deal coolly with a fire, automatically following the series of memorized procedures. So it is with a well-trained surgeon.

Not all the drama in an operating room is of the life-or-death variety. Surgery to remove huge abdominal cysts is exciting to perform and always attracts a full gallery. I once reviewed some of the Clinic's outstanding cases of large tumors of the abdomen and they make fascinating reading. In 1888, for example, Father removed a 65½-pound cyst from the left ovary of a woman who was only twenty-three years old. It was her *second* cyst removal: five years previously, he had taken a 33-pound cyst from her right ovary. He noted that the second one hung down to the poor woman's knees.

In 1920, Uncle Will removed an 82-pound cyst from a

woman who was fifty-three. There had been a gradual enlargement of her abdomen over a period of twelve years. Two years later, he removed a larger one, weighing 100 pounds, from the right ovary of a sixty-year-old woman. Her husband had made her a harness to support the bulk of the tumor so that she could walk.

These are large enough, but the Mayo Clinic record is held by a twenty-three-year-old who came to Uncle Will in 1920 for an exploratory operation. A diagnosis was made that she had an inoperable cancer. Two years later, to his surprise, she was back. Her abdomen was grotesquely enlarged—I'll never forget the picture we have of her. Uncle Will operated again and took out of her right ovary a growth that weighed 139½ pounds. He also drained away about twenty pounds of fluid that had been sloshing around freely in her abdomen.

Before the operation, the woman weighed 277 pounds; after it, she weighed 119 pounds. For doctors who are interested, the strange growth was diagnosed as Concato's disease (polyserositis).

I had one curious experience myself with removal of cysts. Within one week, I removed a 21-pound cyst from the ovary of a seventeen-year-old and a 30-pound cyst from a girl who was nineteen. Both had identical histories, both were active university students and neither had the slightest symptom of distress. Except for their distended abdomens, they would have been unaware of their conditions.

As I have said, no one can predict what the surgeon will find when he cuts through a patient's skin. The insides of people are as individual as are their faces and bodies. One of the oddest discoveries a surgeon can make is that of a certain kind of teratoma. Teratomas are tumors composed of embryonic tissue and when they develop, usually in the ovaries of women or anywhere in the abdomen of men, they can contain hair and teeth and other recognizably human parts. An explanation of this gruesome object is that the person in whom it grows was one of twins, and early in embryonic development the twin somehow stopped maturing and became lodged within the healthy fetus. Later, usually in adult life, the embryonic tissue inexplicably starts to grow again and follows a demented course, neither human nor a true tumor, until removed by a surgeon. They are not pleasant sights but anything you are used to seeing you can bear.

Since I seem to be discussing some of the black side of surgery, I'll deal quickly with that most chilling of news after an operation, which laymen customarily describe as, "There was nothing they could do—he was just full of cancer. The doctor just looked at it and closed him up." It is regarded as a death knell, and it usually is.

When a surgeon opens an abdomen in such cases, he has different degrees of feeling about what he can accomplish, based on tests which have established approximately how widespread the cancer might be. He never operates in a mood of hopelessness, since he expects that even if it is too late for a complete cure at least he can make adjustments which will alleviate the patient's distress for a time.

Occasionally, however, it is clear at once, without biopsies, that the situation is out of control. In the most serious cases, there are thousands of tiny spots on most of the visible tissue: the small intestine, the large intestine, the peritoneum, everywhere. The surgeon closes the incision in heavy silence.

In cases in which the malignant process seems to be confined in one area, the surgeon performs his task of removing it as thoroughly as he can and then must face the almost equally formidable duty of telling the patient's family that the growth was not benign. I always asked the family to allow me to tell the patient the truth about his cancer, rather than pretending that his condition was otherwise. I knew that patients always would suspect it and fret secretly about it, more frightened by the evasions they sensed than they would be of reality. I believe it is best to be aboveboard about cancer.

130

Happily, I was almost always able to accompany the news with statistical evidence that other patients with similar or much worse conditions had been cured, some of them living a normal life span, others enjoying five, ten or twenty years more of health. With the benefits of cobalt or chemotherapy, when necessary, and good aftercare, together with a confident outlook on the part of the patient, apparent miracles are fairly commonplace in modern hospitals. An attitude overloaded with bitterness and self-pity is less conducive to recovery, I have noted.

I would like to see medical authorities bear down on prevention of cancer even more than they are now doing. There are some common lesions which I regard as precancerous and deserving of the closest observation but which some physicians regard as minor, uninteresting difficulties. In this category are first leukoplakia, which are hard white patches on the tongue, lips or oral cavity, which appear most commonly in men over forty, and polyps of the colon and rectum.

As an example of this latter condition, a very good friend of mine came to the Clinic and I removed a polyp from his colon. It was found to be benign, but I advised him that he must have regular re-examinations for the rest of his life: it has been established that there is a 28 per cent risk of new polyps developing in cases where one has been detected, and the possibility of cancer increases sharply.

A few years later he was found to have another polyp, but this time he stubbornly refused to have it removed. I disapproved, but I told him that he could defer surgery only if he was willing to have the polyp examined every six months. "It is bound to become malignant someday," I told him bleakly. He said he would take his chances and promised that he would have an X-ray examination twice a year. Nine years passed before a regular re-examination revealed that the polyp had become cancerous. A resection of the colon was necessary but fortunately the malignant process had not penetrated the wall of the bowel or involved the lymph glands. This would have been the next development if he had missed his checkup. His case demonstrates both the menace of these innocent-seeming polyps and the importance of regular examinations.

Polyps of the colon are rare in young people; about 86 per cent occur in people over fifty. A polyp can be benign for as long as twenty years before becoming malignant but, in my opinion, it certainly will be a cancer eventually. The Cancer Prevention Center in Chicago once noted that in fifty thousand examinations of patients between twenty and seventy-six years of age, polyps were discovered in 7.9 per cent, cancerous polyps in .65 per cent. Advanced cancer occurred in .035 per cent of cases.

The University of Minnesota has a cancer detection unit for women over forty-five and men over fifty years of age. After its first eight years of operation, 8229 people had been studied and one in every thirty-six proved to have a malignant lesion in some part of the body, an incidence of 2.7 per cent. Half of these had been found on the second examination, and were not noticeable on the first. It was found that rectal and colonic polyps are more than four times as likely to become cancerous than lesions found in any other part of the body. A total of forty patients, twenty-two women and eighteen men, had histologically-proved cancers in the rectum and colon; by comparison, fifty-seven had skin cancer, and seventeen, stomach cancer.

I emphasize that the survival of patients whose malignant lesions are discovered in a routine checkup, before there are any symptoms, is three times that of patients who first see a doctor after they have experienced some distress. The evidence is incontrovertible: the older adult who doesn't have regular examinations is jeopardizing his life.

In my early years in surgery, I performed an interesting operation on a Portuguese lady who was suffering from a megacolon, an abnormally large colon as round as a melon. The symptoms justified that a resection be done, so I removed it entirely, six feet of it, and hooked her small bowel to her rectum. Astonishingly, in view of this drastic rearrangement of her interior, she later had a normal pregnancy and gave birth to a son, who became a doctor and came to the Mayo Clinic as a fellow. While in Rochester, he became the father of a girl named Clara and paid me the honor of asking me to be godfather.

There were some operations I preferred not to perform, or even watch—those within the skull. Maybe my distaste for them arose partly from a grisly joke that I heard once and haven't been able to forget. It concerns an old country doctor who was using an auger on the skull of a farmer. The operation was performed in the farmhouse on a very hot day and the doctor had great difficulty because the bedspring would yield when he tried to apply pressure to the auger. He strained and strained to no avail and finally moved the patient to the floor, where he set himself strenuously to his task. Suddenly, the auger slipped through the bone and sunk itself deep in the patient's brain. The old doctor straightened and wiped his brow. "I was afraid of that," he said.

I wasn't too comfortable about performing eye operations either—my own eyes tend to water sympathetically if I even remove a cinder from someone's eye—but I did do circumcisions, although not too gladly. Early in my career, the wife of a colleague asked me if I would circumcise her infant son. I didn't want to admit that I had never performed one but I agreed, reasoning that rabbis with only a fragment of my medical training did them all the time.

I underestimated the problem, I discovered. The baby kept crying lustily and pumping his knees which, since the area of the operation is not too large to begin with, greatly interfered with my ministrations. I had a decent concern that I might remove too much skin and so, with all the contingencies to consider, it isn't surprising that I removed too little. The mother loyally brought the baby back a few weeks later to have the operation done again.

Amazingly, she still had faith in me a few years later when she gave birth to another son. She brought this infant to me for circumcision also but this time I was experienced and equal to the responsibility; I did it properly in one try.

It's remarkable how much confidence some people put in doctors. I had one woman patient many years ago who seemed very agitated the night before I was to operate on her. "Doctor," she said, wringing her hands, "I'll be *all alone!*"

"No you won't," I comforted her. "I'll be there." About four emotions passed across her face before she laughed.

Another time a bellicose patient asked me in a rather arrogant tone of voice, "Did you take care of —— from my home town?" I hadn't the faintest idea whether I did or not, and not too much patience left, so I replied, "If he's alive, I did."

That same friend who had the polyp that turned cancerous once developed a small goiter and I removed it under a local anesthetic. Dr. Edward Judd was my first assistant that day and I remember this friend kept wailing, "Oh Chuck, you said it wouldn't hurt!" We'd give him a little more novocain and after a while he would start complaining again. We managed to persuade him that he was capable of walking out of the operating room, which he strongly doubted, and then he began berating me again. "What do you mean?" I asked him in amazement. "I never said it wouldn't hurt *you*, I meant it wouldn't hurt *me*. And I was right, it didn't."

I remember fondly the exchange with Danny Kaye just before I removed his appendix. He's a frustrated doctor—I think he even went to medical school for a short time—and treating him has some of the aspects of treating an alert colleague. When he inquires about a urinalysis, for instance, he asks about the albumin determination. He diagnosed his own case of appendicitis; he was at Wichita, on a trip in his own airplane, and he simply notified me and then set course for Rochester.

When he arrived in surgery his hand brushed against my surgeon's gown. He recoiled apologetically, "I'm sorry," he said, "I forgot you were sterile." He considered this observation for a moment and then murmured, "What am I saying? He's got *six kids!*"

I inquired kindly, "Any last words?" He wasn't too amused. "I'm scared," he confessed. "I'm more scared now than at any time when I've waited in the wings to go on stage." I signaled the anesthetist to begin, consoling Danny, "Good words. I'll remember them."

I might say here that it never mattered to me, and I doubt if it matters to any surgeon, whether the patient on the table is a celebrity or not. It is all the same when the incision is made. If a surgeon gets excited because he is operating on a famous person, he's in the wrong profession. Naturally, though, it isn't possible to be unaware that the patient is someone special, if for no other reason than that the gallery is packed with nurses and doctors who just happen to decide to watch surgery that day.

It is a different matter if the patient is related to the surgeon. Doctors rarely operate on their own kin, mostly because they know that something can go wrong—it can go wrong even during the simplest and most carefully performed operation—and a man would spend the rest of his life wondering if it would have been different if someone else had done that operation. I have known surgeons who operated on their wives and the wives died; that's very difficult to live with.

Father once was in a serious mood, talking about a patient of his who had died that day. "You know why I like doing hysterectomies?" he asked me suddenly. "Because you never lose a patient." Once he startled some visiting surgeons by telling them merrily that at the end of a hard day in surgery he liked to finish off with about five hysterectomies. He was joking, but I knew what he meant; operations with almost no mortality are much appreciated by surgeons.

Fortunately, I never had a patient die on the operating table. I regret to say that I once did leave a sponge in a patient. Surgical sponges are attached to a ring that a surgeon wears around his wrist, which is a handy arrangement. I once heard of a patient in a distant city who wasn't healing properly after an operation in the pelvic area. When they opened him up again they found the entire ring inside him, together with a number of sponges.

I find that one incomprehensible, but my own miscount of sponges desolated me. It happened during an operation to perform a resection for cancer of the upper rectum. I had two sponges on the end of extremely long forceps, used them deep in the cavity and then withdrew the forceps without noticing that only one sponge was still attached. It is the usual procedure in surgery to keep a careful count of such items as sponges for just that eventuality, but this time something slipped up.

Later, in the patient's home town on the West Coast, another doctor took an X ray and found the sponge in a draining sinus in the pelvis. Some doctors in similar circumstances will say nothing to the patient about the foreign body they have detected but will keep a watch on it, knowing that usually it works its own way out and a second operation to go in for it can probably be avoided. With a second operation, in addition to the pain and expense, there is more likelihood of adhesions forming. This doctor, however, informed the patient of the presence of the sponge and the patient immediately sued me. Eventually the patient was awarded ten thousand dollars, which an insurance company paid.

I am fiercely proud of my profession, and detest the small proportion of incompetents in it as much as any abused patient, but I hold to the old ethical tradition that doctors

9. Joe, Father, me

10. Joe and me at Mayowood, 1912

11. My first man's suit, age seven

12. Father and Mother in the shadows of the patio at Mayowood

should police themselves, and militantly, but in private. Father felt the same way, I think. In *The Surgical Journal* in 1929 he commented on the distasteful picture presented to the public when doctors openly quarrel. During a trial, for instance, at which distinguished specialists were testifying for both parties involved, he noted that both sides became "violently partisan—they left out this matter and that, and entered into the case as if it were a game of football or baseball between college teams. The patient was almost wholly forgotten in the excitement and scramble of the trial."

I found a few small sponges left by others from time to time but on one memorable occasion a woman came to me with a draining sinus in her neck following a goiter operation and I removed a sponge strip that was about two feet long. I can't imagine how it could have happened but I said nothing to the patient and wrote the surgeon involved a tactful letter telling him about it. His pride was hurt, I suppose, for he wrote me back one of the nastiest letters I've ever received.

One time I recall a doctor's error that was impossible to hide from the patient. It happened when I was still on my fellowship at the Clinic and had been assigned to change the dressings of a patient in the Zumbro Hotel. He had had a gallbladder operation somewhere in Illinois, and came to the Clinic because it wouldn't heal. I kept dressing and probing the wound but could find no cause for the difficulty. The patient himself, a stoical fellow, also kept poking at it himself and one day felt something in the wound. He pulled it out, and kept pulling, and pulling, eventually dragging out about two feet of drainage gauze. I wrapped it in a newspaper and deposited it in a trash can. The patient didn't seem perturbed, happily, just relieved to be rid of a nuisance.

Like many other doctors, I would be grateful for clearer guidelines pertaining to the conditions under which a legal abortion can be performed. All doctors are asked to do abortions and the phrase permitting abortions in cases where the

137

"health" of the mother is endangered is medically vague. When you come right down to it, even discomfort isn't healthy; some abortions accordingly are closer to the strict spirit of the regulation than others. It is a difficult moral, legal and ethical decision; I don't think it should ever be left to one doctor alone to make.

Father disliked being asked to perform an abortion when the motive was merely a tardy form of birth control. A patient in St. Marys Hospital once asked him to give her an abortion. He replied with coldness that he would not, adding, "But you go ahead and have the baby and after it is born you and I will take it out to the barn and chop it to pieces."

I never did any plastic surgery but I used to do an operation that I suppose can be called cosmetic surgery. I operated on women's breasts to make them smaller. Some women came to the Clinic with enormous breasts, hanging down to their laps, and they wanted surgery to reduce their size. It presents an interesting problem because the breasts have to match when the operation is finished. I used to cut around the nipples and then use them as a guideline, taking out most of the fatty tissue and shaping what was left. The loose skin later tightens by itself, but in cases of excessive size it would be necessary to move the nipples up and cut away a quantity of skin from the lower half of the breast.

Those were absorbing operations but operations to remove a breast that has been invaded by cancer are massive. There is much trauma to tissues during that surgical procedure and it would seem that the postoperative pain would be intense, but surprisingly it isn't.

The operation requires a long incision, of course, but operations on kidneys have even longer ones. They seem almost to cut a patient in half and can be three feet long. My longest incision, I think, was the time I removed a big ovarian cyst and had to cut the woman from pubic bone to past the navel.

SEVEN

Alice and I went on a Caribbean cruise in 1933, combining it with a visit to the hospitals on the islands and meetings with some of the leading surgeons to talk about what they were doing and to watch them operate. All our vacations, until I retired, were mostly working trips. I naturally wrote to the hospitals in advance, asking permission to be an observer, and this led to one of the most embarrassing incidents of my life.

Our ship had just dropped anchor in the harbor of San Juan in Puerto Rico when we noticed a boat coming our way with a band aboard and crowds of people waving excitedly at us from its rails. They were doctors and their families, we discovered, come to welcome the famous Dr. Charles Mayo. Their consternation when they saw me, instead of my father, was profound. Of course we all had to go through with it gamely, the tours of the hospitals and even a sugar factory, the formal banquet, the speeches of welcome. I felt more miserable than they did and I was grateful when the ship left that evening.

Two years later I was sent to Europe on a clinical trip to discover what surgeons were doing and report back to the Mayo Clinic. Alice came with me and our good friends Dr. James Priestley and his wife Klea. Jim Priestley's great-grandfather, Dr. Joseph Priestley, discovered oxygen in 1774. He got it by heating mercuric oxide and called what resulted "dephlogisticated air." Phlogiston was the name used two

139

hundred years ago for the imaginary substance that was supposed to be the raw material of fire. The property he discovered was named oxygen the following year by another scientist. Jim's grandfather was also a doctor and had practiced in Des Moines, Iowa, at the same time that my grandfather was there.

I had been equipped with a stack of letters of introduction from Father and Uncle Will to outstanding doctors all over Europe. We started our three-month tour in Italy in March, reasoning that it would be warm there. Instead we encountered bitterly cold weather. In Naples, our first stop, we kept warm by sitting in the bathtub all day with the hot water running.

Our routine was that Jim and I would rise early and be at some hospital by eight in the morning to watch the surgery and make rounds, and we would spend most of the day with doctors, returning to the hotel toward evening feeling somewhat worn. There we would find our wives blithely preparing for an evening of festivity, usually arranged by Father's hospitable friends, and we frequently didn't get to bed until two. The next morning our wives naturally slept late, while we hurried off; they were fresh as daisies again when we returned in the evening. Jim and I rapidly began to resemble exhausted combat veterans.

My nerves were quaking anyway as we approached Rome because Father and Uncle Will had requested that I express their appreciation personally to Mussolini for some honor the Italian government had conferred on them. I informed our embassy in Rome to make the necessary arrangements, if possible, and I rather hoped it wasn't.

Through some friends, we were all privileged to have a semiprivate audience with Pope Pius XII shortly after our arrival. We were awed by what seemed to be his genuine humility, despite the austere expression in most of his photographs, and an obvious aura of greatness. On our return to the hotel, I was given a message that Mussolini would see me at Piazza Venezia at seven thirty that evening. I was aghast.

While I dressed in my diplomat's garb of striped pants and a cutaway coat, I scribbled some appropriate comments on a piece of paper and earnestly memorized them, with Alice prompting. I finally felt confident that I had a graceful speech down pat.

Footmen in stockings and britches were waiting inside the palace to escort me up three flights of wide marble stairs and along a huge corridor to a closed door. I drew some comfort in reminding myself that our ambassador surely would accompany me, but I was told at this moment that Il Duce wanted to see me alone.

I received instructions as to my procedure. On a signal, the doors would be opened and I was to step forward and give the Fascist salute. At the other end of the room I would find Mussolini, seated behind his desk near a window. I later learned that this window opened on the shallow balcony from which Mussolini made his speeches to the crowds in the square below. My instructor told me that Mussolini would rise and return my salute, at which I would approach him, stop in front of the desk and salute again.

The door opened and I saw before me an expanse of black and white marble floor, in a pattern of squares, that seemed to stretch for a mile. My apprehension dazed me. I remember thinking wildly that it would have helped me to walk a straight line toward the desk if the squares had been arranged in a line, rather than diagonally. I suppose I saluted at the door, I don't remember, and I walked to the desk and began to salute again. As my arm came up, Mussolini rose and grasped my hand to shake it. I was startled by this, and by my discovery that he was two inches or more shorter than I am, and I am not tall.

He greeted me in English, which he spoke fairly well, and I launched into my memorized speech. After the first paragraph, he interrupted to ask my impression of medicine

141

in Italy. I answered him, saying something favorable, and then opened my mouth to continue my speech. To my horror, I couldn't remember where I had left off. In my confusion, I heard myself begin again at the beginning.

Mussolini listened a moment and then interrupted again to ask about medicine in the United States, and I replied as best I could. In the process, I once again lost my place in the speech. We stared at one another fixedly as I again began the speech from the opening line. When Mussolini cut in once more, I abandoned the project as hopeless. I replied to his query briefly. "You're a busy man," I then said, adding inanely, "and I am too." And with that I shook his hand firmly, said good night and withdrew, forgetting to salute.

It turned out that it was true that he was busy, for that same night he declared war on Ethiopia. I spent the rest of the evening regaling Alice and the Priestleys with my less than polished performance, which gradually appeared comical even to me.

Jim and I were intrigued by the grade of medicine that was being practiced in Europe at that time. Everywhere we went, we made copious notes of points that would interest other doctors at the Clinic. The surgery in Budapest was especially notable, since doctors there were making extensive use of local anesthesia. They even did resections of the stomach and intestine under local anesthesia, which amazed us.

When we reached Vienna, there was an unmistakable feeling of tension and danger in the air, which became more and more ominous as we proceeded into Hitler's Germany. We took time out for a week in Freiburg and Baden-Baden, at the insistence of Jim and myself who were hollow-eyed from lack of rest. Freiburg, which mostly was destroyed by bombings in World War II, was a beautiful old city in 1935. It was there that I announced to Alice that I could remember some of the German I had learned in school and that I therefore would order our breakfast in that language. She clearly was impressed as I told the waiter, "Zwei eis." *Zwei* is German for "two" and *eis*, as I recalled it, was German for "eggs." It must have lost something in the translation: what we were served was two pineapple sundaes.

We caught our first glimpse of Hitler in Munich, when he visited the museum where we happened to be. Alice and Klea were upset by the atmosphere of cruelty around him. Jim and I were shocked too at the doctors we were meeting. Most of them seemed sympathetic to the Nazi movement, and even saluted one another with a hard-edged "Heil Hitler!" when they met around the hospitals. None of us knew much about what was happening, but we took an instinctive aversion to the government. Its ruthlessness showed, we felt, in the attitude of doctors toward their patients. There was an absence of any humaneness or concern, and a disposition to treat patients as objects. We were disgusted too at the custom of scheduling three or four operations at a time, creating an assembly line of unconscious people.

Alice and I took a side trip to Paris, where I looked up my friend Dr. Henri Welti, whose field of surgery was the same as mine. We were fortunate to attend the Paris debut of Lily Pons in the glorious opera house there, and then rejoined the Priestleys in Berlin. Matters in the German capital were the most military and frightening of our entire trip; even patients rose from their beds and stood at attention to return the "Heil Hitler" salute of the doctors and nurses.

Once we attended a German air force show at Templehof Airport, watching it from a table in an open-air restaurant. When "Deutschland über Alles" was played we rose reluctantly to our feet and Jim and I felt that protocol required us to make a halfhearted attempt at the Nazi salute. Klea and Alice flatly refused to do it. I didn't always take a serious view of the gathering menace of the German army, I suppose, because on another occasion I couldn't resist goose-stepping along behind a German army band in a parade that went by our hotel. The Germans really can parade and I had a fine

143

time joining in for a few hundred yards, but Alice didn't speak to me for the rest of the day.

On the boat that took us to England, I came to the decision that the letters of introduction were a hazard to our health, since they had turned out to be the cause of more parties and receptions than we could attend. To demonstrate the firmness of my resolve, I threw them out of the porthole. We were toasting our freedom from the bonds of gracious hospitality when there was a knock at the door. A steward proudly returned all the letters to me, explaining that they had blown back to the steerage deck and been picked up there. I tipped him as though grateful, and concluded uneasily that we had witnessed an act of God. I took care not to throw them away again and they returned with us all the way to Rochester.

In England and Scotland I found the type of surgery that I was accustomed to, and the warm concern for the welfare of the patient that I believe cannot be separated from mere ability if a man is to be regarded as a good doctor. I was grateful to find this again, since Nazi Germany had been a depressing experience. I wasn't surprised after the war at reports that German doctors had performed experimental operations on helpless prisoners; it fit with the callousness that I had observed in 1935.

We spent a good deal of time in London with Archibald McIndoe, who had been in Rochester for some seven or eight years. For a time he and I alternated as chief surgeon and first assistant as we finished our fellowship training in general surgery, and we became close friends as well. He became a top-ranking plastic surgeon after leaving Rochester and was knighted in 1947 in recognition of his contribution in this field. We also saw a good deal of C. Naunton Morgan, who worked at St. Mark's and St. Bartholomew's Hospitals. His special interest was surgery of the rectum and colon and I was finding an absorbing interest in this field.

Jim and I reported on our trip at the next regular staff

meeting of the Mayo Clinic after our return. These gatherings of the staff to hear firsthand about interesting cases within the Clinic and what was happening elsewhere had evolved out of the custom of Grandfather and his two sons of pooling all information. They are always well attended, but never so well as when my father would return from a trip and pack the house.

He assumed that everything that interested him was interesting and proceeded from there, both entertaining and illuminating. He did not limit his remarks to medicine, as so many doctors do during their lives. He told one staff meeting that the Danube is not blue, and never was blue, and all about the growth of socialism in Vienna, and about the poverty of Berlin hospitals after the first war, where he observed that the only antiseptic was a tube of boric acid and the operating table was padded with sterilized newspapers.

At a staff meeting in 1931, he told doctors that water in the state of California had gone down seven hundred feet since pumping for irrigation had been started, which must have mystified doctors new to his eclectic approach, and that the pioneer surgeon Lorenz had such strong hands that he used them to break up the bones of children with club feet and to break bowlegs. He commented favorably on the ancient Chinese custom of a patient paying a doctor just so long as he remains well. It fit with the philosophy of positive health that he preached everywhere. He once complained that "people accept illness as if it were predestined, submitting to it without thought of prevention."

Another staff meeting received the information that Puebla, Mexico, had fifty-three churches and that the original home of Cortez was in Cuernavaca, which had just established ten day-care centers for children of working mothers. Father approved forcefully of day-care centers, and provided reasons.

Despite the successive blows of small strokes and his increasing age, his imagination remained lusty and young, and

145

inspired. "The only thing permanent is change," he used to declare, mildly rephrasing a noble Greek philosopher. In the early thirties, he was indignant at the feeling among his fellow citizens that the United States should collect its debts in Europe and then isolate itself from world affairs. "The sooner this country stops thinking of her bad debts in Europe and devotes some attention to the Western Hemisphere, the sooner we will come into close relationship with many neighboring nations. Then we will have an outlet for our products and they will have an outlet for theirs, for ages." That still makes good sense, and still hasn't been implemented with any true enthusiasm.

Father's mind was a wonder. At random, I can remember that he prophesied in 1920 that the next war would be fought with germs—and it nearly was; and that before surgeries were built with galleries for the visiting doctors to watch operations, Father invented a wheeled platform that served the purpose admirably; and that he joined the Masons, explaining merrily that he wanted "to make sure there'll be someone at my funeral."

He returned one time from a visit to Detroit and reported to a staff meeting that a doctor in that city was having great difficulty in making flaps grow on dry bone. Father was reminded that he had been successful in this twenty years before, when he had three cases where women had their entire scalps torn off while working around belts and wheels. Father drilled down through the outer table of their skulls with a bone drill until there was some bleeding, then drilled again a quarter of an inch away, and again and again until the skull was a mass of shallow holes. Ten days later enough granulation material had seeped through the holes to enable flaps of hair to be attached.

He wandered from this ingenious solution to relate a story about surgery in the days before antiseptics, "when operations were almost as exciting as the tales of buccaneers of the Spanish Main, and the mortality about the same."

Father's sweep of language could be deeply moving. He wrote a memorial in 1927 to a deceased colleague, Dr. Charles Howard Peck: "It is with a sense of deepest personal loss not unmixed with sorrow that I record the passing of Dr. Charles Howard Peck, master surgeon, earnest patriot and distinguished teacher, benefactor of mankind and my friend."

I chuckled at the radio address he made over WCCO in 1928. "I have spoken but three times on the ether waves," he began, "and although I have put many to sleep with ether I have no knowledge of long-distance work. It is easy to dial out before one becomes unconscious."

Though he always took care to be amusing, much of what he had to say throughout his lifetime was prophetic. In 1888, for example, he returned from a visit to clinics doing work on nose, throat and larynx and observed, "Such diseases don't stand alone. . . . No matter how apparently local its manifestations may be, it is becoming clearer with each new advance in medicine that disease tends to permeate the entire body."

During his radio address, he speculated on the importance of films in education, a development which didn't take place until forty years later. "Are we making use of the moving picture in education and in general teaching?" he asked. "Through the eye we receive over ninety per cent of our external impressions."

He also foresaw the evolution of education away from rote memorization. "Too often our best students, without that care given the car in the first five hundred miles, may burn themselves out mentally by the time their school education is complete. . . . To condense education, more time must be devoted to the essentials and the principles, and but little to details which are mentally exhausting and belong to vocational and professional training."

He was annoyed in 1926 that Americans spent more on tobacco, cosmetics and chewing gum than on education, which he thought would lead directly to a substantial number of illiterate citizens taking little interest in the affairs of their country. Which certainly came to pass. "As American citizens," he scolded, "we think too much of our privileges and not enough of our responsibilities and duties."

He also worried about the caliber of men entering medicine, and the narrowness of their outlook once they began to practice. "It is possible that our medical colleges pay too little attention to the public service work in the education of future physicians, all of whom are benefited by community life. Physicians, especially, owe something to the community."

Mayo Clinic in those grim depression years had lean times, but was in no serious difficulty. Father and Uncle Will, having retired before the crash, seemed to be under no financial stress. They continued to buy the best of everything, usually being the first in Rochester to purchase something new. For instance, earlier, Father had the first car in Rochester and bought Mother the first electric car seen there. She drove it down Broadway and hit a horse-drawn taxi on the first day she tried it out; she never drove it again.

The trend that Uncle Will had anticipated in the increasing importance of medicine over surgery was accelerating. During the first five years of the 1930's, 66 per cent of the fellows at the Clinic were in surgery; during the next five years, the proportion decreased to 31 per cent. The great Canadian Dr. William Osler, then professor of medicine at Oxford, declared, "The surgeons have had their day—and they know it! The American St. Cosmas and St. Damian—the Mayo brothers—have made their Clinic today as important in medicine as it ever was in surgery. Wise men! They saw how the pendulum was swinging."

The Clinic was attracting a number of doctors from Europe, who had decided their careers would benefit by Mayo training. A number of them became good friends of mine, spending their Saturday nights and Sundays with us at Mayowood, and later keeping in touch even during the war years when communication was difficult. One such was Erwin Strassmann, who came from Berlin and after a time in Rochester became a citizen. His father, a renowned gynecologic surgeon, had his own hospital in Berlin, and was a close friend of Father and Uncle Will. Piero Frugoni came from Italy to train in Rochester and then returned to become professor of neurologic surgery at Padua, which is a city famous in medical history. A Spaniard, Alfonso de la Pena, went back to Madrid after his Mayo training and later became professor of urologic surgery. And Kenneth Latter, an Englishman who delighted us with his ability to play the piano, returned to his home to be made a professor of medicine. The Mayo influence is world-wide and well represented.

Two good friends of mine, Antonio Mendes-Ferreira and Eduardo Gusmao, were preparing to return to Portugal after their fellowships were completed at Rochester and hospitably threw a farewell luncheon one Sunday at their boarding house. It was a memorable occasion, starting with deceptive simplicity with the usual cocktails and canapés and proceeding from there to many courses of what we were told was typical Portuguese cooking. These staggeringly flavorful dishes were climaxed by what the doctors assured us was a popular Portuguese dessert: fresh strawberries with sugar and ether. Alice politely choked down one berry but I ate about half my portion, and then agreeably finished off with some delicious port wine from Oporto, Portugal. Eventually we floated back to Mayowood and I think I was strongly under the impression that I was able to speak Portuguese as well. We have all remained staunch friends; in fact, I am godfather to Dr. Ferreira's daughter Maria.

Benjamin Spock was also at the Clinic at that time, and quite evidently was excited by his investigation of the proper care and raising of small children. Alice and I were very fond of both Dr. Spock and his wife but I don't recall that we ever asked his advice about our children. It seemed to us that he was having as much trouble as we were handling his own family. He is accused by some of advocating permissiveness, which I don't think is an accurate interpretation of what he recommends. I grinned when I read that he had ordered his eighteen-year-old son Michael to "shave off that beard or get out of the house!"

Alice mostly was raising the children but I took my turn at continuing a Mayo tradition and used to take our sons, particularly Charlie, on my hospital rounds. Patients would say to him, "And of course you're going to be a doctor too?" and Charlie would nod. I kept out of it, knowing full well what it demands of a man to be a doctor with that name.

The children all rode horses from the time that they were small and our family outings mostly were to horse shows, where they won their share of ribbons and broke more than their share of bones. I don't think any of them grew to adulthood without having a plastic surgeon work on them. It seemed to me that they all had a bottomless talent for falling off horses onto crushed rock, or impaling themselves on fish hooks, or knocking out some teeth in car accidents. But they all enjoyed rousing good health, except for Joe who is a total diabetic.

One of the highlights of those years was the sultry, torrid summer day when the President of the United States, Franklin Delano Roosevelt, came to Rochester. Father and Uncle Will had been giving veterans treatment at the Mayo Clinic free of charge, a pioneer effort which eventually flowered into our present network of veterans hospitals, and the American Legion in 1934 wanted to recognize this with a citation and ceremony attended by the President. The two young grandchildren of the Mayo brothers, our daughter Muff and Waltman Walters, were chosen to unveil the plaque in Soldiers Field. At the time, we were unable to disabuse Muff of the notion that the bands, flags, cheering crowds and the presence of the President of the country were all in her honor.

Father and Uncle Will rode in an open car under the broiling sun with the President. They were to go to Mayowood for lunch so the city hastily paved the dusty gravel road that led to the Big House. The asphalt had been calculated superlatively—it lasted for three weeks and collapsed only after the President had returned to Washington. In any case, Father wasn't too cooperative. To the horror of the guard around the President and the officials who had worked out a split-second schedule, Father had the presidential car leave the designated route and drive past the medical research center he was developing. He reported that the President seemed impressed.

After that they arrived at Mayowood and the gentlemen of the party withdrew to have a pre-luncheon drink. Uncle Will suffered patiently while F.D.R. put away five martinis, without showing the slightest sign of them, and then they went in to dine. Young James Roosevelt, I recall, was there to help his father maneuver on his crutches. They worked it out so smoothly that it was easy to forget that the President was a cripple. His affliction was an asset in some ways, I felt; it gave him time to think.

A great friend of Father's, Dr. William D. Haggard, stayed at Mayowood overnight and wrote out some remarks for the President to read at the ceremony. He was president of the American Medical Association at the time, I think. He worked late into the night, which gave Alice and my impish sister Esther an opportunity to play a prank on him. Dr. Haggard was an austere, conventional man, which is probably what tempted them. They sneaked into his bedroom while Dr. Haggard was still downstairs composing the speech and arranged the covers on his bed over an outsized doll belonging to Muff and some pillows so that it looked as if a woman was sleeping there. As an added touch, they found a wig somewhere and fixed its long curls over the pillow.

They waited impatiently, spying through a crack in a door, until almost three in the morning when Dr. Haggard wearily entered his bedroom and paused on the threshold for a long silence. Then he turned off the light and quietly returned downstairs. He slept on the lounge and the next morning complained to my mystified father about the excessive hospitality of the house.

Father was being kept busy in those days coming to the defense of much more than his outrageous womenfolk. There was a great deal of criticism rising against the men who were occupied with research projects at the Clinic. They drew large salaries, just as did the doctors dealing with patients every day, but years were passing and they seemed to have produced nothing. Father made himself an impregnable wall against the protests and refused to harass the scientists in the smallest degree. He maintained, as I do, that a researcher needs time and that some of it is well spent in a laboratory and some more may be even better spent while the man has his feet up on his desk. It wasn't easy to protect the researchers against the complaints, but Father never wavered in his faith in them and in what others were calling "useless" experiments.

He was vindicated a hundredfold in the important work produced by the great bacteriologist Dr. Edward C. Rosenow, who greatly expanded knowledge of streptococci, and most especially by the discovery of cortisone by Dr. Edward C. Kendall and Dr. Philip S. Hench. I can remember doctors saying irritably to Father, "What the devil is Kendall up to anyway?" and Father replying comfortably, "Great things." It certainly was: in 1950, Kendall and Hench won the Nobel Prize for their work. They had succeeded in 1936 in isolating cortisone from the cortex of the adrenal glands. Kendall, a biochemist, and Hench, a rheumatologist, alertly noted that the pain of arthritis was relieved if the patient also had jaundice and, by a painfully slow process of elimination, isolated the chemical agent that was responsible.

Kendall came to the Clinic as a young man and was taken on staff at my father's insistence in order to help Dr. Plummer with his goiter research. Uncle Will had reservations about the Clinic involving itself so deeply in research, but he withdrew them, in the face of Father's enthusiasm. Father was proven right almost immediately because Kendall's first success was to isolate the active hormone of the thyroid gland, which he later called thyroxin. It was fundamental to the understanding of how glands function and also formed the basis for the next advance in the treatment of goiter.

Father stood behind all research at the Mayo Clinic and was unshakable in his confidence in it whether it succeeded or failed. In research, failure can be very valuable; it narrows the field for everyone else interested in the same project.

In one instance, however, success was vital in a Mayo research project: it isn't too farfetched to say that it helped to win the Battle of Britain. It began in the thirties when Ancel Keyes, a great physiologist who headed that department at the Mayo Clinic, got interested in the physiology of altitude flying and purchased a quantity of equipment in order to simulate conditions under different air pressures. When he departed the Clinic to become a professor of physiology at the University of Minnesota, the equipment was left standing idle. I would pass it from time to time and, in my thrifty way, grieve that we could find no use for it.

My first assistant at that time was W. Randolph Lovelace II, who was also a licensed pilot. He and I often talked about the rash of mysterious crashes that were happening all over the world, the best known of which was the one that killed Will Rogers. Another friend, who was president of Northwest Airlines, was also disturbed by these inexplicable disasters and we discussed them a few times. One night, tossing in bed with half my mind on the problem of the airplane accidents, I had the sudden thought, "Pilot failure!" I was so excited that I could scarcely sleep and I hurried to the Clinic the next morning to mention my theory to Randy.

His hunch was that pilots were flying higher in the improved planes of the period and were collapsing because of lack of oxygen. He recalled that he had noticed during a recent visit to Germany that the Luftwaffe was experimenting with 100 per cent oxygen for pilots of bombers. If the experiments succeeded it would mean that German bombers could fly out of reach of the fighter planes of other nations. I remembered the pressurized equipment gathering dust in the physiology department; it was agreed that he would transfer at once to oxygen research.

To assist Lovelace, we recruited a physiologist, Walter A. Boothby, and someone to concentrate on the design of the oxygen mask, Arthur H. Bulbulian. In remarkably short time they had a mask, which fit over the nose and mouth and had a bladderlike bellows that hung down on the chest; the contraption was held on with canvas straps that buckled around the pilot's helmet. It was known as the B.L.B. mask, in honor of the three men who developed it.

After a period of experiments, Boothby and Lovelace were convinced that all passengers and pilots flying at altitudes of more than ten thousand feet should be supplied with oxygen. In the case of cardiac patients, they added, oxygen was especially crucial. These findings are accepted now as routine for non-pressurized aircraft, so that it seems unbelievable that they ever were challenged. But they were.

The team encountered even more difficulty in proving that 100 per cent oxygen was safe to inhale. Some worried that human lungs would not tolerate 100 per cent oxygen without exploding, others that oxygen would cause intoxication and loss of judgment. These alarms were proven to be groundless, but the researchers had less success in getting acceptance for Lovelace's hope that oxygen masks would be supplied from liquid oxygen tanks, using a method of conversion that he developed. Liquid oxygen, plus cotton, was used to make dynamite, which led to the conviction that it was dangerous. Trucks delivering it to the Clinic were marked EXPLOSIVE, an unquiet sight. Boothby was particularly nervous about it.

John Mathis, a young doctor from Pinckneyville, Illinois,

was a passionate supporter of liquid oxygen and he determined that he would prove to Boothby that he had nothing to fear. He went to Boothby's house one morning, summoned him out on the lawn and poured liquid oxygen on a handkerchief. When he struck a match, Boothby fled inside. The handkerchief didn't explode. It burned, as Mathis promised it would. As an experiment it was pretty unscientific but it was certainly dramatic. However, it failed to impress Boothby and he continued to refuse to have liquid oxygen in his vicinity.

It is a pity that liquid oxygen didn't become popular. I think it would be more economical and efficient in hospital use.

Randy Lovelace proved that the B.L.B. mask worked in a particularly courageous experiment. He bailed out of a B-25 at forty thousand feet, a world-record parachute jump that stood for a long time. It was audacious and indisputable evidence that the mask was effective but it almost had tragic consequences. Randy's arm was caught in the shroud when his parachute opened and the glove was torn from his hand. During the slow descent, his hand froze. For quite a time after that, he was crippled.

News of the Mayo Clinic's B.L.B. mask spread to Britain and we received a visit from three leading physiologists. One of them, Dr. B. A. McSwiney, professor of physiology at St. Thomas' Hospital in London, volunteered himself as a subject during the tests. He tried varying the rates of oxygen flow, eating and talking while wearing the mask, trying it at great altitudes. When he finished he proclaimed the B.L.B. mask the most efficient in existence and the one which made the most economical use of oxygen.

Quietly, the B.L.B. mask was produced in quantities. The war between Great Britain and Germany broke out in September, 1939, and several hundred of the masks were shipped in secrecy to England. A year later, when German bombers began high-level raids with the intention of softening England for the invasion, Spitfire and Hurricane fighter pilots in B.L.B. masks rose high to meet them and heroically won the war in the air.

When the United States entered World War II, we were advised at the Clinic that a number of pilots were being lost because of the pressure on their bodies when they pulled out of dives. Our aeronautical medicine branch went into action again and helped to develop a pressure suit with automatic valves that would keep the pilot's blood circulating in his brain and prevent blackouts. In recent years, the Clinic has had an active role in space medicine. I'm gratified that it all began because I couldn't abide that expensive equipment being idle.

The B.L.B. mask fascinated me with its possibilities. I remembered that Hill devised the oxygen tent in 1925 to treat chronic leg ulcers and edema and the open wounds from World War I that had been resisting all other attempts to heal them. The prevalent use of the oxygen tent for the relief of anoxemia of pneumonia had distracted doctors from this original intent, so I turned my attention to experiments with the B.L.B. mask to determine if 100 per cent oxygen would benefit my surgical patients. I installed the equipment in my operating rooms and was soon sounding like a salesman for a sideshow cure-all; oxygen, it seemed, was good for every one of the minor discomforts of surgery and a few of the major ones as well.

It prevented or controlled vomiting, we found, and was particularly useful when operations on the thyroid gland were performed under local anesthetic. It relieved headaches following a spinal anesthetic and seemed to lessen the likelihood or severity of surgical shock. It also reduced gas, which can cause agony in the postoperative patient, by mixing with the nitrogen in the intestines and diluting it. Pure oxygen administered in the B.L.B. mask increases the level of oxygen in the blood by about 10 to 15 per cent, we discovered, and this margin gave us miracles.

One striking example of the benefits of the mask came when it was used on a seventeen-year-old boy who was almost dead from acute rheumatic fever. His temperature had been 104 and 105 for three days and he was delirious and unable to take nourishment. We put the mask on him and his temperature and pulse rate dropped immediately. A week later he was fine and we stopped the oxygen, which was then being used at a concentration of only 50 per cent.

On another occasion I was operating on a strangulated hernia and I couldn't decide whether a segment of intestine was healthy tissue or not. It was very dark and gave me no clue as to whether I could safely drop it back into the abdomen or whether it should be cut out. The usual technique in such cases is to wait a long period while hot packs are applied but I tried giving the patient pure oxygen. The segment returned to its normal color and viability at once.

Pure oxygen was also found to be effective in the treatment of hangovers.

During 1939 we administered high concentrations of oxygen to 1209 patients, with such favorable results that we almost doubled that number the following year. We observed no cases of lung irritation, as those opposed to us prophesied we would, and in the majority of cases convalescence appeared easier and more rapid. There was an added financial benefit: we reported in the *Journal of the American Medical Association* that the administration of oxygen by tent (which cannot attain the level of 100 per cent oxygen) cost the patient from twelve to twenty-five dollars a day, while the B.L.B. mask cost between five and eight dollars a day. The complete setup of the B.L.B. mask was selling for twenty dollars at that time.

Oxygen therapy had a whirl in many hospitals for a time after that, some of them using it routinely after surgery as I did. Gradually, it fell into disuse as a routine postoperative procedure. I expect that it will return some day; surgery pursues cycles, even as women's fashions.

I was gratified in 1937 to be invited to be one of the founders of the American Board of Surgeons. I informed my friends when they congratulated me that I could see no good reason for the selection of me, outside of the good taste of the committee involved. Certification by the American Board of Surgeons was established as much more demanding than the somewhat clubby requirements of the American College of Surgeons. Surgeons are obliged to pass a stiff oral and written examination to be accepted by the Board. I announced that I was lucky to get in as a founder or else I never would have made it.

Father and Uncle Will had bought neighboring homes in Tucson, Arizona, where they could escape some of the bitterly cold Minnesota winters. When they left for their annual visit there in 1939, Mother suggested that Alice and I should inspect the Big House carefully and make any alterations we liked, including major ones. "After all," she explained without fuss, "you will be living here someday and you have a right to fix it to suit yourselves."

The main rooms of the Big House are of such imposing size that the family preferred to gather in the smaller sunny rooms at one end, where Father and Mother had their studies and a conservatory. Alice planned boldly to tear out Mother's study and an adjoining bath, knock out the inside walls of the conservatory and turn the area into a single long room, with a windowed alcove at one end and a fireplace at the other.

My old school, Central, was being torn down so Father imaginatively purchased all the tall carved classroom doors. Under some twenty-five layers of heavy paint, they were Minnesota white pine with a pink-bronze glow when rubbed. We were fortunate to have a master carpenter working for us, Anton Brunholzl, known as Mister Tony by us all. He paneled the entire room with those doors, ingeniously matching the pattern. It created a warm effect that was both inviting, restful and beautiful.

Alice was understandably nervous on the day that Mother and Father returned from Tucson. She anxiously watched Mother's expression as they entered the drastically altered room. My mother said at once, and believably, "I like it, I *like* it! Alice, how clever you are."

That lovely room became the heart of the house for us, Alice in her small green velvet armchair and I settled in my green brocade one beside the fireplace, with the bookcase at my back. A portrait of Mother hangs over the mantel, looking serene and proud with her hands hidden in the folds of the black dress she is wearing. The artist had painted them with their swollen knuckles and she, self-conscious as always at the look of them, had them painted over. At the same time, Mother had the artist paint portraits of Ruth and Alice, both of them striking beauties in formal gowns, and one of me looking serious in my American College of Surgeons' robes. Working from a photograph, the artist did a matching one of Joe. He is tanned and steady-eyed in it, wearing an open-necked tan shirt, and there is something fathomless in the expression. The portraits of Joe and me hang in our library; Ruth and Alice, full length, flank the fireplace in the main room.

Father and Mother were home only a few weeks before they left for Chicago, where Father wanted to attend a medical meeting. It was mid-May, but chilly; Father nevertheless was impatient of overcoats and refused to wear one. He caught a cold and it turned into pneumonia. Mother called us to come at once; he was dying.

The family gathered at Mercy Hospital, Alice and Mother and I and my sisters: Dorothy, who hadn't married; Edith Rankin, who came from Lexington, Kentucky; Esther, who was married to Dr. John Hartzell in Grosse Pointe, Michigan; and Louise, who married quite a few times so I can't remember who was her husband just then. Father was in an oxygen tent and clearly could not last; penicillin, which might have saved him, was still in the future.

Father had a friend who was also consulted as a family doctor, though he was renowned for the pessimistic view he took of all illness. One evening at Mayowood Father had speculated on what would happen if ever he was seriously ill. "I'll be lying there in a coma in an oxygen tent," he decided, enjoying himself, "and you'll call him to come and see me. He'll lift up the curtain, shaking his head, and tell you that the situation is very grave, and then he'll listen with his stethoscope—though I'm damned sure he can't hear a thing—and then he'll shake his head again and say that it is bad, very bad." Father drew breath. "But I want you to know," he told us with a grin, "that no matter how sick I am, I'll hear him and I'll know at least that I'm not as sick as he says I am." And we all laughed.

It was eerie when it happened just as Father had described it. The doctor lifted the curtain of the oxygen tent, shaking his head gloomily and saying the things Father had imagined that he would. I felt an unreasonable burst of encouragement, thinking that maybe it would turn out all right after all. We all looked for Father's lips to twitch, but he was still.

He roused from his coma later and signaled that the oxygen tent be removed. He didn't want to prolong his dying. He looked directly into the eyes of all of us in turn, whispering "Love" to each. Mother was last; he took her hand and looked at her for a long moment and then weakly said, "Love." And closed his eyes. Mother said, after a while, "This is the way he lived, and this is the way he is dying." He remained in a coma until he died a day or two later. It happened on May 26, 1939; he was seventy-three.

We were engulfed by flowers, testimonials, telegrams and mail from all over the world, a weight of mourning that was awesome. Our grief was personal and, for my mother especially, perpetual. She lived three years longer and carried a miniature of Father's face in her palm always, concealing it in a lace handkerchief. She confided in Alice that it helped

13. Me wearing my beer suit as a college senior

14. Marilyn Miller, 1921

15. Marilyn Miller and her sister,
Clair Montgomery, on shipboard, 1920

16. My wife, Alice, as a child dancer (*Bachrach, Philadelphia*)

17. Alice in her wedding dress, June 25, 1927 (*Photo-Crafters Studio*)

her believe that Father was still part of everything she did. During the silent ride on the train from Chicago to Rochester, Mother kept getting up from her seat and going back to stand beside the coffin, returning to us with a composed face only to return to the coffin again a few minutes later.

Father was laid in state at the Clinic for two days, while an endless line of people moved past his bier to pay their respects. Mother stayed up all one night sorting through his letters, burning the angry and unguarded ones and presenting me the next morning with a packet of those she thought should be preserved. Then his body was brought to Mayowood and on the morning of the funeral his grandchildren gathered wild roses in a pony cart and strewed them around the coffin. A close family friend, Mrs. J. L. Hormel, brought a cross of gardenias which was put on top of the coffin and then there was a simple church service, attended only by the family and those very close to us.

After that, Mother, still calm and outwardly in control, called Alice to her and said that we would be switching houses. "You and Charles will come and live in the Big House now, and I'll move into your house." She insisted firmly and the exchange was made a short time later. I think the most emotion Mother permitted herself to show, in her stoic Scot way, was her indignation at the undertaker who trimmed Father's shaggy eyebrows. She loved the tangle of them, a Mayo trait, and fumed when she found them neatly clipped.

Uncle Will didn't attend the funeral. He was dying of stomach cancer and was too weak to leave his bed; in any case, he detested funerals and thought them barbaric. He had visited Mexico that winter and when he returned to the Tucson home he had a mild stomach upset, which he thought was some amoeba he had picked up. He was treated there for a while without improving any so the brothers returned

161

to Rochester that spring somewhat earlier than usual so Uncle Will could have a checkup at the Clinic. The X ray revealed cancer of the stomach, which was ironic because stomach cancer had been his particular field all his life—no one did more operations on stomach cancer than he did.

An operation was performed, which revealed a high-grade malignancy. They did a resection, but it was clear that the situation was hopeless. Everyone knew about it, but we avoided discussing it. After that Father and Uncle Will spent even more time together, talking quietly. Father stayed by him until he was assured that Uncle Will was feeling stronger, at which he agreed to go to Chicago.

Not long after Father died, Uncle Will noted with professional interest that he was becoming jaundiced. He diagnosed it at once as metastasis in his liver. "It has blocked off the duct," he reported in a matter-of-fact tone. "This is it." I gave him a pint of blood, which was the only transfusion he accepted. He could have been kept alive for a time with constant blood transfusions and intravenous feeding, but that wasn't his style. As a little boy he had broken his arm while playing; he walked home stolidly, without tears, to have it set.

He went about his death in the same practical, crisp manner, with no self-pity. First he called a meeting of the Mayo Board of Governors in his bedroom, gave them some policy instructions and made important decisions, such as selecting the people for the Clinic's powerful Fiscal Committee. The mood was businesslike and not in the least sad. Then he summoned the family. He looked dreadfully ill but he was in command. "I know what the problem is and I know the future," he instructed us. "I've had a good life, and this is all right. But I'm not going to have any further medication to keep me going—no more intravenous and nothing else, except some morphine for the pain. I'll say good-bye to all of you now." We said our farewells as he wanted us to, without sentimentality, and left him. Three days later, on my father's birthday, he died.

The curious circumstance that the brothers, so bound together in life, should die within two months of one another is something to contemplate. There seemed something natural about Uncle Will's death, once Father had gone. He lay in state in his massive stone house, which he gave to the Clinic as a meeting place for doctors; it is now called Foundation House. Obedient to her husband to the last, Aunt Hattie, a devout Congregationalist, invited an Episcopalian to join in the funeral service. Uncle Will had never been much of a churchgoer but he kept a nominal interest in the faith of his parents. He was buried beside Father.

The letters of condolence filled mailbags, and it seemed that they kept arriving for months. They ranged all the way from pencil notes on ruled paper from school children to the embossed stationery of the President of the United States.

One eulogy about the Mayo brothers, written nearly twenty years after their death, strikes me as particularly apt. It was written by Ridgely Hunt in the *Chicago Tribune Magazine* during the course of an article on the Mayo Clinic. He wrote, "The gods, not content to have endowed them with great surgical skill, showered upon the two brothers every gift of intellect and spirit imaginable. They were brilliant, witty, modest, courageous, inventive, generous, large-minded, strong—they had it all."

My father was the only hero I ever had in my life. We had never been close, but I felt lonelier after he died. It had been a terrible few years—Joe, Father, Uncle Will. Marilyn Miller had died in 1933, from meningitis that came on quickly after a mastoid; someone notified me, so I wouldn't read it first in the papers. And Sister Joseph died, just a month after Father. She had been superintendent of St. Marys and a former first assistant to Uncle Will. Father, Uncle Will and Sister Joseph often seemed a triumvirate. Very sad years, those.

I greatly admired the style of my father's death, putting aside the oxygen tent, and the similar decision of Uncle Will to die when it was time, without trying to eke out any extra days. When their deaths seemed to them inevitable, they simply died. Their acceptance was stamped with dignity, a quiet conscience, a sense of fitness.

In recent years, medicine has advanced greatly in techniques for resuscitating the dead and maintaining some kind of life in the dying for years at a time. I am inclined to think that we have gone too far in this direction, that we keep alive patients for whom further existence is pointless. We should keep people going only so long as they are productive and happy with themselves, able to carry their own weight as a personality. It is a tragedy to maintain life in an unconscious vegetable, but it is happening in every hospital in the land; it drains the families economically and emotionally, and serves no purpose that I can respect.

A doctor cannot act as God, nor should he attempt to make life and death decisions on his own, but he can consult with other doctors and perhaps with others, clergymen for example, in order to decide that the time has come to discontinue intravenous feeding and let the patient go naturally. I call it "masterful inactivity"; in such cases as when the patient is "alive" only to the degree that he breathes and has a heartbeat but his brain is dead, it constitutes a charitable act.

I have made it clear to all those near me that I want masterful inactivity practiced on me, when the time comes. I want the doctor who is treating me to consult with his colleagues, and when they agree that it is impossible that I can be restored to a sane, conscious degree of health, I wish to be allowed to die. We doctors today are keeping people alive who should not be kept alive, and I don't want to be one of them.

EIGHT

Uncle Will's tough deathbed decisions about the power structure of the Mayo Clinic were to have far-reaching consequences for me. The Clinic's Board of Governors, together with the committees it appoints, forms the supreme authority in the Clinic. The remarkable sacrifice Father and Uncle Will made in shifting ownership of the Clinic from themselves and their partners in 1920 had been proven to be beneficial, though it escaped no one's notice that the brothers continued to dominate the Clinic's development as before.

Uncle Will was chairman of the Board when I was named to it and Father sat as an ordinary member. As a junior member, I kept my peace but observed that Father and Uncle Will worked so smoothly together when matters of policy were introduced that it was evident they had discussed them beforehand and reached agreement. Harry Harwick, the only non-doctor on the Board, had the power of veto because he controlled the purse strings but the rest of us left most matters to Father and Uncle Will.

Then, in 1932, Uncle Will announced at the year-end staff conference that he and Father and Dr. Plummer were resigning from the Board in favor of three younger staff doctors. I think he felt it wise to let the Board get accustomed to self-government, without the towering presence of the Mayo brothers, but in practice the Board remained aware of the opinions of the founders and I don't think it ever carried out anything that didn't have their approval.

It was generally felt around Rochester that Uncle Will reached his decisions after careful weighing of all the considerations and that debate on one of his judgments was somewhat redundant. I can give an example of this. In the early thirties, Rochester was considering the adoption of daylight saving time. Uncle Will heard that the Chamber of Commerce was meeting to discuss the matter and he appeared at it. "You gentlemen realize that whatever you do in Rochester, you are working directly or indirectly for the patients who come here to the Clinic," he began. It was irrefutable; the Clinic at that time was the town's only industry. He continued to say that the patients would be confused by daylight saving time and the appointments would be mixed up. "Gentlemen," he concluded, "for that reason we're not going to have daylight saving time in Rochester." And then he left.

The chairman of the meeting surveyed the silent faces before him. "Gentlemen," he said, "it looks like the only sensible thing to do now is to adjourn."

Similarly, though Father and Uncle Will no longer *seemed* to have any authority in the handling of the Clinic's affairs, they continued to rule. After their resignations, I was named to be a life member of both the Properties Association and the Board of Governors, and could never be dismissed. Uncle Will's two sons-in-law, Dr. Donald C. Balfour and Dr. Waltman Walters, were given the same arrangement. All other members were elected from and by the Mayo Clinic staff doctors for six-year terms.

This was the group that Uncle Will summoned to his deathbed on that July day. He wanted to issue instructions about some specific matters and he told us that he would decide who should serve on the various committees. It was a significant opportunity for me. I had long felt bypassed in the Board's decisions about how the Clinic should be operated. Most of the doctors were older men who had known

166

me from childhood and continued to think of me as too young to be considered. I had the good sense to notice that the Board in some respects was only a front for the real power, which lay with the Fiscal Committee. I therefore stepped forward at the meeting in Uncle Will's bedroom and openly asked Uncle Will to name me to the Fiscal Committee.

I think some of the Board members were astounded that I was so aware of the real authority in the Clinic. Uncle Will stared at me with no expression that I could read and said slowly, "It's true that whoever controls the money, controls the Clinic. If that's what you want, you can have it." I was elated until I heard later that Uncle Will, for reasons of his own, had changed his mind. The Fiscal Committee was headed by Harry Harwick and my name was not included in the members.

It meant for me the beginning of an endless and often bitter struggle with the Board of Governors, during which I often felt the enmity of the majority. I tended to favor expansion sooner than the Board did, believing as my father and uncle did in our responsibility to provide the best facilities available for the patients; when we built, I always urged overbuilding—it seemed logical that the Clinic would continue to grow and that construction costs would also climb. The Board was cautious, and so we fought. I frequently found myself the only voice opposed to a policy or plan, but I was stubborn enough to present my arguments anyway.

My relatives, it seemed, conformed better than I did, with the result that those closed, private meetings of the Board sometimes presented the odd picture of the only successor to the Mayo name locked in a solitary war with the entire Mayo Clinic. I always was outvoted, of course; the sessions were exercises in frustration for me.

My irritation at that time was not enhanced by the Board's

167

indifference to my financial difficulties. Alice and I were living in Mayowood, a home so vast that our children once kept goats in a downstairs room for two weeks before we discovered them. Father had left a $100,000 trust fund to keep up the house, the surrounding buildings—which included several comfortable homes—and 4300 acres of gardens and farm, but rising costs ate it all in a shockingly short time. In addition, we inherited along with the house the tradition of hospitality that my father and mother had established. Distinguished visitors to Rochester expected to be entertained handsomely at Mayowood and Alice and I enjoyed being their hosts, but the expense was fearful. My salary of twenty thousand dollars a year didn't begin to meet these costs, along with educating and clothing six children. In desperation, I began borrowing from the Clinic.

I had some more of my ill-fated schemes for earning extra money. One year I bought a flock of four thousand turkeys— that was the year of a violent windstorm that blew the turkeys against a wire fence and killed them all. I reasoned that there would be a shortage of turkeys, since other farmers had the same experience, so I borrowed the money and bought four thousand more. Incredible as it seems, another storm wiped them out again. My money-raising ventures always turned out like that, every time.

In the spring of 1940, when Hitler swept through the Lowlands and France to the shore of the English Channel, I telephoned my close friends in London, Clifford Naunton Morgan and Archibald MacIndoe, both surgeons and both later knighted for their distinguished careers. I pointed out to them that families were being evacuated from London in the expectation that it would be a battleground, and I urged them to send their wives and children to live with us in Rochester. "It looks like a bad war," I said, and they agreed and accepted my offer.

A short time later MacIndoe's wife and two daughters and

Morgan's wife and son and daughter arrived by plane and moved into Mayowood. It made a lively household: ten children and three women who scarcely knew one another. Even when rationing and our distance from town made matters truly formidable, Alice was a brick and never complained. She always had a serenity in the face of confusion, and a generous spirit.

I was in no position to pay close attention to my tangled household because the European war was beginning to drain our supply of doctors and we were busier than ever at the Clinic. I was intensely occupied with my contribution to the development of colon surgery, a procedure to avoid sacrificing the anus in cases of cancer in a certain region of the rectum. Most doctors removed the anus and performed a colostomy in situations where I was certain it could be avoided, and I was anxious to prove with a weight of careful statistics that I was right.

In some areas, surgery was making strides toward eliminating itself. For example, surgeons in Father's day always removed tumors of the uterus as soon as they were detected, believing them to be precancerous lesions. But evidence was piling up to show that they are harmless and can be safely left, except in cases where they become so enlarged that they press on the bladder or else work themselves into such a position that they hemorrhage.

Similarly with duodenal ulcers, which at one time almost always meant an operation. Medical treatment of duodenal ulcers had progressed to such a point that fewer than 15 per cent of such cases were coming to a surgeon; I was sure that even these few could have been avoided with adequate medical treatment. Speaking as a surgeon, I vastly prefer a medical treatment of duodenal ulcers to surgical treatment, but a medical man I know once elected surgery.

I am almost fanatical on the subject of water as part of the medical treatment of duodenal ulcers. I once told a medical meeting, "I have an ulcer tendency myself. If anyone wants to develop an unusual interest in this subject, I would say: get an ulcer." I maintain that medical treatment which does not include a high intake of water is in error. The water dilutes gastric acids to an astonishing degree.

"I have yet to see a jejunal ulcer develop in a case in which the average intake of water is more than three glasses a day," I wrote in the *Journal of the Kansas Medical Society*. "Manual workers should carry water in a canteen, thermos bottle or jug; the office worker should keep it on his desk and never pass a drinking fountain without leaning over and taking a few swallows."

Water is the cheapest medicine available to man, and the best. I note that constipated people don't drink much water and I am convinced that a higher intake of water would help that condition. Some research on the problems of hangovers also persuaded me that two glasses of water, taken after a party and before going to bed, substantially reduce the discomfort the next morning.

Water intake shouldn't be stepped up all at once, by gulping down three glasses of water in the next ten minutes, but it should be spread evenly throughout the day. It is possible to get sick from an overdose of water, with something called water toxemia, as with overuse of any other normally innocent product. But I felt a duty to prevent the need for surgery on ulcers if I could, so I always stressed water.

"For the next few weeks," I would advise patients, "eat whatever you like, so long as it agrees with you, but don't leave the table without drinking two glasses of water. That will get six glasses of water a day into you and at the end of three weeks your symptoms probably will be gone." A small person can work up to drinking nine glasses of water in a day, a large person up to fourteen; intake to these levels should be increased gradually over a period of at least three weeks.

High intakes of water are helpful in cases of constipation,

as I have said, and also beneficial to the complexion. People tend to forget that much of the food taken into the body is waste and must be disposed of somehow. Water quite literally flushes it away, through the kidneys, bowels, sweat glands and respiratory system.

For less obvious reasons, I discovered that water reduced such conditions as migraine headaches. Patients with chronic migraine usually have highly colored urine, which means they aren't taking in enough water to dilute their kidneys. There is a build-up of waste in the body until the threshold of early migraine symptoms is reached. Acute migraine, as sufferers know, produces agony and even vomiting.

By the way, coffee is not a substitute for water even though it largely is water. I suspect that tea is better and acts in the body much as water does, for which reason I have always considered the English habit of frequent tea times as rational.

I was amused one time when a medical paper I wrote about water was excerpted by a company that bottled pure spring water, and used to promote the product. I had no objection: I believe mightily in water for health.

In this context, everyone who has ever been part of the Mayo Clinic sooner or later encounters someone who thanks him effusively for "the Mayo diet." "Which one?" I always inquire politely. "There are about two million." It is true, a prescribed diet or such diet suggestions as increasing water intake are always part of the treatment of any patient. Mayo doctors are outlining diets all the time and all of these can be termed "Mayo diets." I'm aware that the one the public generally means is some concoction of grapefruit and eggs and steaks, taken for two weeks, which is supposed to reduce weight by up to twenty pounds. It may even be *a* Mayo diet, devised by someone here for a specific patient with a weight problem, but it is not *the* Mayo diet.

I used to note menus with MAYO DIET in big letters, listing

under that heading a variety of items alleged to be part of that diet. I don't think I ever saw two lists alike. I was visiting a USAF officers' mess in Germany in 1966 and saw MAYO DIET on the menu, after a lapse of some years when I had concluded gratefully that it was going out of style. I suspected that the menu was a joke in my honor, but I learned it was serious and a regular feature of the kitchen. I think it ran to fruit and cottage cheese that time, which is harmless enough, in moderation. I assume that someone received such a diet at the Clinic and, when it worked, passed it around to his friends.

I'm resigned to the prevalence of this wonder "Mayo diet" but I am amazed, as are many of my colleagues, at the North American anxiety over vitamins, leading to the widespread use of vitamin tablets. A well-balanced diet contains more vitamins than a person can use—extra vitamins are only indicated in certain unusual cases, on a doctor's advice. I realize that vitamin addiction has a psychological basis in many people and provides them with reassurance that their health is being protected, so I suppose that they fill a genuine need in that sense. If not taken to excess, vitamin pills do no harm: I find the cult strange, and sad.

Crash diets are a more serious matter. The human body can bear an extraordinary amount of abuse but I flinch when people deliberately shock it with such assaults as an abruptly decreased food intake. I disapprove heartily and evidence bears me out that the method has a poor prognosis: people who indulge in crash diets almost invariably put the weight back on in a year.

Patients are always asking doctors what foods they should or should not eat, a question which almost invariably reveals a dietary prejudice. They have heard that cucumber is indigestible, or strawberries lead to hives, and they want confirmation. The underlying factor is the average person's poor understanding of what digestion is all about. The human

172

race as a whole enjoys digestive health, or it would not have survived the capricious food supply available to early man. Man can eat almost anything that grows or breathes.

A mummy was discovered in the Ozark Mountains some years ago and when examined it showed that the feces contained black oak acorns, the fruit of the sumac, charcoal and insects. Herodotus, the world's first historian, records that the slaves who built the pyramids lived on a diet of radishes, onions and garlic. The ancient Greeks ate dogs and foxes.

Man is an omnivore, which means he can eat either flesh or vegetable foods. His digestive system combines the simple design of the purely carnivore animal, whose food rushes through the body, and the more complicated arrangement of the herbivora, whose grass diet must be stored and digested slowly.

Primitive man learned he could tamper with his daily intake of food and indulge himself in fasts for religious reasons, but he never denied himself water. Throughout the history of early man, populations followed fresh water rivers and lakes. The fastest way to starve to death is to be deprived of water.

The digestive tract is an engineering marvel, relying in some degree on gravity and at every point in its length making a stalwart effort to conserve and return to the blood the water that the salivary glands, stomach, intestinal walls, pancreas and lymph have been draining from it in order to function. This thrifty housekeeping relies on a good supply of water, naturally, but plentiful water also presents the intestinal tract with a problem, since it tends to sluice away stomach acids and cause the intestinal fluids to become more acid. A subtle, mindless system of balance and counterbalance then begins to cope with this situation.

Proctology, surgery of the rectum, was just developing when I became a doctor, and I found myself more and more intrigued by the challenges it offered. Newspaper reporters assigned to interview me when I was active in surgery were somewhat at a loss to discuss colon cancer for very long—it doesn't have that wide a public appeal—but I was enthralled by the consummate craftsmanship of man's digestive system. The ramifications go beyond the physical: as psychiatrists have noted, a man's personality and his digestive system form a continuum and if you know a great deal about one area it is possible to make accurate guesses about the other.

I made a study for a paper in the *Journal of the American Medical Association* on the influence of environment on the colon. I noted that alternating periods of constipation and diarrhea are not uncommon, but usually patients see their doctors because of discomfort from one or the other. "You must have the patient's confidence," I observed. "If he says his mother and father had convictions like his, and he doesn't want to deviate, it is not a good idea to start out by dissuading him."

Instead I recommended a line of questioning which would establish if there were periods of insufficient rest, or anxiety, or inability to relax: it is almost certain that one, or all, will be found in the patient's recent past. Digestive symptoms appear on the heels of accidents, a death in the family, unexpected loss of money, property or job, betrayal of a confidence by a friend, migration or change of party, church or occupation. In short, anything which dislocates the personality is practically certain to change the pattern of his bowel movements as well.

Most people are puzzled when they first notice that they are suffering from constipation or diarrhea. They try drugstore remedies and when these are ineffective they begin to wonder if they have cancer. Fear has the instant effect of making the symptoms worse, and the patient is well on his way to becoming a colonic invalid.

"Intrigue and politics," I wrote, "are not physically dangerous to modern man but they may serve as effectively as the mace to produce disabilities." Environmental change is particularly disturbing to bowel function: a girl from a small town who moves into a crowded city is almost certain to be constipated.

Because it isn't considered a dainty subject for conversation and confidences, few people are aware how prevalent are difficulties with the bowel. The relationship with fear is unmistakable, and we live in fearful times. The colon reacts to anxiety as it would to a disease and doctors are confronted by patients who become almost obsessed by their concern for their colons. These are the unfortunates who form a substantial market for the remedies for digestive upsets which are rarely helpful and sometimes are definitely harmful.

"Don't be jocular with the fearful patient," I have warned doctors. For one thing, it may drive him into the arms of the quacks. A thorough examination and an air of sympathy is indicated in such people, I have maintained, "especially if there is a record of colon polyps or cancer in the family history." Patients fall into two groups, those with a sound basis for concern, such as an unexplained diarrhea after a time in the tropics (and these are easy to treat), and those whose judgment is fallacious and imagine that their case is different from any other that the physician has ever seen. This second group is a vexation: they are worthless to themselves, miserable, arrogant, evasive and almost impossible to treat successfully.

Early doctors impressed their patients by prescribing a laxative. From savage to sophisticate, man is awed when a small amount of medicine can bring about a large amount of upheaval. Unfortunately when the colon is emptied by the use of a laxative, it rapidly fills with gas and liquid and the patient is more uncomfortable than before. Habitual use of purgatives is a mistake; it punishes the colon.

Our civilization is generally in conflict with a healthy, regular functioning colon. People bolt their food at odd hours, which results in such unpleasant symptoms that they are

175

convinced they must have a food allergy. Our toilets have faulty design, the handwork of plumbers rather than doctors. They are too high for comfortable, natural defecation. They would be adequate perhaps for people who could relax while eating, sleeping or supposedly enjoying themselves in a leisure pursuit, but this is not a description of the average man in today's society.

Once tension has produced a disturbed colon, the existence of the irregularity will produce more tension, which impedes the health of the colon still further until the patient is alarmed enough to consult a doctor. Some of the suggestions to break this chain are simple: eat more slowly, avoid extreme temperatures of food and beverages (particularly if the problem is too many bowel movements), review eating, sleeping and work habits. Some people fail to realize that they are pursuing a pattern of work and eating and irregular rest which is vicious on the digestive system.

It is an observation many doctors have made, but sturdy blond people rarely seem to have colon disorders with sociological causes. The typical patient whose colon is misbehaving as the result of tension and carelessness is tall, slender and brunet. It is a task of invincible proportions to convince such people that they don't have an organic disease, merely a phenomenon of reflex. They are advised to rest and relax, but very often they can't.

Unfortunately, there are no characteristic symptoms of cancer in the colon. It is possible for even an alert person to have symptoms for a year before going to a doctor. Unfortunately pain, which gets people to the doctor faster than any other symptom, is not often an early factor in colon cancer. My valued friend and colleague Dr. Louis A. ("Gus") Buie, a pioneer in the development of proctology who headed that department at the Mayo Clinic for many years, wrote a definitive book, *Practical Proctology*. In it he mourned, "If there was pain from rectal carcinoma, the story of this disease could be rewritten."

Unhappily for those who have tumors develop there, the rectal mucosa has no sensory nerves. If it did, man would be obliged to empty his bowels continuously to avoid pain.

Routine examinations of persons who considered themselves in the prime of health have too often disclosed advanced colon cancer, even inoperable colon cancer. The tumors that a colon surgeon sees are usually large, involving half to three-quarters of the circumference of the bowel. It is estimated that in up to 40 per cent of cases where colon cancer is diagnosed it is already too late.

This is shocking, and all the more so because 73 per cent of colon cancer locates so close to the anus that it can be detected easily in a doctor's office, using nothing more sophisticated than a finger or a sigmoidoscope. Sixty per cent of these tumors can be seen, with very little difficulty. The yards of upper colon and small intestine folded loosely in the abdomen are rarely invaded by cancer, which tends to concentrate in the fixed portion of the colon immediately adjacent to the anus, those few inches of bowel known as the rectum, the rectosigmoid and the sigmoid. There is a bend in the colon where it joins the sigmoid, which possibly has something to do with the vulnerability of that area, and it also bears a share of the descending colon's function of storing feces. Most doctors assume there is a relationship between the frequency of cancer in this region and the fact that it often is invaded by dry, hard feces.

In his presidential address to the American Medical Association in 1917, Uncle Will said, "Chronic irritation, whether the result of mechanical, chemical or infectious agencies, is the most important of all those precancerous conditions with which we are acquainted."

The sinister cancerous tumor of the colon and rectum is so trouble free that it doesn't even obstruct the passage of feces until it is almost beyond the operable stage. The best-known symptom of its presence is blood in the stools, but even this doesn't always occur, nor is it always to an extent that is noticeable. When it is, alas, some doctors fail to investigate for any condition except hemorrhoids. Dr. Buie states flatly, "To me, rectal bleeding means cancer, until I can prove that cancer is not present."

Another doctor, Dr. Fred T. Kolough of Twin Falls, Idaho, put it succinctly during a medical meeting that I attended when he said that we can best fight colon and rectal cancer with "an alert physician, with a high index of suspicion." Because colon cancer is so unusual in young people, occurring only 2 per cent of the time in patients under thirty years of age, doctors who encounter rectal bleeding tend to think of cancer only when the patient is over fifty and put it down to hemorrhoids in younger people. This has had tragic consequences for a number of young patients.

One of the common misdiagnoses of colon cancer is that of pernicious anemia, which may indeed be the only symptom. If the doctor prescribes iron therapy the patient, unfortunately for a proper diagnosis, responds and feels better. Others have elimination problems of a mild but annoying nature and they purchase home remedies, ointments, suppositories, laxatives or "tighteners." By the time they decide to see a doctor, it is too late to save them.

Eventually there is a "heavy feeling," "a sense of fullness," "soreness on my right side," "trapped gas," or, most significantly, a sensation after evacuation that it hasn't been complete. The symptoms may still be vague and are easily mistaken for chronic appendicitis, chronic cholecystitis or even peptic ulcer. There may also be dyspepsia complaints or a sour stomach, weakness and fatigue. In about half the cases, there is a loss of weight; only in a third of cases is there a change in bowel habits, and this sometimes so slight as to be unnoticed for a long time. Sometimes the change is in the direction of constipation, sometimes it is greater frequency of stools, occasionally it is alternating diarrhea and constipation. Shortness of breath isn't unusual.

Dr. Buie notes that about 66 per cent of patients who later

were found to have rectal cancer complained of burning or soreness. Colon cancer produces intermittent, cramping pain in most cases, but may not. One man of only thirty-two had no symptoms whatsoever, except that he felt a hard mass just under his stomach. It turned out to be a fatally advanced tumor in his transverse colon.

The vagueness of the symptoms presents an exasperating problem for those who seek to establish earlier detection of colon cancer. But we must find an answer because cancer of the colon is common. It represents 7 per cent of all the malignant tumors that affect the human body; every year in the United States it kills the equivalent of a small city's population. Possibly because of misplaced fastidiousness, it receives little attention generally. Doctors must take the leadership in changing this state of affairs.

Colon cancer *can* be detected in its early stages by any wary physician. Despite its catastrophic talent for giving its host little trouble, colon cancer can be diagnosed by careful palpation of the abdomen, roentgenologic examination of the colon after a barium enema and a proctosigmoidoscopic examination. I believe this should be routine procedure whenever a patient has a change in bowel habits, a passage of blood from the bowel, abdominal discomfort, loss of weight, weakness or unexplained anemia. And also, obviously, when an abdominal mass has been found. Sometimes these tests prove negative, but the symptoms continue. The tests then should be repeated within a few months. Cancer detection clinics commonly find no colon cancer on the initial visit but a flourishing one six months or a year later.

Once the lesion has been detected, delay is inexcusable. The cleaning of the bowel will require two days, three at the most, but this must be the extent of the wait before surgery. A curable condition in colon cancer can change in a day to an incurable one.

Almost from the beginning of my career as a surgeon, I was one of a minority who began advocating a procedure known as a one-stage combined abdominoperineal resection. It was my choice when the cancerous tumor was located so low in the rectum that it was impossible to avoid taking out the anus. In a single operation, I would remove the lesion and the rectum, working through an incision in the abdomen, and lead the severed end of the colon through an opening in the patient's side, through which feces would discharge. I then removed the anus, like coring an apple.

Most surgeons at that time made two operations of this because they thought it was easier on the patient. They would cut the colon in the first operation, giving it a new exit; this is known as a colostomy. Later they would remove the tumor and the anus. They claimed that this was better mostly because it was how they had been taught and they knew no other way. As an excuse, they said that it would be dangerous to move the patient during the operation, since they were positioning him differently for each operation. Those of us pioneering the all-in-one procedure found a position, one similar to that used when removing gallstones, which didn't require that the patient be moved. We pointed out that it was more desirable to have the malignancy out of the body sooner, and that the patient suffered less, was a briefer time in hospital and was put to less expense. Most surgeons were indifferent, or else outraged at the implied criticism.

Over and over again at medical meetings, I gave my carefully kept statistics. I could prove that the one-stage was as safe as the two-stage; as the years passed, it gained and could be shown to have a lower mortality rate. I was amazed that some opposition continued even after that, but the one-stage procedure eventually was adopted all over the country. As early as 1953, it was being used three times as often as it had in 1940. Today it is the operation usually performed and the two-stage procedure is mercifully rare. I am pleased that I was able to make a contribution to that state of affairs.

Many patients are devastated by the news that they will require a colostomy. They regard it as both mutilating and revolting, but it isn't as intolerable as it may sound. If the surgeon brings the colon through the abdominal muscle on a slant, the patient can train himself to control emissions almost as effectively as if he still had a sphincter; a tiny bandage over the opening suffices. In 90 per cent of my cases, the patient wasn't obliged to wear a bag; carefulness with diet, avoiding those foods which loosen the bowels, was all that was required.

I was visited one day at the Clinic by an elderly farmer who wanted to thank me for the colostomy I had performed on him. He was one of the few who used a bag and he was delighted with it. "Now when I go to the state fair," he explained, "I don't have to go to the toilet."

In the nine years between 1934 and the beginning of 1943, I performed 296 of the one-stage operations, with a mortality rate of 6.1 per cent. The final seventy-four consecutive operations had no deaths.

In eleven cases, cancer was so advanced that saving the patient's life was out of the question. What surgery I did was designed to make him comfortable for whatever time remained; such surgery is described as palliative. Among the 285 non-palliative operations, more than half the patients had cancer that had spread, with nodal involvement and metastases in the liver; 133 patients were free of this extension. Of the latter group, more than 86 per cent were alive three years after the operation, more than 72 per cent were alive five years after the operation. Where the cancer had spread, the three-year survival rate was 57 per cent, the five-year survival rate 38 per cent.

It has been established that people who survive 5.7 years after an operation for cancer have about the same chance of a normal life span as people with no cancer.

The surgeon has several decisions to make when he discovers that a malignancy has spread beyond the original tumor. If the cancer is very extensive and the growth nonresectable, I felt it wise to avoid the palliative colostomy and resort merely to nonsurgical and dietary palliation. This was also the course I followed when the primary growth was small, but the liver was heavily invaded. Sometimes I would find extensive lesions of the rectum, with ulceration, fixation and hemorrhage, and it would be essential to perform a palliative colostomy, followed by local radium and roentgenotherapy. With this, the patient can live a month or two longer under such miserable conditions, both for him and those in contact with him, that I often questioned my choice of procedure.

There are a great many patients whose condition puts them in a borderline area—the resection will enable them to gain weight and feel better for a short time. The surgeon performs the operation with a better spirit; about half will die in six months and none will live beyond two years, but the extra time gained has not been all wretched. Many people can live for a considerable time even after the surgeon has observed metastasis in the liver. Without the stimulus of the parent malignancy, cancer in the liver grows slowly.

I made a study of 334 post-mortems performed at the Clinic over a five-year period after patients died of cancer of the colon and rectum. Sixty per cent of them had lesions which had spread. I was interested to know whether the secondary cancers had been easy to locate during the original surgery and I was relieved to learn that they were. Only 18 per cent of them had escaped detection by the surgeons. Metastases in the liver can be minute and surgeons sometimes are guessing that they are there: I found that in 91 per cent of the cases where it was suspected that the liver was affected, the surgeons were right.

Then there is the brighter side, even of colon cancer. I received a letter one day from a woman in Kansas who said I had performed an operation on her for cancer of the colon twenty-six years previously. She was almost eighty, she wrote, and "you saved my life. My blood pressure, urine and heart are perfect, so the doctor said. I take care of old people."

Despite the importance of the colon, life can go on without it; the kidneys can replace the function of the colon as a salt balancer in the body and other parts of the digestive tract will accommodate themselves to the colon's role as a temporary storage plant. The colon, for those unfamiliar with anatomy, is about five or six feet long and is part of the large bowel, extending from the junction of the small intestine at the ileocecal valve to the rectosigmoid, which joins to the rectum. The rectum, which is some four to six inches long, is the passage leading to the final inch of the digestive system, the sensitive anus. Though I once described myself as a "general surgeon with a particular interest in the territory between jawbone and anus," it was the lower part of the colon which increasingly absorbed my interest as I matured in my profession.

I noticed early in my career that colon and rectal cancer, and cancer of the stomach, tend to be hereditary. I searched the records of 438 families who had visited the Clinic and my tedium was rewarded by positive proof that cancer in these areas are much more prevalent in some families than the normal incidence allows. Also, I discovered that cancer and polyps in the colon are chiefly male afflictions; the incidence in men is almost twice as high as that in women.

So much of a doctor's work is routine and anticipated by his training and experience that it is more stimulating than we usually care to reveal to have a patient with an unusual medical problem; the Mayo Clinic possibly has more than its share. The rare medical condition poses a challenge to a doctor's expertise and imagination; chances are that he will be talking about it whenever he exchanges banter with cohorts for years to come; it will be the subject of a paper in some journal and maybe an illustrated lecture. Some of the zeal with which he faces every working day arises from his hope that he will encounter something incredible; it keeps up his spirits even when a patient starts off, "Doctor, I just feel tired all the time. . . ."

I therefore have my own fond recollections, usually in the nature of an oddity obstructing the intestinal tract. Most often such blocks are composed of tissue of the texture of elastic but in 2 or 3 per cent of cases it is something else. Once we encountered a seventy-one-year-old man who complained of a sharp pain in his abdomen of twenty hours' duration. An operation revealed that a loop of his jejunum had turned itself 180 degrees and somehow wedged itself into his peritoneal sac. A fifty-six-year-old farmer told us he had been drinking beer steadily for sixteen hours; his innards were in such a tangle that we removed eighty centimeters of small intestine before we straightened them out.

Then there was the six-year-old boy with a cramping pain and violent vomiting. In the surgery it was discovered that a loop of ileum was twisted and his bowel kinked by a firm scar. But the one who stands out is the two-year-old who ate dirt. Before his mother brought him to the Clinic he had vomited twice, bringing up a large amount of dirt, and then he went into shock, with a high fever. It was obvious that an intra-abdominal catastrophe had occurred.

We gave him transfusions and intravenous feeding and antibiotics for five days and then operated, finding a hole in his bowel and a knot in his intestine that had become gangrenous. I tried, but I couldn't untie it and I was forced to cut it out. I removed 105 centimeters of intestine from that tiny person, or about 50 per cent of his small bowel. The final act of the drama lasted throughout the next two days and nights when student nurses, orderlies and whoever could spare a moment held a pressure gauze against a fistula, a seeping of his fecal material, until his ileum was restored to normal.

18. Alice, Ned, Charles and Muff

19. My morning pike catch at Deer Lake, Minnesota, 1933

20. Alice and her horse, Sherry, in 1933

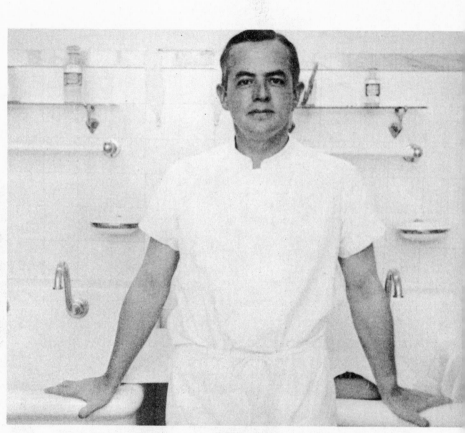

21. Me in 1934

A great many two-year-olds eat dirt without such terrifying consequences. This one, we discovered, was unlucky enough to be born with a rare mesenteric defect, which collapsed under the load of dirt.

There are also the eccentricities that nature arranges, such as the wanton duplication of some part of the gastrointestinal tract, a duplication that leads nowhere. Most frequently abnormalities of this kind are found in the small intestine. One doctor had a patient with three colons, who managed for years with this profusion of equipment.

The symptoms of such an error are the same as those of obstruction. Secretions accumulate in the blind duplication and eventually enlarge it, causing pain. One patient who came to the Clinic was a woman of twenty-seven who was in trouble because she had two colons. Seven years before that, she had an appendectomy for a gangrenous appendix and the surgeon discovered that she had another, healthy appendix besides—and two uteri. For balance perhaps, there was but one kidney.

During the embryonic development period, the human intestine goes through a wide change in position before it settles into the orderly ganglia of its adult position. By the time the embryo is ten millimeters in length, the umbilical loop has been so busy that it already has turned 90 degrees counterclockwise from its first position. This squirming movement is typical; the cecum doesn't arrive at its proper place in the lower right corner until the baby is a year old.

Sometimes this intestinal rotation fails to take place, or is imperfect, or gets twisted on itself. Somewhere early in the child's life, some surgeon will sort it out and replace it where it belongs. Occasionally an infant is born with his intestinal tract outside the body, covered by a moist, thin membrane which will dry and tear within a day or two if surgery is unavailable. It is best to operate within an hour or two of birth and tuck the miniature organs in under the baby's fascia and skin.

My curiosity once led me to collect information about a little-known but apparently safe technique for relieving a patient bloated with gas: the principle is, you stick a pin in him. English doctors did a version of this a century ago and I knew that farmers pragmatically aided bloated cows by jabbing a penknife in their colon. The gas is let off spectacularly and at once; the animal leaps to its feet, restored to its normal size. I read that when this was used on a person in the nineteenth century, gas came out with such force that it blew out a candle. Doctors used a trocar, which is like a slender skewer, or a hypodermic needle. The trocar was better because the gas could escape more rapidly through the larger opening.

Some of these tales of bowel puncture are hair-raising for a modern surgeon. It wasn't unusual at one period for doctors to puncture bowels to let out the feces, when some obstruction prevented normal elimination. It worked and there was little infection, which is a wonder.

The human intestine is made of curious resilient material and heals better and faster than anything else in the body. A woman whose bowel was punctured twice died the next day of a heart attack, affording her doctor an opportunity to remove the bowel and examine it. He found that it had no leak in it, even when he inflated it under pressure. A Boston doctor once fed a woman beef tea through a tube he plunged into the lumen of the bowel. The patient could keep nothing in her stomach and intravenous feeding had not been devised. The experiment suffered a setback when bits of meat in the tea plugged up the tube, so the doctor substituted choice rye whiskey diluted with three parts of water. The woman complained of the pain, so he abandoned his enterprise. There is no further report of the patient, but she would have suffered astonishingly little damage from this zany procedure; the bowel reseals itself promptly and the peritoneum seems to be able to handle what small seepage does occur.

NINE

On Pearl Harbor morning I was in the St. Paul Hotel in St. Paul, Minnesota, attending a medical meeting. Like all adult Americans, I have an imperishable recollection of the moment when I heard the news; for me, it came from the hoarse voice of a newsboy selling papers on the street. I remember thinking, "I'm forty-three, that's still young enough to go."

My best plan, it seemed to me, was to recruit an entire staff of nurses and doctors at the Clinic and present ourselves as a package to the armed forces. I went back to Rochester to begin on this private enlistment program; it soon was known as the Mayo Unit. While it formed, I continued to work desperately hard. We had been short-staffed before Pearl Harbor but the situation was worsening rapidly.

Alice was under considerable strain herself. She had undertaken to head Rochester's Bundles for Britain project, a roundup of clothing and other supplies for bombed-out civilians, and her enthusiasm and diplomacy were making it a great success. I wasn't seeing much of the children, though Muff, Charlie and Ned now trailed around with me on rounds from time to time. "Like children on a farm," someone has said about the Mayos, "they learn as they go along." On fine Sunday afternoons during the summer, Alice and I would gather up the five children and escape to a cabin in the woods about a half-mile from Mayowood, but well hidden. This was about the only private time we ever had as a family;

six days of the week, I left for the hospital at six thirty in the morning, always the first doctor to arrive, and I returned home in the evening, usually with guests.

Alice was running a shop in town where clothing and other items were assembled into the Bundles for Britain packages. Her sixth pregnancy was slowing her down somewhat, so she turned the project over to one of our British guests to run. In a tactful move to ease the burden on Alice in view of my imminent departure, the wives had left Mayowood and were living in town.

We rarely saw Ruth, the widow of my brother Joe, even though she and their two sons were living in their home on the property. Four years after Joe's death, Ruth had met a patient at the Clinic named Paul Meserve. He was a former actor turned landscape gardener and looked her up at the suggestion of a mutual friend during his convalescence from a severe attack of jaundice, brought on when a surgeon in his home town had accidentally cut his common duct while operating on his gallbladder. He and Ruth were much attracted to one another and married in 1940.

It was about two in the morning in February, 1942, when Alice and I were awakened by an agitated telephone call from a woman who was staying the night with Ruth and Paul. She said she had heard a shot from their bedroom and would we come at once. We hurried over and found Ruth breathing her last; she had shot herself through the head with Joe's pistol.

Paul told us what had happened. They had been quarreling violently; as I have said, Ruth was a tempestuous woman. She threw her wedding ring into the fireplace and then ran into the bedroom. When Paul followed her, she opened a drawer and snatched up Joe's pistol. "If you come near me," she screamed at Paul, "I'll kill myself." He didn't believe she would carry out such an extravagant threat and he was anxious to take the gun away from her, so he moved into the room. With that, she put the gun to her head and pulled the trigger.

We were almost too shocked to think, but Alice remembered the children. We found the two boys asleep in their beds, wrapped them in blankets and took them just as they were to Mayowood. David, the adopted son, was eleven, and Bill, the child Ruth had borne with such courage and patience, was seven. I don't recall that we even discussed it—it was taken for granted that we would raise Joe's boys along with our own brood.

We buried Ruth next to Joe in Oakwood Cemetery. It sickens me that those two passionate and vital people should both have died so brutally, so senselessly, and so soon.

Alex, our youngest child, was born in April and I left a few weeks later for Washington for preliminary training. Alice remained behind with the eight children, dispersing Charlie, Ned, Bill and David to Culver Summer Camp when school ended. Joe couldn't go because of his strict diabetic diet.

Jim Priestley and I were assigned to Walter Reed Hospital to learn something about medicine in the military and we arrived in Washington in time for one of the city's mind-dissolving heat waves, which compare favorably with those of equatorial jungles. I had brought only six shirts with me and in two days I sweated through all of them. Laundry facilities were meager, so I washed them myself and ironed them to my satisfaction by putting them between two boards under my mattress and sleeping on them.

Alice came to visit me once, bringing Muff with her. Muff was fourteen that year and it was their first trip together. I gathered that they cemented a friendship during the long train ride that survived considerable stress later on. Muff already was showing signs of being a highly individual person; she was intense and candid, with the cool nerves of an aerialist.

After three months in Washington, Jim Priestley and I returned to the Clinic to await further orders. They didn't come until January, 1943, when the Mayo Unit was activated as an affiliate of the 71st General Hospital and posted to a staging area in Charleston, South Carolina, with me as unit director. I was given the rank of lieutenant colonel and asked to bring the unit up to strength, which meant recruiting office staff and corpsmen and training them. We had only the nucleus, the sixty-five doctors and seventy-five nurses from the Clinic. Some aspects of the arrangements mystified me, such as the daily marching we were required to do. I couldn't see the relevancy of nurses and doctors drilling on the parade square and slugging across country over marshes and fields.

We were also perplexed at the lack of medical supplies for training purposes. In order to demonstrate to the corpsmen how to give an injection, we used an arrangement of tubes attached to lemons and grapefruit.

I had one stroke of luck, or so it seemed at the time. I encountered a civilian clerk in a general's office who showed amazing ability to cut through the ennui of red tape and get things done. If I wanted to have someone commissioned, he could do it on the spot. I persuaded him to join our unit, suggesting that he get himself the rank of captain. He managed that with ease and thereafter my paperwork was done with dazzling efficiency and speed.

Months and months passed and this man had obtained his own promotion to major when I came to realize that he was a queen homosexual. The amazing ease with which he processed requests was due to the network of homosexuals in the armed services, who helped one another. And all nine of the office staff he recruited for me were homosexuals. I still don't know how it could have taken me so long to notice, since I saw them every day, but I think it proves that I'm a farm boy.

My first reaction was the mortified concern that strangers would think that I had surrounded myself with homosexuals because I was one of them. Then I began the task of weeding them out, with some regrets because they were really good typists. I strained over the wording of the letters to their parents, selecting the vaguest phrases I could devise—"unfit for service," I think—in order to explain why the young men were being released, without being too specific.

I assumed that we would be in South Carolina for only a short time, so I gave orders that the wives should stay at home. As the months passed, more and more wives began arriving until they all were there, with the exception of Alice. In the spring I gave up my attempt to set a good example and sent for her.

We found a two-room apartment, with an antique chaise lounge that the landlady told us had been at the signing of the Treaty of Ghent. Alice, who preferred soft green shades for upholstery and drapes, was amused by the strawberry pink and turquoise blue decor and referred to it as our "ice cream soda place." We were delighted as truant ten-year-olds on a spring morning to be away from our boisterous family and the big house, and had a happy time together there. Alice was obliged to cook, for the first time I think, and rose nobly to the challenge of the closet-size kitchen equipped with a two-burner gas range, a portable oven and only one pot, a three-tiered steamer.

Once or twice we got away to New York for a weekend to see some of the Broadway shows. One night, by waiting until almost curtain time, we were able to get two tickets cancelled at the last minute for *There Shall be No Night*, starring Alfred Lunt and Lynn Fontaine. The seats, we discovered, were in a stage box and from this excellent vantage point we could see that the photographs on the grand piano throughout the first act were of Father and Uncle Will.

The play was about a doctor in Finland during the Russian invasion and both the theme and the pictures of the Mayo brothers prompted me to send my card backstage, with a note expressing our appreciation of the great performance the Lunts were giving. An usher hurried to us a few minutes later with an invitation to come backstage, and we went, feeling shy and out-of-place as you do in such circumstances.

Lynn Fontaine put us at our ease immediately, by recalling that she knew a medical school classmate of mine, a Dr. Mark Nesbit in Madison, Wisconsin. She asked him to examine her eye, which had a minor infection, and he was doing so, she told us, when Alfred Lunt strode into the room from his bath, dressed simply in his skin. He was oblivious to his own nudity, and concerned for his wife, while she made a gracious introduction to the flustered doctor. We laughed at her story and had a relaxed, gay visit with them, possibly because we found we were all from the Midwest.

Alice could stay with me only a month and then had to return to Rochester and all the children. She had four at home, Joe and Bill attending public school and little Maria and Alex still under school age. David, Charlie and Ned were attending the Episcopal Military School at Shattuck, about sixty miles from home, where they became permanently antagonistic to military life, and Muff was at the feminine version of the same school, St. Mary's Episcopal School.

All that summer I made so many trips to Washington begging for our posting that the Surgeon General's Office issued a special order that I wasn't to come again. The one cheerful note was the arrival of Sev Olson, who later became a professor at the University of Minnesota School of Dentistry. He put himself through dental college by having two bands and when he enlisted in our unit he brought along an entire orchestra. We trained those musicians as corpsmen, and they were good, and by a feat of legerdemain we managed to purchase their instruments as part of our medical supplies. We were the only hospital unit anywhere with a full band concealed within it.

As the unit grew, it was divided into two parts. Jim Priestley took half, the 237th Station Hospital, and was sent to Utica. I remained in Charleston as executive officer of the other half, the 233rd Station Hospital. We divided the band between us, fairly.

In July, Alice telephoned me that my mother was dying. It wasn't unexpected. She had been suffering from leukemia and was in St. Marys Hospital when I left Rochester. For a year before that she had been growing steadily weaker, though she never complained. The children used to visit her often in Ivy Cottage and Alice and I usually dropped by in the evenings. Mother never referred to her ill health during our times together, though she must have been distressed at the large swelling that was developing in her neck. Instead she pressed me to tell her what was happening at the Clinic and about my work. I used to mix her an old-fashioned, a strong one; she was drinking for the first time in her life. We would talk shop, glasses in hand.

My cousin Johnny Berkman was treating her and he decided that she should go into St. Marys for radium therapy. The Sisters there adored her and fussed over her affectionately. Until almost the end, Mother remained conscious and rational and seemed to regard her coming death as a matter of no great importance. Consistent with her character, she was practical about accepting something that couldn't be changed. She died in July and I arrived home in time for the funeral. We buried her next to Father, under the common headstone that covers the four graves of the Mayo brothers and their wives.

Mother left us a bundle of letters to be read fifteen years after her death. When the time came, Alice and I took them with us in our boat and read them slowly as we traveled on the Mississippi. Alice cried like a child over some of them, those that expressed Mother's loneliness and longing to be closer to her busy and important husband. Others were full of wisdom and sweetness, and her love for us all. They are remarkable documents, but very private.

I returned to Charleston and my impatience at what seemed to me a waste of the excellent Mayo doctors and nurses stalled there was mounting uncontrollably. I was already aware that I was not cutting too successful a figure as an Army officer. Red tape irritated me, the slowness to make decisions and the stupidity of some of those decisions made me fume openly. It is not too surprising that my rebellious and candid person was kept in out-of-the-way places most of the war.

We finally moved out of Charleston in late November, 1943. We assumed that we would be sent to the European theater, since it was handier to the eastern seaboard, but instead we were loaded into trains and sent across the country to San Francisco. It was all secret, of course, but in the railway station at Chattanooga I encountered an old girl friend who was dispensing coffee and doughnuts to the troops. She promised to telephone Alice and tell her that I was headed for the Pacific.

We were collected at Camp Stoneman, waiting to sail. Christmas Day was a lonely strain, though I was one of the lucky ones who got a call through to home. I had picked up a heavy cold, which kept me coughing and resulted in a nasty thrombosed pile. There was some talk that I wouldn't be well enough to sail with the unit, so in alarm I hurried to the dispensary and mixed myself a batch of strong cough-suppressor, terpin hydrate and codeine. I had just swallowed some of it when a colonel came into the room. "How did you get that liquor?" he said with gusto. Before I could explain that it looked like gin, but wasn't, he up-ended the bottle and drank deeply. He woke up about twenty-four hours later, when the effects of the codeine had worn off.

The medicine also worked for me and I was allowed to leave with the rest on the converted liner *New Amsterdam*, which was so fast that we didn't need an escort. The provisions weren't too plentiful; we dined only twice a day and when water supplies ran low halfway across, we were obliged to wash and shave in salt water. After twelve days of evasive action and a stop in New Zealand for water, we arrived in Australia. I went ashore with the gift Alice bought me in Charleston, something she thought no one should go to war without—a folding camp chair. I emphatically agree with her assessment of war. The chair became my favorite possession and I carried it everywhere throughout the twenty-three months I served in the Pacific.

The two predominantly Mayo Clinic units, mine and Jim Priestley's, had been reunited before we sailed, which meant that we had two bands to offer for the entertainment of the crowded, apprehensive troops who made the crossing on the *New Amsterdam*. The bands continued to be in demand for concerts at the staging area at Hern Bay, just outside Sydney, Australia, where we awaited transport to New Guinea. We began to perceive that the bands were precious to our morale, and an excellent item with which to barter, so when we had to climb down the rope ladders from the deck of the transport ship to the heaving little landing barges below, the lightly-laden officers gladly volunteered to tote the instruments.

We were landed on a dark beach somewhere in New Guinea in the finest tradition of such maneuvers, which is to say that no one expected us or had the faintest idea why we had come. We borrowed two tents for the night and I discovered the next morning that we were supposed to be thirty-five miles away, at Nadzab in the Markham Valley. The 5th Air Force, which had the most extensive landing strips and deployment in the world, had its base a mile away; its men would be our patients.

I got in a jeep and found our location; a portable hospital had been unloaded there in crates, but the Air Force already had plundered about three-quarters of it. I left a guard to protect what remained and went back for my unit. It was decided that the nurses would remain behind while we doctors and corpsmen worked with the engineers to set up our quarters.

We pitched tents in the kunai grass of the valley, which grows to a height of fourteen feet and harbored the scrub typhus bug which caused a distressing disease. We also discovered, promptly, that a certain tree with runny red sap caused severe dermatitis. Our tents had no floors, rain came through the closings, which had not been provided with flies, and we had to keep our shoes in tightly closed boxes every night to prevent their being covered by fungus by morning. This was the rain forest, we were informed; the annual rainfall was 197 inches. After the first day, we believed it.

We were notified that the replacement for our pilfered hospital was on the way—in three different ships. We agreed that this practically guaranteed that they would unload at three different ports, and that one of them would be in Iceland.

We noted another unusual feature of the location chosen for us: across the river was the 5th Air Force's bomb dump, the largest in New Guinea, where five-hundred-pound bombs were stored. It seemed a curious neighbor to have chosen for a hospital. Luckily it never was bombed during the time we were there, but the frequent alerts and blackouts kept our interest in it from flagging.

Because of the rain, flash floods were not uncommon. I helpfully pointed this out to the engineers, but they continued to put the pipes that carried our power under the stream, rather than suspending them over it. As a result, we frequently were without power while repairs were being made. The most spectacular flood victim was our chapel, which was flattened to bits one night. The conditions seemed to benefit the local population of scorpions and tarantulas, however; we found them in our beds and water bottles.

The engineers brought bulldozers to our site and we all pitched in to help clear the ground, some of the doctors exultantly driving the behemoths. After months of waiting, our hospital and equipment arrived and we could provide a fine quality of medicine and surgery for the men of the 5th. My role was mostly confined to administration and Carl Schlicke headed the surgery. He had two operating rooms with cement floors, one of them air-conditioned, the insulation ingeniously being sawdust packed between double walls. Our most grisly and sad cases were the pilots and other crewmen who were torn up by antiaircraft fire and crash landings. The majority of our work was the usual run of health problems found in any community, with a few heads damaged by falling coconuts for variety.

Four months passed before we moved out of the tents into frame quarters. We had a struggle putting them up, since the timber came from Australia and was as impregnable as iron. When we tried to hammer in the nails, they bent over like butter. Later, when the unit moved out, we were shocked by the order that all the nails had to be removed and used for crating our material for our next move, to the Philippines.

I wrote Alice that I was sharing two-roomed quarters with Bill Howell, a doctor from the Washington Clinic. We had a sitting room and a bedroom, in which I rigged up a workable indoor toilet. We added decorative touches, such as sacksack concealing the tin in the sitting room (sacksack is woven palm leaves left on a long stem) and green burlap for partitions. We soon were entertaining a stream of visitors, come to inspect what was being called the "Mayo Clinic." From them we learned that Jim Priestley and the 237th Station Hospital were having an equally miserable time. They had been posted to Finschhafen, near the coast but still part of the rain forest. The soil under them had a coral base, which meant that water couldn't drain away; most of the time they were up to their knees in tan gummy mud and for days at a time no one could get in or out.

I was enlivening my stay at Nadzab by wangling rides in the bombers when they went out on combat missions. I don't know if I ever was shot at, the engines made such a racket, but it was exhilarating to buzz the tops of the jungle trees. After a few missions, three or four, the brass heard about it and grounded me.

I was pained to notice that the crates in which our supplies had been shipped were deteriorating and vanishing, even though they obviously would be needed to take our equipment out of there. I pondered on this waste for a while, and began to devise a scheme whereby the crates could be converted into mess tables or desks once they were unpacked. I worked it out in some detail and sent an outline of my plan to my good friend Jay Hormel, of Austin, Minnesota, a member of the meat-packing family.

He set it along to Donald M. Nelson, chairman of the War Productions Board in Washington, and Nelson replied warmly that the Office of the Surgeon General and the Navy Bureau of Medicine and Surgery were favorably impressed and would be discussing the possible designs that could be used. None of the dual-purpose crates ever turned up in my part of the war, but I haven't stopped thinking that it was a practical idea. Keeping crates in continual use has obvious advantages in a war, where the movement of materials is costed in blood, but I can see peacetime uses as well. For instance, summer cottage supplies could be shipped in crates that convert to ping-pong tables, and back to crates again in the autumn.

To my own amazement, I found myself writing poetry in my letters to Alice. The verse was rudimentary, with overtones of doggerel, but it served my embarrassed purpose, which was to tell her that I loved her and missed her, and was proud to be serving. I am an inarticulate man on subjects that move me deeply; only Alice would appreciate how much feeling lay behind such lines as

> Wish you were here so I could nudge,
> and wink and smile at your funny face. . . .

By June of 1944, we were getting a number of patients who had heard of Mayo Clinic units in New Guinea and asked to be sent to us from forward areas. My complaining about the dust in the surgery had won for us macadam for the main roads in the hospital area and the traffic was heavy; we had about five hundred patients. I set up monthly Nadzab Valley medical meetings, attended by all the doctors in the area to discuss interesting cases and exchange information. The resemblances to the Mayo Clinic's style of operations were growing, and I was working on schemes to interest doctors in staying in the service after the war. I wrote Alice, "If the war lasts long enough, you won't have to worry about my getting home—they'll kick me out to keep me from bothering them."

Every now and then Carl Schlicke let me operate with him as his first assistant, which amused us both, since he had served as my first assistant in Rochester. "Didn't know I was so versatile," I wrote Alice. But mostly I just watched and heckled. The medical teamwork was a joy; we all worked beyond our strength in the warm bath of mutual endeavor and sacrifice that typifies wartime service. I used to speculate that after the war I wouldn't return to the frustrations of Rochester but would take the Nadzab people, intact, to a new location in a warmer climate and start my own clinic.

Friends were sending me newspaper clippings from the United States that tended to dramatize what I was doing in New Guinea. I felt sheepish about the exaggerations and wrote Alice, "My plan as directing surgery has been to leave the surgeons pretty much alone, only entering when they ask for advice or help. I have confidence in them, and they have proved worthy of confidence. Any one of them can operate on me anytime, and therein lies the answer."

Some distinguished visitors were turning up at the 5th Air Force's base, and usually made a side trip to see us. My friend Charles Lindbergh was in the vicinity for a while, acting as liaison between airplane manufacturers and the pilots

199

who flew the aircraft. He was involved in listening to complaints and praise for the new fighter, the P-61, which had just been delivered. I talked Colonel Jim Guthrie into taking me for a ride in one and we soared over mountains and clouds for a time and then dove straight down for six or seven thousand feet, pulled up and rolled over. I got out tottering, but grinning from ear to ear.

We were grateful for the USO entertainment that came our way. Jack Benny brought a troupe on July 25, 1944, and I went to the Air Force base to ask him to include our hospital. He said he would, and we eventually became close friends, but there was one problem—his singer, Martha Tilton, had a sore throat and probably couldn't take part in the show. I informed her gallantly that I would fix her sore throat. She came with me in a jeep and I found the complicated throat-spraying machine that we had in the hospital. I'd never used it; in fact, I'd never sprayed a throat before. She arranged herself where the patient was supposed to sit while I kept up a banter, trying to figure the thing out. I deduced that I would have to put my foot on a pedal to get pressure in the spray nozzle, so I did so. Unhappily, the nozzle wasn't aimed too well and the disinfectant was sprayed liberally all over the front of her dress.

In the awkward moment that followed, I explained that I was a surgeon, not an ear, nose and throat man. Miss Tilton smiled sweetly, murmuring, "That's obvious." I finally did manage to spray her throat properly and it was effective because she later sang for our patients and was a delight.

Our band played for Jack Benny and he was so impressed with the musicians that he would have no other for all his shows in the area. We never ceased blessing the good fortune that delivered them to us, ever since our discovery that other units would pay in goods for a concert. We shipped them out for miles around and they returned with window screens, provisions, movies. The nurses were almost as helpful. I instructed them to scrounge things we needed at the hospital in return for dates with the Air Force and it turned out to be a beneficial arrangement. The rarest and most valuable commodity in New Guinea was liquor, since General Douglas MacArthur had decreed that it was to be a dry war, but thanks to the band and the nurses a little bit came our way for entertaining.

Jack Benny promised me that he would look Alice up if ever he was in the vicinity of Rochester. I always instructed States-bound guests to do that, with the result that Alice had so many people calling on her that she found the simplest way to handle the situation was to give a big party every Saturday night, inviting over some of the other wives who were alone. The arrangement had some disadvantages however, since Alice was growing alarmed over stories of how thin and exhausted I was. I decided to stop complaining to her about the ghastly food we ate, the bully beef we called "Red Heart No. 2," the tinned scrambled eggs and, a gastronomic disaster, tinned scrambled eggs with ham. Instead I emphasized what dietary highlights came our way, such as on the night that Sev Olson came back from Australia in a "fat cat" troop carrier and brought us meat and fresh vegetables and thirty gallons of fresh milk. We gave twenty gallons of it to the enlisted men and kept ten for ourselves. It was the second time I had had a taste of milk since arriving in New Guinea. We had a good meal the night one of our nurses married an Air Force man. We celebrated by drinking our ration of beer for the week, despite the failure of our refrigerator due to a flood disrupting our power —a pilot consented to take the beer to a great altitude and fly it around for a while until it was sufficiently chilled.

In mid-October I was given a week's leave in Australia and when I returned I found that the 233rd had been absorbed and now was known as the 247th General Hospital, with me as chief of surgery. There was also a letter waiting for me from Alice, saying that some friends of ours were pulling strings to have me returned to the States. I cursed my thoughtlessness in mentioning to her that some officers were returning home, and how I envied them as I saw them off, and hurriedly wrote her that all such efforts were to cease at once. I sent another letter to the general involved, requesting that he ignore any requests of this nature. Rumor had it that our hospital would be attached to the Air Force and moved to Manila and I wanted to finish the war with them.

I tried to explain this to Alice. "We have many officers and men in the ranks who want and look forward to the same thing," I wrote. "I don't want to take any advantage which is not available to them. I think too much of the morale of the individuals with us." I ended, in case this was in doubt, "I do love you," which was true.

I was envious of Jim Priestley, who had landed in the Philippines with a surgical team and was working in the front lines. My share of the war seemed tame and forlorn, in comparison.

About a month after my letter to Alice, I was advised that General Somervell wanted to see me at once, in Washington. He was head of personnel on the General Staff, under which the Medical Department serves. Alice was notified that I was on my way and she was waiting when I got off the aircraft. She later admitted that she expected I would be crisp and splendid in full uniform. Instead I wore fatigues and a leather jacket and looked exactly how you would expect a man to look after fifty-four hours in a bucket seat. Besides the rumpled state of my clothes, my skin was yellow from the atabrine we took to prevent malaria and I was thirty-four pounds lighter than when I left the States. For an instant, Alice didn't know me.

I learned that my protests had been in vain and I was being offered a post in Washington for the rest of the war. I turned it down firmly, for the reasons I had given Alice: I wanted to stay with my group until the end. They told me that I could take as long a leave as I liked—I think they were shocked at my appearance—but I decided that two weeks was plenty. It seemed to me that any more would have been unfair. Alice and I had a second honeymoon in New York for a while, seeing the shows, and then came to Rochester so I could visit with the children.

Alex was a stranger, a small person who could walk and talk instead of the baby I had left. Maria still says that her childhood memories always are of me in uniform, which must have stemmed almost entirely from that visit. The others were a handful for Alice to supervise: Charles and Ned and David had been sent to my former tutor, Edward Pulling, who operated an excellent prep school, Millbrook, in New York State; it hadn't worked out too well for Charlie, probably because brothers shouldn't be in the same school together, so he went to Hill School, my old nemesis, after a while, and David transferred to a school in Asheville, North Carolina, that had a sports program that suited him. Bill, my brother Joe's natural son, was difficult to raise, possibly because of the two shocks he sustained when small in the deaths of his parents; David, his older adopted brother, was a model of tact and thoughtfulness. Muff also had changed schools: she now went to Gulf Park in Mississippi because it had facilities for her to take flying lessons. She resembled my brother Joe in many respects, being constantly in hot water with the authorities and on the verge of expulsion. Alice spent so much time pleading with the staff to give her another chance that when Muff finally did graduate, dressed in her gown and mortarboard, she left the procession of graduates and walked over to where Alice was sitting and laid the diploma in her lap. "This is for you, Mother," she told her. "You earned it more than I did."

While I was in Rochester, Ingrid Bergman came to town to head a bond drive and I was invited up on the platform with her. She's a beautiful woman, unaffected and glowing, but she is tall, and I am not. I found a small stool, set it down beside her and stood on it to kiss her cheek.

I returned to New Guinea just before Christmas, taking with me two silver cups that Alice deemed appropriate for Bill Howell and me to use for our drinks. I also had a duffel bag that contained a case of Scotch and a case of bourbon. I tagged it "FOR MALARIA RESEARCH" and never let it out of my hands. I was in Camp Stoneman in San Francisco for two weeks waiting for transportation until I learned the local ground rules—the WAC in charge of putting personnel on the planes was responsive to gifts. I found three pairs of nylons for her and was on the next flight out, clinging to that duffel bag. I knew I was going to be the most welcome returnee in the history of war.

One bottle broke, a great tragedy, but we divided the rest equably, with the patients assigned one quarter of the supply, the enlisted men another quarter, the nurses a quarter and the officers a quarter. To simplify the arithmetic, and for other reasons, I took out one bottle for myself.

Shortly after my return, I was transferred to the 237th Station Hospital at Finschhafen as its commanding officer. I hated leaving the good comradeship at Nadzab but I had the consolation of knowing that the new group was also full of my friends from the Clinic. They were arranged on the landing strip when I arrived and greeted me with the information that once again the ingenuity and determination of the American enlisted man had proved equal to the challenge of a crisis situation: Finschhafen had its own still in almost continuous operation and the product was deemed drinkable, since no one yet had died of it.

I settled in with many happy distractions. My brother-in-law John Hartzell turned up in a Navy ship that was anchored nearby and for several days we enjoyed a family reunion. One night I went to a movie with him and some others from his ship and I forgot to wear the nuisance leggings that our regulations required after sundown. A guard stopped me and would have turned me away but I informed him levelly that I was in the Navy, and therefore not subject to that order. He decided not to argue the matter and after that our band usually saluted my entrance with a rousing "Anchors Aweigh."

Soon after Irving Berlin arrived with the show *This Is the Army*, with a huge cast that had been traveling some twenty thousand miles around the Pacific entertaining the troops. I thought at first it was a dismal waste of money, especially when I found we would have to enlarge our stage for the performance, but it was a night of theater that I'll never forget, and worth every penny it cost. I wrote Irving Berlin to that effect, and received from him a gracious note saying it was the finest letter of appreciation that he had received in the three years he had been touring.

The war in Europe seemed to be drawing to a close and we listened to the short-wave news avidly. The Russians were only eighty-five miles from Berlin, I heard one morning. I calculated that this is about the distance from Rochester to Minneapolis, which bolstered my optimism. The news in the Pacific was better too, with a landing on Luzon just above Bataan without a loss of life and our Navy roving the China Sea without encountering the enemy. I seemed to have more time for myself, despite my increased responsibility, and I got to work on a medical paper on the changes the profession must make to meet the demands of the times. I heard from Harry Harwick at the Clinic that a postwar expansion in the educational program was planned, and I wrote him that I approved and also suggested a housing development where the young doctors and their families could live. I also sent a letter to the Clinic's Board of Governors, urging that we launch a new fellowship program leading to a degree in medical administration, just as the existing degrees in medicine and surgery. I'm a passionate advocate of group medicine—I think it is the proper direction for medicine to take—and it seemed to me that many experiments with group medicine failed because of faulty business setup and administration. Mayo Clinic, whose success rested so soundly on good administration, seemed an obvious place to offer such an education.

My spirits and health improved at Finschhafen and I realized I even was enjoying myself, except for missing Alice. I wrote her that no one ever had a "better, sweeter or more adorable wife than I have." I found that I also was in love with the sound of her name and I wrote her at length about that. She was writing me on an almost daily basis too, and had some flattering things to say about me.

A new base surgeon arrived in late February, read my medical paper on future developments and told me it was filled with dynamite and too controversial to accept. I told him I neither liked innocuous papers nor the authors of them, and we glared at one another for a time in heavy silence. He decided he would send the paper up the chain of command without comment.

My former base in the Nadzab was being reduced and the patients were coming through our hospital, together with the doctors and nurses, the latter bound for Manila. Tales from people who had seen the Philippines since our landings were filled with the horror of the destruction there, the buildings flattened, the harbor filled with debris and half-sunk shipping. Clearly, though, it was developing as the medical base for our stepped-up assaults against Japanese-held islands and, eventually, against Japan itself. We felt more and more frustrated and bypassed in Finschhafen and longed to be on the move. I could only chuckle at Alice's laments that the children weren't a huge success at school. I wrote Muff consoling her that she probably had all the right answers on her examination paper but the teacher had misread them, and to Ned suggesting that he aim for third from last in his class, instead of second from last.

I heard on the short-wave on April 13 that President Roosevelt had died. I had not approved of many of his policies and certainly not of his third term—my family demonstrated, I think, that a well-built organization doesn't collapse when an individual leaves—but I felt stricken at his death. His efforts at developing internationalism in his countrymen and founding the world organization for peace seemed to me remarkable, particularly as he had held the view as a younger man that Americans should never fight on foreign soil.

Late in April, Jean Young, who headed our nurses, heard that I had been promoted to colonel. She encountered me outside the church, where I was looking for someone who had just been promoted to major. I had his oak-leaf insignia with me and I was polishing it absently, talking about his good fortune. Jean said, "Why don't you shine your insignia? You always go around unpolished." She whipped out a handkerchief and started rubbing my insignia while I chattered on. When she stepped back, I discovered she had managed to pin my colonel's eagles on me, which was the first I knew of the promotion.

We heard about Berlin's fall and the death of Hitler on May 2, and about Mussolini. It was almost ten years from the day I had met Mussolini in his palace, and now he hung by his heels. We also had good news in the Pacific: the landings in Borneo, the capture of the airfield in Okinawa, the air raids over Japan, the advances on Mindanao. I wrote Alice that I would be home soon; I had been saying that for a year and a half, but now it looked as though it was going to happen.

One morning I acted as first assistant to my good friend and former first assistant, Ed Judd. He was doing a difficult case, a complicated duodenal ulcer, and I remembered an operation developed by his father, Dr. Edward Starr Judd, who had trained me. The procedure had become known as the Judd pyloroplasty and I showed Ed how his father used to do it, cutting out the anterior wall ulcer, taking out most of the pyloric muscle and closing transversely in order to enlarge the stomach outlet. He did a beautiful job, and we were both caught by this pure example of the links between our families: my father had trained his father, his father had trained me, I had trained him—would he train my sons?

We all felt strangely depressed when V-E Day finally arrived, much as we had been looking forward to it. There was no celebrating; the day went on as usual. We were despondent to be alone now in a dirty war while others would soon be home, and we were surprised and ashamed at our own selfishness. I contrasted our glum mood with the gaiety I could picture in Times Square and Piccadilly, and I recalled the confetti and jubilance of the crazy night I spent in New York when World War I ended. We were dispirited in New Guinea for a long time after V-E Day, and stopped listening to news broadcasts. I wrote a poem:

> I herewith take a liberty
> Quite unauthorized to me
> Proposing medals soon be struck
> For those who in the rear are stuck,
> For some of us who fail to see
> Where is our utility.

I got the news that Jim Priestley and some others from the Clinic had been awarded Bronze Star medals. I rejoiced for them; they had been handling combat casualties and worked almost around the clock, and deserved the honor.

Our morale lifted at the end of May, when we were ordered to pack everything and sail for the Philippines. We were loaded into an LST which we were told was only a year old but seemed closer to the century mark; it had taken part in some of the landings in the Philippines. The crew was so young that the oldest officer on board was only thirty-two, and the captain was twenty-six. We grew to like them very much, which was fortunate since we were together for a

22. Alice, Christmas 1936

23. Me driving horse and sulky at Mayowood, 1936

24. Alice and me in our riding habits, 1936

25. Dr. C. H. Mayo and Dr. W. J. Mayo receiving honorary doctors of law degrees at Villanova, 1937 (*United Press International*)

These two made The
Clinic a perpetual thing

26. Left to right: Alice, Maria, Muff with Bozo

27. Alice in 1939

week at anchor waiting for the convoy to assemble and another twenty-eight days crossing the Pacific. The convoy could move only as fast as the slowest ship, and that was us.

It didn't help any that we seemed to drift from harbor to harbor after we arrived in the Philippines, sometimes traveling in the exact opposite direction from the one in which I knew our destination to lie. Once I discovered that the other half of our outfit, which was on board another ship, was about to sail away with a convoy bound in another wrong direction. By pleading with the Port CO, I rescued them and they crowded aboard our ship.

Our first stop had been Subic Bay, where the captain said he wanted to take on fresh water, and also visit his brother-in-law. I decided to let our men go ashore and it took them about fifteen minutes to find the local whorehouse. Someone from the ship saw them lined up patiently and told me about it. I had been walking on the beach with Fat Gal, the cocker spaniel that Bill Howell inherited in the Nadzab when her previous owner, a fighter pilot, was killed. I pondered the situation and then opened a case of prophylactics and distributed them impartially to every man who had left the ship, without inquiring whether there was a need or not.

We finally dropped anchor near the location where our hospital was to be set up and I went ashore to reconnoiter. My long experience in the forces had prepared me for the discovery that we were vaguely expected at a little town, Bauan, near Batangas, and would have to move our supplies by truck. I returned to the ship and the captain tried to run the LST up the beach so we could let down the ramp and unload. After the third fruitless attempt, night fell on his efforts and we had to wait until dawn. I suggested then that we move our men to the rear of the ship, lightening the prow, and he made the beach on the next try. I modestly offered to switch jobs with him, which he took in good grace.

We started to rebuild our hospital on this new island, sleeping in and under the trucks until we got enough tents up and then progressing to the sturdy portable buildings that would enable us to take in patients. The condition of the civilians around us was appalling. They were so hungry that we used to clear the scraps from our plates and give them to the children, rather than dump them in the garbage barrels. It ended up, of course, that we left the best pieces of food for the children and ate little ourselves. The desperate shortages of goods meant that thieving was essential to life; we had to keep a guard on everything, even the jeeps. Our band instruments had begun to wear out, so we sent for new ones, and when the cases arrived they were empty. We never did understand how the natives managed that theft, but we sent for more and they got through. The inflation was shocking, three to five dollars for a meal worth a few cents, six dollars to rent a horse-drawn cart to go a mile.

Bauan turned out to be on high ground about two miles from a fishing village, colorful with those outrigger canoes that the Filipinos handle with such dexterity. Jim Priestley had helped pick the location, which we thought was ideal; our task was a sobering one, to prepare for some of the hundred thousands of casualties that we expected when we would land in Japan. Jim and I worked together on the plans for the spacious surgery in prefabricated buildings and the rows of tents that would shelter the patients. We picked a scenic location for a section of doctors' quarters, to be made of bamboo; the one we would share would have a glorious view of sunsets, which we had discovered were spectacular in that country.

Once I made a trip to Manila to get a pump for our water supply and check on the progress of our nurses. I was aghast at the desolation of that ruined city, the rubble choking the streets, the bridges out, the rough treatment our men accorded private property. I returned despondent.

I had complained lustily about the mosquitoes in Finschhafen, which were so thick they darkened a room, but I was even more disturbed when planes sprayed our area in the

Philippines with DDT. I noticed that it drove away the birds, as well as the insects, and I wrote Alice, "In the plan of nature with everything having a purpose in the long run, DDT over large areas must not be good. But maybe the war won't last that long." I take satisfaction in having foreseen that state of affairs described with alarm twenty years later by Rachel Carson in her book *Silent Spring*.

I was also disturbed at the shocking waste and carelessness that seem to be part of most large, unorganized undertakings. Filipinos unloading our equipment, for instance, habitually tossed it off the trucks with abandon and once broke every X-ray tube in a crate, at a cost of seventy-five dollars each.

We had little to do, outside of a few victims of accidents in jeeps and a stray gunshot wound—our soldiers weren't too skilled at discerning the difference between a Filipino and a Japanese sniper and were still firing at what they supposed were enemy targets, sometimes hitting one another. One afternoon Jim Priestley, Ed Judd and Ed Weld—all Mayo Clinic alumni—were in a four-wheel-drive jeep with me at the wheel. I wanted to cross a stream, which meant driving down a steep bank, across the shallow water and up the other side, and during this maneuver Ed Judd fell off and landed in the water. I looked back at him sitting there indignantly and called out, "That isn't very kind of you, leaving me in rough straits such as this." He laughed, after a while.

As invasion time approached, I was given a new posting, Surgical Consultant to AFWESPAC (Air Forces of Western Pacific) and moved into Manila. One afternoon when I was working, with my feet on my desk, a young ensign doctor arrived and said he was taking care of a patient named David Reyno—or trying to, since Reyno would have no doctor except Dr. Mayo. Would I come?

I set off at once. Reyno had been our houseboy, the most extraordinary servant anyone ever had. Alice found him through an agency and he moved into an apartment in Mayowood with his wife and baby, and served us with a loyalty and devotion that were embarrassing. He insisted on being my valet, brushing my clothes and laying them out, and even trimmed my hair. He assumed some other duties that were unusual: he would pick up our guests in town in a chauffeur's uniform, drop them off at our front door to wait for a mystifyingly long time while he raced around to the rear, changing into his white houseman's coat as he ran, and then he would open the front door and suavely usher them inside. After he served the cocktails and dinner, he would change into a dinner jacket and play the violin for our guests, though we never asked him to. We were helpless during these enforced concerts, since it was unthinkable that we should hurt his feelings.

When I enlisted, Reyno announced that he would enlist as well and accompany me to war as my orderly. This plan proved unfeasible, since he was unable to get into the Army, but he joined the Navy when he heard I was in the Pacific. He bid farewell to his babies, now grown to two, and set off confidently to find me.

On my way to see him, I was informed by the ensign that Reyno worked in the officers' club at the Navy base and had a possible slight stroke. I found him asleep when I arrived and I put my hand over his mouth and pinched his nose to wake him up. He was ecstatic when he saw me, ordering drinks all around to celebrate our reunion.

After the war he turned up in Rochester in full splendor, as the Philippines consul. I cannot imagine how he persuaded Manila that Rochester, Minnesota, was in urgent need of a consulate, but he did. He drove out to Mayowood in his station wagon with the Philippines crest on the doors and explained with dignity that his new duties would prevent him from working for us full-time. It was arranged that the consul would be available only half-days, to serve dinner.

He was busy at the consulate, as it turned out, since his Spanish made him invaluable to the many South Americans who visit the Clinic. He had one habit that Alice found disconcerting: whenever anyone from the Philippines arrived in Rochester, Reyno would put them in the station wagon and drive them to Mayowood, where he showed them around with proprietary pride.

My job in Manila seemed to me mostly make-work, with tours of the facilities that led inevitably to recommendations that would be ignored. I was depressed, and even more so when Alice wrote me that my close friend Alex Steward, godfather to our youngest child, had been killed in a car accident.

Whenever I could, I visited the site where Jim Priestley was directing the hospital building. Rain had slowed down the installation, and I had a tense confrontation with engineers bent on simplifying their task by leveling the Filipinos' farms and groves. Happily, one of their officers was also a farm boy and we arranged to do as little damage to the countryside as possible. The cement floors had been poured and the prefabricated walls were going up. I was gratified, but wistful; I felt ineffectual. To cure my malaise, I wrote medical papers on such subjects as the helpfulness of light plaster casts over a certain kind of abdominal wound and a different method for performing colostomies. The service regularly turned these down, but it gave me practice.

I ran across an odd story about one of our men who had been in a Japanese prison death camp. He managed to build a radio in his mess kit, hooking up in series sweet potatoes with copper and aluminum connections to take the place of a battery. And it worked, though I never would have believed that anyone could get juice like that from a vegetable.

When the atomic bomb was dropped on Hiroshima, I wrote Alice: "The news of the new atomic bomb and its destructive power was revealed via radio yesterday and this morning . . . I hope it will bring about an early surrender. If it is a fourth as good as they say it is, it certainly must shorten the whole affair." It couldn't come too quickly for me; my morale was slipping fast. In the same letter I said, "I wonder how much attention will be paid to recommendations I made. To me, it would seem that what I have to suggest is too logical to be acceptable."

On the day that the Manila newspapers headlined THE WAR IS OVER! while spent bullets were falling like rain from the G.I.'s firing deliriously into the air, I sat down and wrote a request for my separation from the services. I had determined to stay in until the end, and I had done it. I wrote Alice angrily, "I'm not one damned bit interested in remaining in what to me is such a screwed-up medical organization, where politics and lack of leadership on principles and policies and indecision exist."

When V-J Day was proclaimed, scarcely anyone in Manila paid attention. We were all trying to get home.

I was still in Manila, fuming, in September. I put in the time one afternoon by visiting New Bilibid Prison, where we had a station hospital to take care of captured Japanese and collaborators, the latter mostly Filipinos. I saw the prison's prize catch, General Yamoshita, a dignified six-footer wearing awkward boots. His poise impressed me, and his skill as a military strategist; he held out in the mountains of the Philippines until his government surrendered and came out with only forty thousand of his original army of a quarter-million. They all came out suffering from malnutrition, and about 10 per cent had tuberculosis. General Yamoshita was later condemned as a war criminal and hanged.

Our hospital was finished and functioning in the main for the normal kinds of illness and accidents to be found in a peacetime population. When Americans released from Japanese prison camps began to arrive, surprisingly few of them needed hospitalization—only 320 out of the first batch of 4500—despite the desperate conditions under which they existed for years. I noted to Alice, "One of the best means of propaganda to raise morale is to exaggerate what, of course, is a deplorable condition and to magnify atrocities."

One of the returning prisoners was Jim Keeley, who had been a fellow at the Clinic; he had been in Japanese camps in Mindanao and Japan for thirty-nine months. He reported that the average weight loss at the camp where he was the doctor was forty-five pounds, but the Japanese had begun feeding the prisoners much better rations early in August—before the bomb was dropped, which is interesting—and some were approaching their normal weight already.

One day we joined a party made up by the Red Cross and went to Corregidor, the scene of one of our earliest defeats. We walked around on the rock, sickened by the dripping debris, with thighs, hips, ribs and skulls littered in it.

Late in September I got news that I was about to be sent home by plane. Just as I was made sure of it, a friend of mine, Louis Vaughn, got word that his wife had been in an automobile accident and was in serious condition. His need was more pressing, so I switched priorities with him and got away, finally, a week later, by boat. They gave me a farewell send-off that almost made me miss my midnight sailing. I was the last person aboard, carrying an assortment of gear, and I couldn't find a place to sleep. Someone said there was an empty bunk in a lower cabin, so I made my way there in the pitch dark. It was stifling hot and, in feeling over the three-decked bunks for the empty one, I discovered to my embarrassment that I was groping over naked bodies. There was much complaining, but I located an empty berth and discovered in the morning that I was sharing my quarters with twenty-one others, most of them former prisoners of war.

The diet on the ship, because of the prisoners, leaned to ice cream by the quart. By the time we arrived at San Francisco nineteen days later, the man in the berth above me had gained so much weight his bedsprings were giving way. I telephoned Alice in Rochester and said, "I'm back." And no one, anywhere, was gladder than I.

TEN

The war ended, for me, on November 7, 1945, the day I arrived home in Rochester. I picked up my discharge at Camp McCoy in Wisconsin and went back to surgery at the Mayo Clinic. I had been worrying that my technique was getting rusty during the three years I was mostly an administrator, but I was grateful to discover that surgery is akin to those muscle-memory skills, like bicycle riding, and it came back to me with astonishing rapidity.

I admitted freely, now that I was back, how much I had missed surgery. Our unit had so few operations scheduled that I didn't want to hog what work there was, but I felt restless away from it. It didn't help any that one of the few operations I did as a chief turned out to be not exactly necessary. It happened while we were still in Charleston and I was sitting in the Officers Club one day, when the officer of the day got a call that the wife of a noncom had arrived in emergency and required an appendectomy. He asked me if I would do it, and I said sure. It turned out after I took it out that it was a normal appendix.

The Clinic was still short-staffed for some time after the war, waiting for our doctors and nurses to trickle back from the services. We all worked hard, I especially. I felt I had to make it up to the exhausted few who had stayed behind in Rochester throughout the war and somehow met the needs of a rising number of people coming to the Clinic. In comparison, I had been loafing for three years so I felt somewhat

216

mortified as I hastened to take my share of the load again.

My problems over money seemed to be worsening. Higher costs in every area were making it impossible to run Mayowood and keep up the Mayo tradition of hospitality there, but I could not abandon either. As quietly as I could, I sold off pieces of the land, which never failed to grieve me. It was forbidden that Clinic doctors should have an outside income, but I was growing desperate.

I saw my opportunity one day when talking to my friend Ed Noble, who had come to Rochester as a patient. John Edward Noble was a remarkable man. He bought a company that made little round candies and had the idea to put a hole in them and called them Life Savers. With the fortune that ensued, he purchased a radio network then known as the Blue Network and renamed it ABC. On this occasion when I was visiting him in his hospital room, Ed was grousing because he couldn't listen to his network while in Rochester.

"Why don't I start a radio station here and we'll affiliate with ABC?" I suggested. "Then you can hear your network any time you come." He thought that was a fine idea, so I went ahead and borrowed the necessary money. We put up four 350-foot towers in a field near Mayowood and called the new station KLER. Alice was named president and took offices in town, with a staff of about eighteen people. Fearing the wrath of the Clinic's Board of Governors, I kept in the background as much as possible. My only overt connection with the station was that I was a member of the board of directors.

We hadn't been running long when the local newspaper reported at some length about Rochester's new radio station and made prominent mention of the Mayo name: mine, to be specific. I waited, knowing that a terrible row with the Board was in the offing. Associates urged me to head off the storm by selling the station at once, but I wouldn't back down. My position wasn't too vulnerable, since the Board couldn't fire me.

I was notified that a special meeting had been called to discuss the matter of my association with the radio station and that I was to attend. That day I took my time with my patients and arrived a half hour late, and the fight began. I remember telling the Board in some heat that no one there knew how much money my father had left me, or about the condition in his will which was financially disastrous for me, or about the poor trusteeship of that will, or what I held to be poor trusteeship. The plain fact was, I continued, that I was heavily in debt and obliged to sell my land to keep from sinking.

They all expressed amazement, maybe most of it genuine, and asked why I hadn't sought to have my salary raised. I pointed out that my position at the Clinic was a delicate one, and I didn't like coming cap in hand to the Board. They knew my salary and they knew how hard I worked, and surely they could guess what it cost to entertain visitors to Rochester on the scale that was expected. The outcome of all this was that the Board gave me a substantial raise in salary and an expense allowance to relieve to some extent the high cost of hospitality at Mayowood.

With that done, the Board advised me to get rid of the radio station at once. I replied that I would not, and took that opportunity to point out that Harry Harwick, a Board member and the Clinic's financial administrator, was also on the board of directors of radio station KROC, my chief rival in Rochester. This was an awkward coincidence, but the Board got around it by telling me that Harry wasn't a doctor and therefore wasn't robbing patients of some of his energy and concentration, as I was. This was rubbish, in my view, since it pretends that a doctor who has any interest outside his practice is less capable as a doctor—while I hold that the reverse is more likely to be true. As a compromise, in view of the tension that was being generated, I agreed to resign from KLER's board of directors. I held firm in my resolve not to

218

part with the station. The meeting finally ended and we went our ways, all of us feeling mangled by the encounter.

Alice continued to run KLER for about three years, until it was purchased by KROC. We made no profit on the deal, my luck being consistent in that regard, but for a wonder we didn't lose either. It compares favorably with such ventures as the bull terriers, the turkeys and—ah, yes—the fig orchard. Someone told Father about the fortune to be made from figs, with some growers receiving incomes of around fifty thousand dollars a year. He was delighted to hear about this effortless wealth, so he purchased 114 acres of fig orchard near Fresno, California. The fig market promptly went to pieces, leaving me with expensive trees to maintain at a loss. For a time we had hopes that oil could be located on the property, but these proved misplaced.

Few people knew about Father's will at the time of my battle with the Clinic's Board, but it later became public knowledge by way of the front pages of newspapers. Father made out his will in 1929, at the time of his stroke, and it was never altered in the succeeding ten years he lived. Since it was composed at the time of the stock market crash, which took ten thousand of my precious dollars with it, Father understandably was anxious to protect his family from the treachery of investment in stocks. He therefore stipulated that the money left us was to be held by a trust company and invested in bonds only. Our inheritance would be the yield from these bonds. He named some of his friends to act as trustees of his estate, Harry Harwick among them. As it happened, all the trustees were busy men and I don't think it is unfair to say that they had little time to give to our affairs.

The estate was complicated. Joe and I were named as co-owners of Mayowood, with a $100,000 trust fund, in bonds, to operate it. Since Joe died three years before Father did, this half of Mayowood passed to Ruth and then, after her death, to their two sons. In addition, my four sisters, Joe's family and I all received varying amounts of money, depending on our needs. I received $120,000, but Joe's portion was slightly larger because he was still in postgraduate study when the will was drawn up; my sister Dorothy, who later was killed in a car accident, had never been stalwart—I think her share was larger as well. All this money, by the terms of the will, went into bonds and earned us 5 per cent interest annually. Father didn't want to spoil us.

The remainder of Father's estate was left to the Mayo Foundation, and when I last heard about it, it was *earning* more than a million dollars a year. Uncle Will left an even larger estate; Father was the more unrestrained of the two in money matters. Uncle Will's two daughters were left with comfortable amounts far in excess of ours, but then there were only two of them and six of us. The bulk of Uncle Will's estate also went to the Mayo Foundation.

It didn't occur to me until after the war that it had been a serious error on the part of my usually astute father to restrict us to low-return bonds. Esther was the first to realize this. Some banker friends of hers in Grosse Pointe were shocked when she confided in them the terms of her inheritance. They urged her to try to change the will, pointing out that the return from a partial investment in stocks would give her a handsome income. She began pressing me to do something about it but I was very reluctant. Inherited money is pure gravy and I had done nothing to earn it; there seemed something decidedly ungracious about complaining that it should be more.

Eventually, for the sake of all of us but mostly my children who would inherit those bonds, I approached the trustees. I reminded them that the will had been written at the time of a stock disaster, when stocks clearly were a frightening investment, but that the economic situation had greatly changed. I was sure that they agreed that Father would not have wished to see his family deprived of the considerable income that we could receive from converting some of the bonds into stocks. It seemed to me that the role of the trustees of an estate is to carry out the intention of a will and to act in the best interests of the people concerned. The trustees refused, taking the position that the will could not be changed despite altered circumstances.

I fumed about this in growing exasperation. I had been named to the board of trustees of nearby Carleton College, and a few other organizations with investment income, and I learned that it was customary to put about 65 or 70 per cent of this into stocks and the rest in bonds. I realized that it would be healthy to change the ratio from time to time but that stocks would probably always predominate. The post-war boom had begun and none of us could partake of it, because of that will.

Esther continued to plead with me to take action and I finally determined to try to break the will. Immediately, the situation grew even more unpleasant. I had to have the agreement of all the heirs and Joe's son, Bill, by this time a young man living in Minneapolis, went to a lawyer who advised him for some inexplicable reason to oppose the suit. I was amazed, but Bill would not yield. I knew I no longer stood to gain much because I could see that the legal fees would be enormous—lawyers will eat you up, cold turkey—but I decided to go ahead. I sued the Minneapolis Trust Company, holders of the trust through the First National Bank, Minneapolis, Minnesota. The trustees and Bill Mayo lined up together against me and I lost the case. I think the court was influenced mainly by their opposition. We appealed the judgment and were gratified to have it reversed by a higher court. I was right in my pessimism about the legal fees: they amounted to forty-seven thousand dollars.

But it was an important victory, and not only for the beneficiaries of Father's estate. The case established a legal precedent that I'm told has enabled a number of people to obtain sensible adjustments to a will whose intent is warped by changing conditions. I still think it was the duty of the estate's trustees to instigate the suit themselves, as a demonstration of their concern for our welfare. After the appeal verdict was handed down, we converted a large part of our trust funds into stocks and immediately improved our incomes. The failure of the trustees to act cost us many, many thousands of dollars.

In the period after the war I found myself involved in national affairs to a greater extent. While I was still in the Philippines, the American Legion had asked me to serve as assistant chief medical adviser on its National Medical Advisory Board and I did so for more than twenty years. In 1946, President Harry Truman invited me to be a member of his Special Committee to Study Medical Problems and I also was named chairman of the Special Medical Advisory Group of the Veterans Administration, and held that post for seventeen years. I think the most important good that I accomplished, or helped to accomplish, was in the location of the mammoth veterans hospitals that were built all over the States. Politicians put pressure on us to build them in truly odd locations, obviously reflecting some inner need, but we ignored them and stubbornly put the hospitals where they were accessible to the greatest number of veterans and their families. I take great pride in my contribution to those decisions.

The American Legion medical group would meet on the same day, or the day following the Veterans Administration group, for the convenience of a few of us who served on both, and we counted it a shining achievement that we were able to provide our veterans with the best medical care in the country, living up to the motto "Medical Care Second to None." In view of the difficulties in persuading doctors and nurses to work under a civil service kind of setup, it is perhaps surprising that the quality of medicine should be so high; but it is, it is truly a wonder.

I was also editor-in-chief of a medical journal, *Postgraduate Medicine*. A businessman, Jacob G. Cohen of Minneapolis,

Minnesota, and Dr. Arthur Sullivan of Madison, Wisconsin, came to see me in 1946 and told me they were launching the publication in order to print articles that would keep the general practitioner informed of developments in medicine that would be helpful to him. They asked me if I would like to be editor-in-chief and I said sure. We worked out an arrangement so that I could fulfill my function from my desk in Rochester. The magazine's editorial staff in Minneapolis is headed by Sylvia Covet as executive editor, and Dr. Morris Fishbein, the celebrated doctor-author who gave leadership to the American Medical Association over a long period, is a contributing editor.

In 1957 we were honored to receive the American Medical Writers' Association Honor Award "for distinguished service in medical journalism."

Mr. Cohen and Dr. Sullivan died in 1951 and 1954, respectively, and in 1966 their widows decided to sell the magazine to McGraw-Hill, Inc., one of the largest publishing firms in the world. *Postgraduate Medicine* continues to prosper under the new management, and the circulation continues to rise in a gratifying manner. I appreciate this all the more because I have been on the payroll ever since my retirement from surgery in 1963. Out of deference to the Clinic's rule against outside income, I accepted no salary as editor-in-chief for the first seventeen years of the journal's existence.

In between all these varied activities, I was working a twelve-hour day as chief of a surgery section at the Mayo Clinic. I continued to perform the assortment of operations which come the way of the general surgeon, but my special interest in cancer of the colon gradually attracted a greater proportion of such cases. Eventually a third to a half of all the surgery I did was to resect colons because of a malignancy.

My confidence in my judgment was being bolstered greatly as statistical evidence continued to demonstrate more and more convincingly that I was right in the early stand I took in favor of my one-stage procedure. As I described before, the procedure used almost universally when I began in surgery was to perform two separate operations when cancer occurred in the lowest portion of the colon, the first a colostomy and the second tumor and anus removal. I knew my figures had to be unchallengeable if I hoped to have the one-stage operation accepted and I sweated over them.

One of the difficulties was that statistics on hospital deaths from the two-stage operation were kept in a curious way. If the patient died after the first stage, the colostomy, the death was not counted as being the result of a two-stage procedure. Only deaths after the second operation were attributed to the two-stage procedure. Until I established that this gave an unreal picture, deaths from my one-stage operations were being compared with only a fraction of the deaths from the two-stage one.

I was under considerable attack during the first five years that I stuck to the one-stage procedure and awaited follow-up studies. Some called it heresy. One time I was called to consult on a case and recommended that the patient have a one-stage procedure and the medical man was so shocked he blurted out, "Oh, don't do *that!*" I told him mildly that he hadn't followed the development of this operation as closely as I had, which was certainly true since I was one of the few men who were engaged in developing it, and that it was preferable to the two-stage.

Like my colleagues, I had been trained in the two-stage procedure but one afternoon I fell to wondering why the two operations couldn't be combined. I reasoned a person is like a twelve-cylinder car that can withstand being hit softly many times—why not hit just as softly, but only once?

I got into many arguments at medical meetings about that operation from doctors who had never seen it or paid much attention to my reports. But many doctors came to watch what I was doing and I think some were impressed. I could do six of those combined one-stage abdominoperineal resections in a day, using a good, experienced first assistant in the role of second assistant. The initial part of the operation would go slowly while we worked deep and sometimes blindly in the abdomen, but the anus removal took only ten minutes.

Surgeons in most places began to prefer the one-stage after the evidence established that it was safe. The postoperative death rate of 6.5 per cent compared favorably with that of the two-stage operation, and the survival rate of some 60 per cent five years after the operation was about the same. The major improvement was in the patient's time, money and pain. I took a five-year period from the beginning of 1945 to the end of 1949 and surveyed 1400 lower colon operations. The two-stage patients were in the hospital an average of forty-three days; the one-stage, an average of fifteen days.

The one-stage procedure now is the operation of choice in most surgeries, but there are still many two-stage operations that I don't think are necessary.

My success in establishing that the one-stage was a safe procedure encouraged me in an even more controversial development beyond that operation. Removing the anus and the precious sphincter always distressed me and I often wished that I could somehow avoid this mutilation. I progressed from this to wondering if the surgery manuals of the day were justified in declaring that the anus must be removed when certain conditions are present. Could they be wrong?

I must backtrack a bit to explain the prevailing status in lower bowel surgery. When surgeons began developing bowel surgery in the nineteenth century, working without modern anesthesia, or knowledge of how to maintain fluid balance to counteract the immense loss of blood involved, or technique for thoroughly cleaning the bowel beforehand, they nevertheless evolved sound procedures which form the basis of all such surgery a century later. In those days as now, cancer in the colon located three times out of four in those few

225

inches between the sigmoid, where the descending colon kinks and turns toward the rectum, and the anus. They endeavored humanely to remove the tumor without sacrificing the anus. To them we owe the ingenious "pull-through" operation, dating from 1888, in which the tumor and the rectal tube containing it is cut out; the free end of the sigmoid is pulled through the sphincter or the lower segment of the rectum and allowed to heal there without stitches.

But in 1908 a surgeon named Miles became convinced that cancer anywhere in the rectum or rectosigmoid spread downward and to the side. Whenever a tumor occurred in this region, which is only inches from the anus, he felt that it was obligatory on the surgeon to remove the anus to protect the patient from a recurrence of cancer. No one doubted that Miles was correct until 1932. Then Dr. Wayne Babcock of Philadelphia questioned the necessity to be so thorough. His challenge, and that of his colleague, Dr. Harry Bacon, and the work they did in support of their view, passed almost unnoticed for ten years. Then I began to wonder the same thing. When I was sure enough in my own mind, having established to my satisfaction that colon cancer spreads upward much more readily than it does downward, I worked out a way of performing a low, low resection, leaving in the anus and sphincter and avoiding a colostomy. What faced me, as I well knew, was a five- to ten-year wait until I could be sure of my results.

My decision rested on distances that were measured in centimeters. If the lower borderline of the tumor lies five centimeters or closer to the dentate—that is, notched—margin of the anus, the surgeon has no choice but to remove the anus with the tumor and perform a colostomy. It would be disastrous to refrain from doing what is still called the Miles abdominoperineal resection, taking out the sphincters, rectum, rectosigmoid and lower part of the sigmoid, together with the pelvic mesocolon, levator ani muscles and perirectal tissues. There is too much danger that these parts will be contaminated by very low carcinoma.

No surgeon at that time, or this, disputed that the anus could be saved if the lesion was located eleven centimeters from its dentate margin. In such cases a comfortable radius of tissue can be removed with the tumor to give a generous measure of safety, without having to sacrifice the anus. However, I contended that a surgeon was justified in preserving the anus when the cancerous tumor was as close as six centimeters to the dentate margin of the anus. On this five centimeters of rectum I staked lives, and my reputation. I could not have gone ahead, holding my nerve together during the long wait for a volume of case histories to be assembled, if I had not considered and investigated every aspect with the utmost caution. To me it was never a gamble, or I wouldn't have done it: it was a sure thing that would take time to prove.

I was supported by the good goal, to give patients a better life after the operation. I hoped my work would act as a deterrent in some of those surgeries where doctors were removing the anus as a matter of routine when I felt it wasn't necessary. It is easy to take out someone else's anus: the surgeons seemed to have an easy conscience about what they were doing. But I wouldn't have slept well, if it had been I.

The low anterior resection that I helped develop to save the anus was difficult to perform, being much deeper into the pelvis than surgeons were accustomed to going; Mayo's low, low resection, it was called. The V Mueller Company made special instruments for me to my specifications: clamps and scissors with foot-long handles. I had to reach into what amounted to a Black Hole of Calcutta, a narrow space packed with contents that never see the light. Women were easier than men in this surgery because they have a wider pelvis and I could sometimes remove the uterus to obtain a better view of what I was doing. The operation was impossible on obese people; I simply couldn't reach. I also had to contend with the vagaries of the human pelvis, which is as individualized as the human face.

The operation could never have been developed without superior anesthetics that kept the patient absolutely still. The slightest cough or strain from the patient would result in a tangle of the exposed intestines or damage from the various instruments bristling in the wound. It could never have been done without modern methods of maintaining fluid balance in the body throughout the operation and good blood replacement afterward. And it would not have been possible without the improved techniques for preparing the bowels for surgery. At the Mayo Clinic we restrict diet for two days before the operation to liquids and such foods as result in a minimal residue. The rectum is irrigated twice a day and, on the morning of the operation, washed until the water returns clear.

I made use of every improvement that came along. Each one contributed to the success of the surgery as much as I did.

Except for such delicate moments as when the cut ends of intestine are being joined, surgeons can handle the contents of the human abdomen with a familiarity verging on heartiness. They pack aside the movable parts casually, piling them on sterile gauze squares, and probe around with their hands, making blunt dissections with their fingertips to free some of the lower colon that adheres to bone. Every organ is as recognizable by touch as the contents of the surgeon's own pocket. Whenever the abdomen is opened for any reason, the surgeon takes advantage of the opportunity to rummage over the liver and to check for any gross abnormalities. It's a startling sight for the uninitiate—a man's hand buried to the wrist in someone's living guts.

The surgeon gives the cancer he has removed only a

glance, knowing that the pathologist will give him a full report in a few minutes, but he can guess a good deal about it. If it has grown so that it covers three-quarters of the circumference of the bowel, it is probably about eighteen months old, which is the queen of spades. More than a third of all tumors removed from the colon are in this advanced category.

The pathologist comes back into the operating room carrying the tumor in its dish. He speaks from the door, to avoid approaching the sterile area around the operating table, and announces in a voice that echoes metallically in the tiled room that it is a grade three carcinoma with involved glands. He sounds businesslike and detached, but he knows that what he is saying is that the patient is dead. The anesthetist continues to squeeze the rubber bag that pumps oxygen into the patient's lungs, the surgery section gently and carefully completes the operation with all its skill, the relatives are sipping coffee in the hospital cafeteria and assuring one another that everything will be all right, the intensive care recovery room awaits. But there will be a funeral in six months, or a year. It's a sad business.

My grandfather made a sound observation about cancer before the turn of the century that has been helpful ever since in enabling surgeons to guess the likelihood that the cancer has metastasized in cases where they can see none. He said if the tumor "grows away from you," the crater-type that goes through the wall of the bowel, it is exceedingly dangerous. But when the tumor "grows toward you," the proliferative type that goes into the lumen of the bowel, its growth is slower, it is more contained, and there is a better chance. Sometimes the sight of the latter tumor even when it is advanced gives the surgeon hope that it has been stopped.

Every surgeon has known a few cases in which recovery could be classed as a miracle. I always remember the young man, only twenty-three, on whom I operated in 1937 to remove a shockingly advanced tumor in his upper rectum and rectosigmoid. I performed a sigmoid colostomy on him which I described in my notes as palliative, done only to ease his final few months. After the surgery he had Roentgen and radium therapy and we sent him home, a terminal case.

Twenty years later a questionnaire was sent to his home from the Clinic. Though it was worded discreetly as an inquiry about his health, we really wanted to learn how long he had survived in order to assemble some mortality statistics. To our astonishment, the patient filled in the form himself. He told us cheerfully that he was in splendid health, except for the odd cold. I remembered the case because of his youth and I was dumfounded. I used it after that as an example for patients and their relatives who are in despair.

Cancer is fast-growing in young people and the survival rate in the under-thirty group is a little lower than the overall average. I studied 126 cases of patients under thirty who came to the Clinic to have cancerous tumors removed from their colons and rectums—one was an eight-year-old girl— and found the survival rate was a discouraging 54.4 per cent. However, the operation is worth doing on patients who are over eighty. I have noted that people who arrive at an advanced age show ability to withstand bodily trauma much more than most doctors believe. A man who arrives at eighty has an average chance to live six more years, which is a considerable period. A person can enjoy a lot of sunsets and apple pie and laughter in six years. I looked over 154 case histories of patients over eighty who had colon cancers removed at the Clinic, most of them also suffering from such old-age diseases as poor hearts and hypertension, and found our three-year survival rate was a respectable 46.9 per cent.

It wasn't understood in Grandfather's day when such surgery was performed that instruments could become contaminated by touching the tumor and then would spread the malignancy throughout the incision. Before this was known, there were even cases of sutures becoming infected and causing cancer to recur along the suture line. Uncle Will was one of the first to publish warnings about this hazard, urging surgeons in 1913 to handle tumors with care to avoid breaking off cells that would seed themselves in healthy tissue.

Surgeons today treat tumors with the same respect that they would accord an unexploded grenade—which it is, so far as the patient is concerned. The lesion is never disturbed until the veins draining it have been clamped off and then a wide block is taken with the growth—parts of the peritoneum, the body wall or any organs that can be sacrificed safely if they have touched the growth.

I was obliged to wait for three years before I could begin to collect the survival statistics that would establish whether or not I was justified in performing the low, low anterior resection rather than an anus removal. During that time almost nothing in medical literature supported my conclusions. I faced the opposition of almost all the leading surgeons of the time who specialized as I did in colon and rectal surgery. It was a grim wait, but the early follow-up reports seemed to indicate that cancer was recurring in my patients at a rate not much different from recurrences among those with colostomies.

I continued with what I was doing despite the storm of criticism, for I am a stubborn man when I have made sure of the rightness of my cause. When five years had passed I had a small group of cases that I could demonstrate to my colleagues as proof that tumors as low as six centimeters from the anus did not always justify removing the anus. I knew my figures would be doubted and challenged, so I prepared them scrupulously. I began to deliver papers about my cases to medical societies all over the country and to have reports published in medical journals. Though I was braced, the disapproval I encountered was sometimes hard to take.

In those early years of the operation, at a time when I and a few finally-like-minded colleagues at the Clinic had performed it for controversial-area tumors only sixty-three times, our survival rate was only 4 per cent lower than the survival rate obtained by surgeons who removed the anus in such cases. "I know of extremely few people, including myself, who would not be willing to take this four per cent chance in order to keep the anus, rather than have a colonic opening," I used to comment. With more cases and the steady improvement in antibiotics, anesthesia and such factors, I was able to report after 476 such operations at the Clinic that the survival rate was almost exactly the same as that obtained by the old-style surgeons. I published the new figures as fast as they were gathered by the Clinic's Section of Biometry and Medical Statistics and I made my point plainly. On one occasion I said in a speech about the low, low anterior resection, "Before World War II, I sacrificed many rectums unnecessarily, feeling that I was doing the correct thing because that was what I had been taught. Now I am firmly convinced that I was wrong."

Finally, a great many surgeons began to believe that they were wrong too. By 1951, the proportion of colostomies being performed in the United States was a third lower than it had been a decade before. I took a mild kick at those colleagues who were still unconvinced in a paper on *Principles in Surgery of the Colon:* "There are as many methods of performing a particular surgical procedure as there are surgeons doing them," I wrote. "Each surgeon has his small or great prides and prejudices. It is important in the development of a man as a surgeon or as a physician that proper evaluation be made by virtue of clinical travel and study. It is an easy thing to sit back and delay such travel and study from year to year, until the practitioner becomes hidebound by self-induced provincialism."

I think most surgeons now preserve the anus whenever

they can, but there are still a few who do the same operations today as they did twenty and thirty years ago, as though nothing had been developed in the meantime. I was still addressing myself to this band of rigid, narrow men in the final paper I prepared before my retirement from medicine. I read it in the spring of 1963 at a meeting of the American Proctologic Society in San Francisco and it was published six months later in *Diseases of the Colon and Rectum.*

I reported that in my lifetime as a surgeon I had performed 424 low anterior resections without colostomy on persons living in the United States. Their average age was fifty-nine and men slightly outnumbered the women. Among those whose lesions were in the controversial band, the survival rate was 60.77 per cent. That's as good a survival rate as surgeons can provide by removing the anus, so I am proud of that work.

Surgery has now gone as far as it can in saving the lives of people who have cancer in their colons or rectums. Graphs at the Clinic showing postoperative mortality of the more than one thousand patients we have treated surgically for such cancer show a skidding downward line: I drew one in 1951 that was like a ski run, with about 18 per cent of patients dying in hospital in 1936 and less than 2 per cent dying in 1950. That's about as safe as such major surgery can get.

As Dr. Louis Arthur Buie observed in his book *Practical Proctology,* "there are few fields of surgery in which greater perfection has been attained than that of the management of malignant lesions of the colon. . . . Fantastic operations are performed."

The next development must come from the physicians who examine patients for the vague and misleading complaints that colon cancer produces. We surgeons cannot improve the survival statistics any further. We are up against the brick wall of too-late diagnosis. The great progress in the struggle against cancer in this region will be made by those who find a method of early recognition. About 12 per cent of people have potentially malignant lesions in their colons or rectums at some time in their lives. I think we must endeavor to find those lesions, which often are polyps, and remove them before they become cancerous. It is the best hope we have at this time for reducing the number of deaths from colon cancer.

ELEVEN

General George C. Marshall wrote to me on September 5, 1951, asking me to leave almost immediately on a month-long trip around the world to inspect American medical installations in the Far East, Middle East, Mediterranean and European areas. The Korean war was on and there had been some rumblings of difficulties. General Marshall was Secretary of Defense at that time, but he was succeeded the following week by Robert Lovett, to whom I would make my report.

My colleagues at the Clinic generously agreed to take over my duties, so I was free to accept. On the morning of September 20, I began operating at seven in the morning, performing a total colectomy, a skin graft, an ileostomy and a hysterectomy in the next three hours. My plane left shortly after eleven and I was joined in Seattle by Dr. W. Randolph Lovelace II, the gallant and brilliant surgeon who had been my first assistant before developing the B.L.B. oxygen mask.

Randy had left Rochester after the tragic deaths of two sons from polio, and he founded the Lovelace Clinic in

Albuquerque, New Mexico, with his uncle. He was chairman of the Armed Forces Medical Policy Council of the Department of Defense and accordingly was my partner on the trip. For the first ten days or so we were joined by Dr. Leonard Scheele, Surgeon General of the U. S. Public Health Service. We were accompanied from time to time by assorted doctors, diplomats, government officials and Pentagon brass. Alice came along too, as far as Bangkok.

We hopped from Alaska to Japan, where General Matt Ridgeway politely asked me what I was doing there. The trip had been arranged so hastily that he wasn't clear on what it was all about, so I explained our mission. I was grateful that President Truman had just recalled General Douglas MacArthur, not a favorite of mine since an incident in New Guinea when he refused a visit to our Surgeon General Kirk to the Philippines. He wired General MacArthur for permission to visit the Philippines. MacArthur replied by wire YOU WILL NOT COME, and General Kirk thought that there must be some misunderstanding, so he repeated his requested invitation. He was sent another wire: YOU WILL NOT COME. YOU WILL NOT COME. I think he hated medics; he was always locating hospitals in rice paddies.

A B-17 took Randy and me to Korea, where we took one horrified look at a Korean government hospital that I charitably could class no better than eighth-rate, and then spent a week at the admirable United Nations front-line first-aid stations and collection hospitals. They were part of a relay system, to give the wounded preliminary treatment before flying them to the big hospitals in Japan. The helicopter airlift from the battlefield worked so well that some of the most grievously wounded were in surgery a half hour after they were hit. This was making a big improvement in the mortality figures, since for the first time in warfare doctors were getting severed arteries in time to save the soldier's life, before his body emptied of blood. In Korea, getting to the first-aid station alive was practically a guarantee of survival. In

World War I, the mortality among those who reached first-aid stations alive was 8 per cent. In World War II the mortality fell to 4.5 per cent, but in Korea it was about 2 per cent. Of every thousand men still alive when they reached the first-aid station, 980 of them would live. It was extraordinary, in view of the damage a land mine, for instance, can do to a human being. We were sickened by the violent mutilations we saw, boys blinded and crippled for life. One night stands out in my memory when I watched surgeons in a tent trying to save two young marines who had been lacerated by land mines. Both had been hit in the abdomen, genitals, chest and legs and their intestines were full of holes. During the long fight for their lives, they were given twenty-three pints of blood. Toward dawn, they died. It made you want to weep, but they got great surgery—as good as anyone could get, anywhere. And it was within the sound of guns.

It is interesting to compare the combat statistics of Korea and the First World War. During the year and a half that the United States fought in that bloody war in the trenches, our forces suffered 334,000 casualties, of which 39,000, or nearly 12 per cent, were killed. During the first year and a half of the Korean war, the States suffered 104,383 casualties, of which 18,000 were killed, or 19 per cent. This doesn't count the 13,000 listed as missing in Korea during that period. I couldn't avoid noticing that while we doctors had improved methods of treating the wounded, manufacturers of war machines had made even greater progress.

On my way to an exceedingly far forward first-aid station, the helicopter transporting me flew over the battle lines. I tried to get a look at this, the genuine thing, but a panorama view of war doesn't offer much. In New Guinea, it was all noise and jungle and in Korea noise and mountain. Later, when I landed for my inspection of the front line installation, my curiosity was fully satisfied. The post was being shelled at quarter-minute intervals and there were several hits during the time I was there.

We stopped off on an aircraft carrier, the *Boxer*—landing on a heaving flight deck is quite an experience—and then proceeded to Tokyo. The vast and excellent military hospital there was complaining about its supply of whole blood for transfusions: there was either too much or none. Matters were so desperate when Randy and I arrived that we donated a pint each on the spot. Most of the blood was coming from the United States, where it was being collected by the American Red Cross. It seemed to the people in Tokyo that the Americans at home were showing callousness in not keeping their blood bank well supplied, but in my opinion the Tokyo hospitals themselves were at fault, at least in part.

To save time and trouble, they were using whole blood rather than plasma. Plasma has a long shelf-life, but whole blood deteriorates after a few weeks. In Tokyo, it had been decided that the three weeks after the date it had been collected was the allowable period that the blood could be used; after that time, they dumped it. I protested, assuring them that blood four weeks old was also safe, and after a great deal of discussion it was agreed that this was true. Accordingly, it was ruled that blood would be stored for four weeks before being thrown out, but there was a peculiar rider—United States soldiers were not to receive any of the blood older than three weeks. It could be used only for Japanese, and other nationals. I didn't protest, since four-week-old blood is acceptable from a medical standpoint, but I didn't like the connotation.

Also, it annoyed me that in spite of the severe difficulties in the blood supply, no one proposed that an appeal be made to Japanese citizens for donations. There could have been no reason other than racial bias, but it made no sense to me as a doctor. Blood is blood, and that's a medical fact. Plenty of white Southerners have been saved by Negro blood, though they never knew it.

It added to the poor picture of my countrymen that I was getting when I discovered that six Japanese artists were being paid $150 a month, for all of them, to draw medical illustrations. They were doing beautiful work at that atrocious low pay scale. I remember a drawing of mosquitoes that was in the realm of fine art.

We spent a day visiting Hiroshima, which was just beginning to lay out new streets six years after the atomic bomb had vaporized the middle of the city. The States had built a fine hospital on a hill outside the city and it was filled with the ghastly victims of fire and radiation. The scars on faces and hands that had been exposed to the blast were hideous beyond description. I have never seen anything comparable.

We flew from Japan to Thailand and in Bangkok I attended a cocktail party in the Chinese pants and shirt and bare feet that seemed appropriate. Randy and I toured the good, clean, efficient hospitals and addressed Thai doctors, Randy speaking about war medicine in Korea and I about research and developments in medicine in the United States. The doctors feted us with a lunch of aged eggs, shark soup, a twenty-day-old pig cooked whole (we ate the skin first), snipe (bones and all), and something spicy, hot and delicious cooked in a coconut.

Alice returned to Rochester and Randy and I boarded a KLM plane to take us to Saudi Arabia, touching down at Calcutta and Karachi on the way in weather so stifling hot that we were grateful for the cologne the stewardesses sprinkled on our heads. Our destination was the new American base just being built at Dhahran, under an agreement with King ibn-Saud.

We had been at Dhahran only a few days when we were requested to visit Emir Saud Ben-Abdulla Jiluiwi at once. His back was hurting him and his son had an upset stomach, so they desired that the famous American doctors in the vicinity should attend them. It was the humane, decent thing to do, and also diplomatic, since the emir's province included much of the oil fields.

A DC-3 flew us into the desert to Hofuf, an ancient city near an oasis within rings of white walls. We were met at the luxurious airport by a Cadillac convertible with sand tires, driven by an imposing Arab in flowing robes and a white headdress. He drove very fast to the gates of the palace walls, scattering goats and camels in the courtyard, and we were escorted to our rooms inside, which we discovered were air-conditioned to a glacier temperature and equipped with modern baths. The floors everywhere were piled with many layers of marvelous rugs.

We found the emir seated next to a table on which there were five telephones. We felt his pulse, listened to his heart, and looked wise. Randy thought his trouble might be a disk, so we arranged to have a supportive belt fitted the next day. The son's problem was of a more delicate nature, mainly to do with his sex life. I think we prescribed a green elixir, made by Squibb, for the emir, and sympathy for the son.

The emir spoke no English, so an Arab crouched in a kneeling position before him translated for us. The room was huge and strange to our eyes, but beautiful. The emir clapped his hands and his advisers entered in their Arab robes and sat silently in a row. He clapped his hands again and a huge Arab came in with an ornate brass teapot that had a long, slender spout, and he was followed by another servant with the cups. The interpreter tasted the tea first to protect the emir if it was poisoned, then the emir's cup was poured and then ours. We almost gagged; the tea was like hot perfume.

I finally finished the sickly stuff and held out my cup to return it, which was a mistake. The servant promptly filled it again and I had to drink that too. I discovered that it was the custom if anything was left in the cup to empty the dregs on the Oriental rugs. I was horrified that priceless rugs should be given such treatment, but the interpreter assured me that it was good for them. I certainly wasn't going to dispute that. The emir's chieftains all were armed with wicked shining sabers and kept looking at Randy and me with hot eyes.

That night a banquet was served. The chef had cooked three desert sheep, whole, and I was interested to observe that they had heavy tails, in which I was told they could store water. His Highness put a toothpick into the eye of one of the sheep and passed it to me. It was an honor to be singled out for this delicacy, so I was obliged to eat it. I got it down somehow and hastily took up the glass of milk placed before me to wash away the taste. It turned out to be sour camel milk.

A man with a fan stood behind every diner to discourage the millions of flies, and a waiter was assigned to every platter to flick away the flies with a napkin. We were told that it is possible to tell how long a man has been in an Arab country by the way he bats flies off himself. My approach wasn't casual, which marked me as a newcomer.

After the dinner the emir asked us what we would like to see, and I answered, "The harem." This wasn't allowed, so we settled for a tour of the primitive attempt at irrigation, a four-mile chain of goatskin buckets, the stables and the native market. As a lifelong lover of good horses, I found the stables intriguing. They were well kept and the horses were hobbled by a chain anchored to the ground, possibly against theft. The market was gaudy with noise, smells and colorfully dressed Arabs. We watched the moneylenders at work with their buckets of silver dollars and eased our way through the narrow, jammed streets to a goldworker's shop. He was making bangle bracelets for a sheik, our guide explained. He had five finished and was just hammering the sixth. I wanted them for Alice, so I pleaded with him to sell them to me; the sheik could wait, I argued, but I was leaving the next day. He was convinced and I bought them all for less than $120. I think he charged me $33 an ounce for the gold, and it was pure gold, and 10 per cent more for his craftsmanship. It was one of the best transactions I ever made in my life: when I presented them to Alice, she put them on and as near as I can recall never took them off.

When we left the next day, with many flowery compliments on all sides, we were each given a silky Oriental rug by the emir. We urged him, if the back didn't improve, to visit a specialist in the States. His Highness promised that he would and later, I believe, came to Rochester.

After Saudi Arabia, we flew to Cairo where NAMRU, the Naval Medical Research Unit, established in 1945, was doing impressive work in the study of parasitic diseases and their carriers. There were fourteen professors from various United States colleges and universities on the staff and they were training a hundred Egyptians in the control of such diseases. The Rockefeller Foundation was paying for a significant research project to determine the effects of modern sanitation methods in the deserts. To make it a scientific study with a control group for comparison, two similar towns were selected and one of them was provided with wells dug deeply and according to the recommendation of sanitary engineers. In this town, the placement of outhouses was regulated by the experts. The other town was left as it was, and the engineers were awaiting the lapse of sufficient time to show convincingly that they had been able to improve the health of the native population.

We touched next at Cyprus and then flew to Ankara, Turkey, where doctors showed us a new method for quick diagnosis of cysts and intestinal infection. I made a note of it to take back to the Clinic. Randy bought an enormous copper tray in the Turkish market. We were beginning to resemble a traveling bazaar rather than two doctors on a serious expedition. We landed at Athens for only minutes, which enabled Randy and me to establish a world's record for fast visits to the Acropolis, and then went on to Tripoli. The American base there was vast, and contained a race track and a stadium. We also visited the market, where I was unable to resist purchasing a natural Tunisian rug for only fifty-seven dollars.

We went on to Casablanca and Rabat, by a rough air trip; the latter was in difficulty because of divided authority between the army engineers and the construction company building the hospital. I think it was in Casablanca that the brilliant simplification of my wardrobe failed me for the first time. I had brought only one pair of socks and shorts and one shirt, all nylon or drip-dry, and I would rinse them out each night. The nuisance involved was more than compensated by the pleasure of traveling light and I grew inured to the lifted eyebrows of hotel maids or palace servants who discovered my laundry drying in the bathroom. In Casablanca, however, it rained walls of water all through the night and when I awakened in the morning my clothes were still wringing wet, and I had to wear them in that condition.

Our next stop was in Germany, at Wiesbaden, handy to a large grouping of NATO installations. We spent hours being briefed on the problems of the area, one of which was the fluctuation in the requirements for hospital beds. I thought a sensible solution to this would be to design hospitals in such a way that they could be converted to barracks and back again, as needed. The proposal was a blood relative of the suggestion that I made while in New Guinea that the Army and Air Force should use dual-purpose packing cases, to be convertible when empty to desks or mess tables. I like continuity of usefulness and feel baleful at the sight of waste.

We went to Paris, where I was unenchanted at the cost of food and drink, and studied the fascinating experiments there to lower body metabolism by chemical means, and then flew to Stockholm, where Swedish doctors were involved in the study of blood volume and its relationship, for instance, to work. I was surprised to learn that blood volume doesn't increase with body weight. We stopped briefly in Copenhagen and London and then flew home to report to the Pentagon.

I am an inveterate shopper, as my parents were, and throughout the trip Randy and I had been unable to resist hurrying directly to the nearest native market or department store whenever we could spare a few minutes. I had made a few impulsive purchases: a Moroccan rug, a German camera, tripod, binoculars and hunting rifle, amber beads and Jensen jewelry for Alice from Denmark, perfume and a four-hundred-day clock, Swedish carving knives and surgical instruments.

I descended from the plane looking like a refugee who had fled with all his household possessions. The odd-shaped bundles and bags I carried almost obscured my vision and I was impeded further by a cane with a sharp point that someone had given me, which I thought gave me a dashing, continental traveler look. I was unaccustomed to the cane, however, and somehow managed to tangle the point of it in my trouser leg and then into the ground, rooting myself to the spot. To get free, I had to put down all the parcels and wrench the cane loose two-handed. The loss of dignity was considerable, but I had the consolation of being excused from paying duty, since I had been on government duty.

Randy and I gave our recommendations to Robert Lovett, the Secretary of Defense. We had lists of various kinds of supplies that some of the hospitals had been unable to receive and an outline of the dual-purpose hospital-or-barracks we envisioned. We presented some proposals to meet the problems of the Tokyo hospitals over blood supply, suggesting that donations be regulated according to need. Over-collection of blood at unplanned intervals, we stated, was producing the feast-or-famine effect in Tokyo's blood bank.

I got back to Rochester on October 31, forty-one days and thirty-six thousand miles from my departure. For a while afterward I devoted some time to stoutly defending against all slights the medical care our armed forces and veterans were receiving. There had been a charge in the *Reader's Digest* just after the war that the country was giving third-rate care to its 2,500,000 disabled veterans. I can't be sure whether this was true or not at that time, 1945, but I could state with truth that veterans hospitals after that met the top standard, and were particularly admirable in the handling of the mentally ill, amputees and paraplegics.

I was sensitive to the suggestion that veterans hospitals were a version of Medicare, the opening wedge in the socializing of medicine. I am opposed to Medicare in any form—I don't think it is needed and I think it has a damaging effect on the quality of medicine—so I wrote hotly in the *American Legion Magazine*, "I have been closely associated with the Veterans Administration medical program on a voluntary basis since World War II and I have generally approved of it. I could not have approved if I believed that our veterans hospitals represent a trend toward socialized medicine.

"In fighting socialized medicine, we doctors have not just been fighting a word. We have resisted proposals which, in our opinion, have boded ill for patient welfare and have threatened to bring about deterioration in medicine and injury to the doctor-patient relationship."

The year of my round-the-world trip, 1951, was also the year I began what has been a very happy relationship with Mutual Benefit Health and Accident Association of Omaha, Nebraska, usually known as Mutual of Omaha, and United Benefit Life Insurance Company, referred to generally as United of Omaha. I accepted an invitation to serve on the Board of Directors and took a prominent role in the fight against Medicare waged by the American Medical Association and insurance companies, and other interested groups, for many years. I made several trips to Washington to discuss my point of view with senators and congressmen and gave many speeches on the subject around the state.

I was in Washington in 1966 on such a mission, talking with some senators whose number included Senator Eugene McCarthy from Minnesota. He told me that it was Hubert Humphrey's birthday, so I went over to the vice-presidential offices to pay my respects. We have been warm friends for many years, though he knows I don't vote for him. In politics, I describe myself as a nonpartisan who always votes

Republican. Alice, however, voted for Humphrey and canceled my vote, which amused him.

Jim Barrett, of Mutual of Omaha, was with me in Washington and he advised me that Hubert Humphrey was so busy I would never get in to see him, but I wanted to try anyway. I was pleased when I was ushered into his office at once and we had a fine chat. He gave me a bracelet with the vice-presidential crest on it for Alice and asked me to come along with him to the White House to have lunch with Lyndon Johnson. I declined, since I had invited Alice and Jim Barrett and Andrew Haley to lunch with me at the hotel.

We were sitting in the hotel dining room a little while later when there was a telephone message for me. A voice said, "This is L.B.J. and I want you to come over for lunch. All you have to do is walk across the park, you're right across from the White House. Hubert is here, and we'd like to have you join us." I said I was in the middle of lunch with some friends and I didn't think I should change the arrangement. "It isn't wartime, or I would drop everything and come," I told him. "I hope you understand." The President graciously said he did and I asked him to give Hubert birthday greetings from me and we hung up.

I went back to the dining room and told Jim and Andy about the caller. Jim was aghast. "We've been trying to get into the White House for a year," he exclaimed, "and you calmly turn down the chance to talk to the President about Medicare!"

"Would you break an engagement with me if the President asked to see you?" I asked innocently. Of course they had to say no.

V. J. Skutt, the president of Mutual of Omaha, came to my office in the Clinic in 1963, shortly after I retired, and asked me to be the company's chief medical consultant. It is a big job and I felt I had enough to do, so I refused him. He persisted, giving me all sorts of reasons why I should, and I kept saying no.

We were still deadlocked as dinnertime approached and I am constitutionally incapable of going off to a meal without asking visitors to join me, so I invited him to dine at Mayowood. He accepted and brought along two dozen roses for Alice. I knew when I saw them that I was finished, and I capitulated soon afterward.

Just about the time of the round-the-world jaunt, I seemed to be getting into a lot of diversified activities. I already was a member of the Board of Trustees of Carleton College in Northfield, Minnesota, succeeding my father to that post soon after his death, and in 1951 I was made a member of the Board of Regents of the University of Minnesota, following in Uncle Will's footsteps. The University of Minnesota is the third largest in the United States, with forty-five thousand students the last time I looked, and it is rated among the top ten on the continent. I take special pride in its fine medical school.

Starting in 1953, I was also the medical adviser to Northwest Airlines, Inc. It was a helpful liaison during the period when the Clinic's Board of Governors grew so concerned at Rochester's failure to have a commercial airport that we built our own. The railroad was wearing out, having a rough bed and tracks that were 80 pounds rather than the necessary 120 pounds. It has since been abandoned but during the years of its decline the Clinic pressed Rochester's civic administration to build an airport and met with refusal. It cost us millions, but we provided one ourselves and later turned it over to the city. My friend Bob Hinckley, who was chairman of the Civil Aeronautics Board, came to Rochester to dedicate it in a ceremony replete with modest understatement. We thought it tactful not to stress too strongly the unusual feature of the airport: that it had been built by a group of doctors in private practice.

It was a marvel of convenience, being only five minutes from the Clinic. We rapidly discovered why airports rarely are so handy, as soon as the heavy, noisy airplanes began to drone almost stack-high over our hospitals on their descent to the runways two miles away. Eventually the city closed that airport, using the land for housing and the Mayo High School, and built another one eight miles away. Nowadays nearly 20 per cent of the Clinic's patients come by air; the rest use automobiles and bus connections from railway stations some distance away.

My relations with the Clinic's Board of Governors were improving perceptibly with my increased stature outside Rochester, though this was perhaps a coincidence. Though we tangled more rarely, disagreements were by no means unknown. I was opposed, for instance, to accepting money from the government to support the Clinic's research projects. I took the position, perhaps archaically independent, that people should undertake research primarily because they wanted to help patients, even if it meant some sacrifice. It was a good measure of a man's intentions to avoid subsidizing him lavishly. I was overruled on this, and the Clinic is still accepting government subsidy; I doubt very much that my father and uncle would like it any better than I do. Happily, though, my major fear that the research money would attract to the Clinic a disproportion of doctors primarily interested in research was proved to be groundless. We still get enough of the kind who are in medicine to take care of people, and they counterbalance the others.

I'm not opposed to research, but I resist the tendency of my profession to value it above care of patients. Some colleagues seem to regard doctors who spend all their time with their patients as second-class citizens, reserving their respect for those doctors who produce research. This is arrogant and errant.

I clashed with the Board of Governors again when we received a proposal from pharmaceutical houses and related industries, offering grants for Mayo doctors engaged in research allied to their own needs. The Board decided to refuse the grants, which seemed to me an inconsistent way to

247

behave. I pointed out that medicine owes a great deal to the efforts of such companies and there seemed no logic in accepting research funds from the government but rejecting research funds from private industry. One Board member explained with a sniff that it was tainted money and I retorted furiously, "You mean, 'tain't enough." Still, I was outnumbered when the vote was taken.

I had much more than losing debates with the Board to occupy my attention in those years. My vigorous, enterprising and highly individualistic brood was rounding into its teens. Long observation has led me to the conclusion that it is impossible for parents to raise a child without suffering the odd headache and heartache, and Alice and I had eight children, counting Joe's, each one of them strong-willed, intelligent and interesting. I'm reminded of the ancient Chinese curse: "May you live in interesting times." The only one of the lot who was wholly agreeable and reliable was David, the son my brother Joe adopted.

Muff's life has been the most colorful, deserving of a book of her own. She was eighteen when she went to a private school in Brussels, where we had arranged that she would live with the headmaster. She decided that she couldn't stand it, so she somehow managed to get her tuition and board refunded—which is no small feat—moved out and enrolled at the University of Brussels.

All through 1947 and the following year we would get letters from various people telling us that Muff had disappeared again, or that she was rumored to be hitchhiking in Spain. When she came back she said she wanted to be an actress and she joined the Neighborhood Playhouse in New York. It was a method school. We went to see her perform one time, and she was a bloodhound in one play and a football in another, but she seemed to be having a fine time.

Gabriel Pascal, a movie director of undeniable verve, had arrived in Rochester for some surgery and we invited him to Mayowood for dinner. He announced in his passionate Hungarian accent that he loved Mayowood and would stay, which he did. We fixed up a gardener's cottage for him and his young wife Valerie and they lived there for three months. He was a great walker and a great sun bather; we used to encounter him in the woods striding along in the smallest of bikinis, displaying a considerable amount of hairy pelt. Valerie and Muff became close friends and Gabriel informed us that Muff must come to Hollywood with him and become a star.

Muff quickly discovered that her main function as a guest of Gabriel in his elegant Beverly Hills home was to be his errand girl, so she moved out and stayed with friends of ours, Pauline Hemingway, second wife of Ernest, and Laura Archera, who later married Aldous Huxley. Muff landed a part in a Jennifer Jones movie: she was the panting on the sound track when Jennifer was chased by dogs. Then she got a job that she described as being a hostess, which alarmed Alice into flying to California at once. Muff was a cocktail waitress, Alice informed me by telephone. We persuaded her to quit by promising to subsidize her, and she moved into a cottage on Malibu beach, got engaged to someone in the film business whom we liked very much, broke that off and then got engaged to Geordie Hormel, whom she had known all her life, and broke that off and fell in love with a young Swiss named Claud.

The Hormels advised us that Muff had bought an Arab horse, saddle and trailer and with Claud had departed to see Indian country. Geordie recovered nicely: he later married Leslie Caron. Alice turned sleuth and telephoned the school superintendent of Taos in New Mexico, giving him the description of Muff, the trailer, the horse and the yellow convertible she was driving. Not surprisingly, the equipage had made an impression on him and he was able to tell her that Muff was visiting the Honorable Dorothy Brett, an artist who had a studio nearby. Alice had a hunch that Muff would go there because she remembered describing the studio to her, and telling her that she had met Frieda Lawrence there, the widow of D. H. Lawrence. One of Alice's most vivid memories of an afternoon spent with Frieda Lawrence was the box of priceless D. H. Lawrence manuscripts, loosely stacked, that she kept casually under the coffee table.

We brought Muff and Claud home, and I took an immediate dislike to him, which increased as our acquaintanceship progressed. They announced they wanted to be married, which depressed me considerably. I asked her to wait for six months, during which time I suggested that Claud absent himself from Mayowood, from the continent even. Muff agreed, and I think that was the winter she spent as postmistress on an Indian reservation. She took the Arab horse with her and when the temperatures dropped below zero at night she would bring him in to sleep in her kitchen.

Eventually she went to Europe after Claud, met his wealthy parents, meat packers with luxurious homes all over the place, and told us that she and Claud were going to be married. I had no interest in the enterprise, but Alice went and arranged what she later reported was as good a wedding as she could put on, given the circumstances of the small French village where it took place. I gather that the wedding was a disaster of unapproachable dimensions. On the day of the ceremony, Muff's beloved little dog was run over and killed. She carried violets and cried all through the wedding.

After that they built a boat at Claud's family home in Beaune and lived on it on the Mediterranean for the next five years. It was a forty-two-foot sailing yacht, a lovely thing, with a Ceylonese for crew. They had no income, so they lived out of the sea and spent something like seven cents a day each for their needs.

During all this, I had anticipations that some of my sons would become doctors. I never said so, since it was none of my affair, but I wished for it strongly. It is a demanding life, but it gives the man who rises to its requirements the occasional moment when he feels worth while, and that's hard to come by. Charlie went to Hill School, then changed to Millbrook and picked St. Olaf's College in Minnesota next. I thought Princeton would be a fine idea, but he said he would choose his own schools in the future and he wanted a small college where he could be himself. He was making the discovery that the Mayo name presented some discouraging problems, in terms of people's expectations and close interest, and he wanted privacy. Some thought it odd that he chose St. Olaf's, rather than Carleton in the same town, since I was a trustee of Carleton, but Charlie is his own man and had his good reasons.

Ned went to Millbrook too and then startled us by deciding to go to Bard College in New York, an arts college that stressed dramatics and things like that. He stayed there only six months and then joined the Coast Guard and served a three-year hitch, which included time in the Korean war. When he got his discharge he enrolled at the University of Minnesota and in 1957 graduated *cum laude*. His major was anthropology and his minor, art, which didn't quite meet the requirements for premed education so he went back to the university and finished another course. He then was accepted at two medical schools, one of them my alma mater, the University of Pennsylvania.

Ned is evasive, but Alice was convinced that something was said to Ned, during his preliminary visit to the campus, that crushed all his ambition to be a doctor. It might have been a comment about the Mayo name, and what great contributions it promised. I've had experience with that sort of remark and it does have a depressing effect. Whatever happened, he returned home and said he would never be a doctor. Instead he wanted to direct documentary films and he went off to Mexico to learn about it. Muff was there, getting her divorce from Claud, to my great relief, and she kept house for him.

Charlie had persevered in his decision to be a doctor and he was accepted at the University of Pennsylvania when he finished at St. Olaf's. He was married there in his sophomore year to Caroline Johnston, known to us as Cari, whom he met at St. Olaf's. She helped with expenses while he was in medical school by teaching school. They have three children now.

Joe also talked of being a doctor when he was small and making rounds with me and his older brothers, but when he left Millbrook he decided on veterinary medicine instead. He went to the University of Minnesota but didn't do too well, being under some strain because he had just been married. He had three children and then there was a divorce, but in the meantime he went to Winona Teachers College and graduated there in biology. He always had been drawn to animals so he managed the Mayowood farm for a while; then, when his marriage broke up, he went back to school and got his bachelor of science degree and found a job as curator of the zoo in Topeka, Kansas.

Bill Mayo, Joe's son, went to a New England prep school and made Princeton, which frankly delighted me. He was the only one to show any desire for my old college. He hated Princeton, though, and left after two years, transferring to the University of Minnesota. He married a girl with a Ph.D. in chemistry, which provoked a number of people to remark drolly that a Mr. Mayo was married to a Dr. Mayo. He didn't finish at Minnesota, and now is a businessman in Denver, with two children. David, the older son of Joe, went into the Navy and was married in 1958, dying of pneumonia the same year. I was in England when it happened and I was desolated by the news. He was only twenty-seven. It is terrifying to contemplate a fate so mindless that three people in a small family of only four would die young.

Alex and Maria, our youngest, seemed relatively sedate, though Alex had rebelled against his New England prep school and was attending high school in Rochester. Maria went to one of the best prep art schools in the country, Cranbrook near Detroit, where she did very well. My sister

Esther Hartzell kept an eye on her and invited her for weekends at Grosse Pointe. One time, Maria told us, Esther was unable to pick Maria up personally so she sent a police car. I blame all my children's eccentricities on Esther, though Louise, the maritally-minded sister on the West Coast, is not exactly predictable. I don't suppose it has been a deterrent to their development as individuals that I have been in some kind of hot water all my life, fighting for unpopular causes or being lighthearted in the presence of solemnity. Alice set a different kind of example: she was intellectually curious about art, history, literature and theater, and drew the children with her enthusiasm to appreciate craftsmanship in all its forms.

I rarely saw the children while they were young but they tell me now that the lasting impression they have of my paternity is insistence on honesty. I have almost fanatical regard for truthfulness and I stressed it in all my dealings with them. Ned recalls the occasion when I drove all of them to a local fair and the man at the gate wanted to let me go through free. I insisted on paying, which so astonished the children that they blurted out the confession that they had been getting into the grounds for nothing all week long by sneaking in through a culvert. I was distressed and lectured them heatedly on the economics of running a fair, and how money from admissions could make or break the operation. Ned said they never used the culvert again and always paid their own way.

I once was asked my advice on raising children by an innocent reporter who clearly knew nothing about me or my family. I side-stepped the question adroitly by suggesting that the wallpaper in children's bedrooms should be patterned with slogans. I thought it would be beneficial to character if the first thing they saw in the morning and the last thing at night was "Honesty Is the Best Policy."

On the medical side of my life, where I am on firmer ground, I found myself more and more absorbed in the

1950's by the problem of diverticulosis and diverticulitis, the former the forerunner of the latter. Few people have ever heard of the disease, possibly because it was unknown before this century and still isn't diagnosed more than a fraction of the times it occurs. A diverticulum is a pouch pushed out of the bowel, almost always the sigmoid portion, something like the bubble that develops in the weak spot on a bicycle tire when it is overinflated with air. Usually diverticula occur in clusters and the patient is said to have diverticulosis; when the pouches fail to empty themselves of feces and become infected, the disease is known as diverticulitis.

Doctors still don't know whether diverticulitis merits concern; it is pretty well established that it isn't a condition leading to cancer. I'm convinced that it is hereditary. My father had it—at the autopsy, his colon looked like a bunch of grapes—and I have it. We think about one in every ten adults over the age of fifty has at least one diverticulum.

In severe cases, the congested diverticulum can obstruct urinary function, causing urgency and frequency of elimination and if the bowel perforates, there will be traces of feces in the urine. More often the disease shows itself in a pain on the left side, low down, that can be piercing and stabbing or a long, dull ache. There is abdominal rigidity and there may be nausea and vomiting.

If the patient recognizes these symptoms early enough, he can be over the attack in twelve to twenty-four hours by taking antibiotics and a liquid diet, preferably water or tea, and staying in bed. If the symptoms are ignored, the patient is in for real trouble. Solid food will cause solid feces, which will aggravate the infection and congestion in the diverticulosis. I have removed colons with diverticula so solidly packed with dry feces that they were like concrete, and they can stretch to as large as eight millimeters in diameter. A surgeon has to proceed gently because the strained tissue is so thin it can perforate very easily.

Diverticulitis is usually found in association with constipation, and with obesity. People who have what is called an "irritable" bowel, with irregular bowel habits, mild abdominal discomfort, flatulence and nausea, are frequently found to have diverticulosis. It is advisable to keep weight down, strive for regular bowel habits, drink plenty of water, avoid enemas. I used to recommend that patients shun nuts, coarse food and fruit with large seeds in it, but I no longer think it matters much what is eaten, so long as the patient is aware of his early symptoms and calls at once to alert his doctor.

TWELVE

Late in the summer of 1953, I was deep in someone's abdomen one morning when I was notified that our state's senator, Edward Thye, wanted to speak to me on the telephone. I couldn't leave my patient so I asked him to please call back and when he did so an hour or so later, I was deep in someone else's abdomen and had to request that he call again in the afternoon.

When we finally spoke, he said he wanted to extend an invitation to me from President Dwight Eisenhower and Secretary of State John Foster Dulles to be a member of the United States delegation at the eighth plenary session of the United Nations, due to convene in a month.

I was dumfounded. I think I asked first of all how much time would be required away from Rochester and Senator Thye replied that the session would last about three months. I explained that I would have to check with my colleagues, since they would have to fill in for me during this extended period, and then I inquired how it happened that I had been chosen for this honor. Senator Thye extolled my virtues for a decent minute, as the situation indicated, and happened to say that the U.S. delegation is always balanced politically, with an equal number of Democrats and Republicans. He and John Foster Dulles had looked me up in *Who's Who* and discovered that I was listed as a Democrat, which was perfect: I would round off the Democratic representation.

I said gently, and regretfully, "I must advise you, Senator, that *Who's Who* is in error. I consider myself a nonpartisan politically, but I always vote the Republican ticket." There was an awkward pause and then Senator Thye said that he would call me back.

When he did, he sounded jubilant. John Foster Dulles and President Dwight Eisenhower wanted me anyway, even if I was a Republican. Word of the invitation had spread quickly through the Clinic and I already had been assured warmly by other surgeons that they would take over my duties, so I was free to tell Senator Thye that I could accept the honor. I was extremely pleased about it, but alarmed in almost equal measure. I knew about as much about the United Nations as the next man which was nothing, and a glance at a list of the member nations revealed a sizable number that I had never heard of.

I wrote nervously to Henry Cabot Lodge, the U.S. ambassador to the United Nations, "I only hope that I will be able to contribute something. At the moment, I am wondering what will be my capability in such an august group." In my official reply of acceptance, I said, "I only hope that I will be able to fulfill the obligations it imposes. At least, I'll do the best I can."

Alice had been interested in the United Nations from its conception and during the time she was running the radio station she became well informed about it. She therefore coached me most helpfully and I also read everything I could

28. Family portrait in 1941:

Mrs. Mayo (Alice)

Maria   Alex

Bill✓   Muff   Joe

Charles   David✓   Ned   Me

Bill and David (who died in 1958) were the children of my late brother, Dr. Joseph G. Mayo, and his wife, and were brought up by Alice and me at Mayowood, the family home. This photograph was taken at Mayowood

29. Alice in 1949

30. Adlai Stevenson, Alice and me during the 1952 presidential campaign. (*Northwest Airlines photo by Don Bero*)

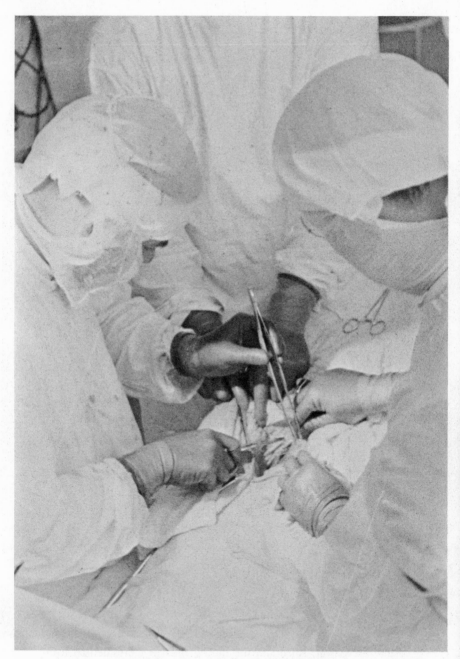

31. A few of us at work at the Mayo Clinic

find about the United Nations, cramming like a schoolboy against the moment I would report to the U.N. headquarters. I received some kind letters of congratulation from such people as Harold Stassen, then director of the Foreign Operations Administration, the president of my Princeton class, John ("Heinie") Leh, and Hubert Humphrey, who wrote graciously, "The president has again exercised good judgment. Minnesota has been honored, and America will have an excellent representative in you."

I had some vague idea that my duties would be light, giving me ample time to arrange to meet with doctors in the area to exchange ideas and watch them in surgery. Alice and I both looked forward to the Broadway shows; I avoid the ones with a message, but I really enjoy the musicals and comedies. It proved to be a monumental misconception: during the time I was in New York, I never worked so hard in all my life. I was so exhausted that I frequently fell asleep in a chair in the delegates' lounge, and I saw only two shows in all the months we were there. I didn't visit a single hospital, and the only doctors I met were those who came to the United Nations Building.

I discovered that the United States delegation to the United Nations is planned with considerable sophistication. It has ten members, who are guided in every detail by the State Department, following the policy decisions set by the President and the Secretary of State. The group of ten always includes the Secretary of State and the U.N. ambassador, plus two senators one session, and two representatives the next session, one from each party. The fifth is usually a governor or ex-governor of a state, and then five alternate delegates are picked from private citizens. But there must always be a woman among the delegates, and sometimes two; one delegate must be colored and one must be a Jew. It is called defensive diplomacy; the presence of these had helped the United States in some tense confrontations, without a word being spoken.

257

John Foster Dulles was a quiet, fatherly man, very impressive in his firmness and conviction but not very easy to talk to. I never noticed that he had much humor, but he must have had some or else the job would have killed him. Henry Cabot Lodge, the U.S. ambassador at the eighth U.N. session, was more affable but had large areas of sensitivity. It was important to be careful of his feelings and to defend him vigorously when he felt injured.

The other delegates when I served were Mrs. Frances P. Bolton and James P. Richards, from Congress, and the retired governor of South Carolina, James F. Byrnes; the alternates were Rev. Archibald J. Carey, Jr., a redheaded Negro who was a Chicago alderman and minister of the African Methodist Episcopal Church in that city, the late James D. Zellerbach, a San Francisco millionaire who then was board chairman of Crown-Zellerbach Corporation and later ambassador to Italy, Mrs. Oswald B. Lord, a leading figure in human rights causes who was born Mary Pillsbury in my home state, Henry Ford II, president of the Ford Motor Company, who arrived at the U.N. with a low opinion of its usefulness but departed an enthusiastic supporter, and I.

Jimmy Byrnes was known to be a hot segregationist, so the wily State Department offset any poor impression this might make on African nations by making his adviser a Negro woman lawyer. Byrnes took this gracefully. They used to drive to the United Nations in the same limousine and he would help her out and hold doors for her with perfect correctness.

I think most of the alternates shared my expectation that there would be little for us to do, other than slip into the vacant chair when the regular delegate wandered off for a moment. We were disabused of this dreamy concept on the day we arrived. We learned that the U.N. General Assembly had seventy-three subjects on its agenda and these, together with membership on ten different U.N. committees, were parceled out equally among us all. Alternates were expected to attend as faithfully as the regulars, and to research and become thoroughly familiar with a dozen complex situations. Most of us had to prepare major speeches on one or more vital issues, though Dulles and Lodge carried the main load in this department.

I was honored by being chosen to attend sessions of the U.N. Political Committee, one of the most important at the United Nations. The agenda included the Moroccan question, the Tunisian question, Burma's complaints that Nationalist China had troops on her border, Korea and disarmament. I was also named to the U.N. Third Committee, which occupies itself with social and humanitarian issues. For a small-town doctor from the Midwest, it meant a lot of homework.

In addition to these matters, I had been entrusted with the terrifying responsibility of making one of the key speeches at the Political Assembly. The United States stood accused by Russia of waging germ warfare in the Korean war, which had just ended. The Russians were showing what they called proof, thirty-six confessions signed by American fliers and a film which included five fliers making verbal confessions that they had dropped bacteria over Korea on orders from their U.S. commanders. A number of nations were convinced by this evidence, and it was vital that the United States answer the charges during the United Nations sessions.

The speech on germ warfare had such grave implications internationally that Henry Cabot Lodge naturally felt it should be made by him, the U.S. ambassador to the United Nations. The State Department strategists differed, however, and decided that the medical aspects of the situation could best be handled by a doctor. They agreed that the doctor selected should have an impressive reputation that would carry weight all over the world. They then recommended me: Chuck Mayo, one of the Rochester Mayos.

I was innocently unaware of the back-room maneuverings that had preceded Senator Thye's telephone call to me when Alice and I arrived in New York and settled our belongings in a small suite in the Vanderbilt Hotel. The Vanderbilt was owned by the family of Bill Manger, who had been a fellow at the Mayo Clinic, but we chose it for an even more compelling reason. The government would pay for the delegate's hotel room only at the Vanderbilt. The modest expense arrangement was that the government would pay fifteen dollars for the room for those staying at the Vanderbilt and nine dollars a day with no hotel payment for those staying elsewhere. Henry Ford didn't care—he stayed at the Pierre—but we did. Meals, tips, laundry and personal calls were paid by the delegates, so that I went into the hole financially to a considerable extent. I took meager comfort in my discovery that the government on occasion shows vigilant concern for the public purse.

The State Department began briefing me about the germ warfare charges almost as soon as I had unpacked. Exhibit One was the Russian film, which had been captured in India; it had been shown to packed houses in Italy and Africa and other places, with great success from the Russian point of view, but I couldn't honestly see how anyone but the most gullible could have been persuaded by it. It showed what was described as canisters of germs falling from U.S. planes, some enlargements of the alleged bacteria—which looked like no bacteria that any doctor ever saw—and a strikingly crude lab where these germs were said to be examined. Most of all, there was something unnatural about the pilots themselves, even allowing for the taut circumstances of their helplessness.

Some fliers had been released from prison camps a few weeks previously and returned to the United States, where they promptly repudiated their confessions and claimed that they had been obtained under pressure. I never doubted that they were telling the truth. Their appearance in the Russian film was radically different from the way they looked in films

260

taken on their return. During the so-called confessions, they were stiff, glazed creatures, almost unrecognizable from their normal expressions and voice mannerisms.

I studied all the material the State Department had assembled relative to the charges of bacteriological warfare and brainwashing, and consulted myself with colleagues thoroughly familiar with Pavlov's experiments on the conditioning of reflexes. The best known of these, I think, is the series the great Russian scientist performed on dogs. First he made a small hole in their jaws so saliva collecting in the mouth would drip through and then he invariably sounded a loud bell just before feeding the dogs. The animals at first salivated only at the sight of the food but eventually they would salivate at the sound of the bell, whether food appeared or not. It has become the classic experiment that demonstrates how vulnerable to clever manipulation are both animals and people.

The State Department then helped me draft the crucial speech that I was to make in the U.N. Political Committee. The speech dominated my days and I thought of little else. Ideas for improvements in it would come to me while shaving and I was always jotting phrases down on random scraps of paper. Every alteration in the speech, however minor, had to be submitted to the State Department for approval, a process that caused days of convulsions in the in-out baskets. By the time the revised version had been accepted and returned to me, I would have several more changes ready. I wore myself out shuttling back and forth to Washington for consultations, put a severe strain on the secretarial pool, the supply of rubber stamps and almost all the available patience by rewriting the speech fourteen times. At last, I was satisfied—or at least convinced that the State Department was on the verge of dropping me off the Brooklyn Bridge.

The Russians had launched the big guns of their germ warfare charges in March, 1952, when they circulated in the

United Nations confessions of complicity handwritten and signed by U.S. fliers, among them two marines, Colonel Frank H. Schwable, of Arlington, Virginia, and Major Roy H. Bley, of Cabool, Missouri. These two were released on September 3, 1953, the day of the armistice, and in San Francisco on September 25 made lengthy statements declaring that their confessions were false, obtained by a scientifically planned system of brainwashing, and that the U.S. had never waged bacteriological warfare in Korea.

The two marines were filmed while making these statements, and their stories were shocking. We made the film available to United Nations delegates at a special screening. Schwable said that he had been kept in solitary confinement for more than a year. Because of his high rank, his captors were particularly anxious to have him sign a declaration that bacteriological agents were being used by his government against Koreans. The pressure on him was intense for eight months. He was kept filthy, frightened and starved, and wakened at hourly intervals by a flashlight shining in his eyes. He was never allowed to lie down, but had to sit at attention with crossed feet, until the strain on his muscles made sitting still an agony that became continuous. He was interrogated by two Chinese, working simultaneously, who varied between threats and offers of warmer quarters if he cooperated. With winter coming on, and his hands already frostbitten, Schwable was convinced that he would be allowed to freeze to death if he didn't cooperate. His mind dulled by hunger and exhaustion and fear, he eventually gave in and began drafting false statements.

Bley, a wing ordnance officer, had been captured with Schwable. They had been on a noncombat mission and inadvertently flew behind enemy lines. As a wing ordnance officer, he could be expected to know every weapon used by the Marine Air Wing and so he was a valuable prize for the Chinese. They worked on him with friendliness while he recuperated from his wounds, then broke it to him that he would have to admit that he had participated in germ warfare. When he refused, he was put into a solitary cell and forced to sit with his legs crossed for several days, then moved to a rat-infested cave with a wet mud floor. Next he was locked in a cage only four feet high and compelled with a bayonet at his back to stand in a hunched position for several hours every day. Five days later, his diet was reduced to one cup of water, one cup of rice and one cup of cabbage or turnips daily and he was placed in another rat-infested cell, where he saw no one but the guard who fed him, for five weeks. Then he was worked over daily with fists and rifle butts for the next ten days, and when he still refused to make the confession required of him was placed in an unheated mud hut—in the middle of January—wearing nothing but a light POW uniform. Incredibly, he continued to hold out for some time after this, despite being starved for a forty-eight-hour period and kept at attention day and night for long periods. Eventually, he succumbed and wrote the confession that they wanted.

On October 26, 1953, I was ready to give the United States answer to the germ warfare charges. The speech was to be made in the room where the Political Committee met. The United States representative sat between Great Britain, on his left, and the U.S.S.R., on his right. Some U.N. delegates are very sensitive about status, and in order to avoid charges that some country had subtle superiority in the seating arrangements, we used to move over one seat every day.

I went in early, when the room was deserted, and sat there alone in my appointed chair trying to calm my nerves. My throat was dry, so I reached for the pitcher of ice water at my elbow and started to pour some into a glass. My hand was shaking so hard that it was impossible to aim the pitcher properly, without risking spilling the water, so I went to the back of the room where there were extra pitchers and glasses and tried again. I still couldn't control the shaking well enough to pour the water, so I finally went out into the corridor, found a water fountain and got a drink that way.

There wasn't an empty seat, or a sound from the tense audience, when I began to speak. "The question before us," I said at the start, as clearly and firmly as I could, "the charge that the United States forces engaged in bacteriological warfare in Korea, plainly involves the honor and integrity not only of my country and her soldiers, but also of the United Nations itself, under whose banner sixteen member nations fought in Korea. . . . It is not a pretty story that confronts us. It is a story of terrible physical and moral degradation. It concerns men shaken loose from their foundations of moral value—men beaten down by the conditioning which the science of Pavlov reserves for dogs and rats—all in a vicious attempt to make them accomplices to a frightful lie."

I traced the history of that lie, from a trial balloon by the North Korean Communists in May, 1951, that even was ignored by Moscow radio, through the steady build-up of charges regularly denied by the United States, by Trygve Lie, Secretary General of the United Nations and by the U.N. commander-in-chief in Korea. The Communists refused a U.S. offer to have the International Red Cross make an independent investigation, and voted in a block against the U.S. motion in the United Nations calling for an impartial investigation by Egypt, Brazil, Pakistan, Sweden and Uruguay. In the meantime, Andrei Vishinsky, the Soviet representative at the United Nations, had circulated the signed U.S. confessions and the Peking-made film of the Americans confessing had been translated into several languages and given world-wide distribution. Then the Korean war ended and the returned fliers repudiated their confessions, which had been the most important and publicized feature of the Communist case.

I then described what some young Americans had endured at the hands of their captors, starting with Schwable and

264

Bley and Col. Walker Mahurin of the Air Force, who agreed to write a confession only after eight months of brutality and solitary confinement. And about those Americans who held out: Lt. James L. Stanley, interrogated and tortured for four months and once placed before a firing squad; Lt. Francis A. Strieby of the Air Force, shackled hand and foot with festering sores at wrists and ankles, who took a punch at the five guards who were beating him up; Lt. Robert C. Lurie, interrogated more than fifty times; Lt. Joseph E. Moreland, who was told his little daughter in the United States would be executed; Lt. Edward G. Izicky, left in a hole five feet long, four feet wide and four feet high for a week, without food or water. None of them signed a confession. No one knows what goes into a man to keep him from cracking under that kind of pressure, but it is awesome.

The torture of brainwashing, I explained, is more subtle and prolonged than the medieval rack and thumbscrew, and intended to be more terrible in its effect. It requires long-term deprivation for a prisoner, so that a dry crust of bread or a few hours' uninterrupted sleep becomes a great event in his life. "The total picture presented is one of human beings reduced to a status lower than that of animals; filthy, full of lice, festered wounds full of maggots, their sickness regulated to a point just short of death; unshaven, without haircuts or baths for as much as a year; men in rags, exposed to the elements; fed with carefully measured minimum quantities and lowest quality of food and unsanitary water, served often in rusty cans; isolated, faced with squads of trained interrogators, bullied incessantly, deprived of sleep and browbeaten into mental anguish."

The Communists used Pavlov's studies of conditioned reflexes to complete the destruction of human will. By worsening living conditions at every refusal to cooperate, and improving them slightly whenever there was a sign of yielding, resistance soon was equated with death in the mind of the exhausted man, and surrender with survival. "If anything is surprising to me," I added, "it is that so many of our soldiers—both those who confessed and those who did not—although for months they were treated like animals or worse, somehow continued throughout to act like men."

At least 107 captured fliers were accused of taking part in germ warfare. Forty refused to sign any confession; of the 36 who did sign, all under duress, some 20 were subjected to what can be fairly called extreme and prolonged physical and mental torture. The remaining 31 were advised that they were war criminals, without rights under the Geneva Convention, and 14 of them were confirmed as dead, with 17 listed as missing.

I closed by asking that the sworn statements repudiating the confessions should be submitted to the plenary session of the United Nations, to counter the false and cruelly-obtained confessions presented by the Russians. The U.S. had decided that formal resolution would be superfluous, in view of the damning evidence we had presented.

My life became a tumult of press interviews and radio statements, and telephone calls from friends who offered their congratulations, and a landslide of mail that was too much for the U.N. secretary I shared with another delegate. To stave off chaos, I sent for the dependable and resourceful Effie Shoholm, my secretary at the Mayo Clinic from the day I joined the staff. She tried to keep some of the newspaper clippings for me, which ran to medical metaphors. Victor Cohn's story in the Minneapolis paper was headlined: MAJOR SURGERY ON REDS; DR. MAYO CREATES STIR AFTER ATROCITY SPEECH. The New York *Herald Tribune* described my language as "surgically precise," and added, "Seldom has there been as coldly documented a disclosure as this." The Washington *Star* editorial said, "Dr. Mayo has used words as a scalpel, grimly factual words, to lay bare the malignancy and malevolence of the monstrous Kremlin," and the Philadelphia *Inquirer* said, "Dr. Mayo brought a surgical decisiveness to the bacteriological warfare lie."

Time wrote that I "had inscribed in the record a new and unforgettable chapter in the black chronicles of Communist treachery and brutality." A story in *Reader's Digest* some time later, titled *Is the State Department Failing Us in the Cold War?* answered its own question in the affirmative, with the reservation that my speech on brainwashing was "one of our few outstanding propaganda successes."

Alone among American publications, *The Nation* was critical. "It seems a little callous to parade the misery of five brave but not invincible men in order to convince those who were never in doubt," it said. I agreed with the sentiments, but there were plenty in doubt and it had to be done.

A former classmate at Princeton noticed an unflattering picture of me in *Time* and wrote from Texas, "If you look like this now, we are no longer friends."

Some people took offense at my references to Pavlov and somehow construed them as an attack on Pavlov on the grounds that he was an active plotter against the United States, and freedom. On NBC radio I tried to clear up this misconception. "Pavlov was a great scientist," I said, "and his work is still highly respected all over the world. What I said was that the Communists seem to have taken his principle and perverted it by applying it to human beings, and conditioning for their own political purposes. Communism and honest science just don't mix."

Dr. Paul Dudley White, President Eisenhower's personal doctor, wrote me a warm note and asked for extra copies of the speech and John Foster Dulles sent a letter commending me for a "very fine public service. Your presentation of the bacteriological warfare matter was masterly."

But the Communists were not among those applauding me. Joseph Malik was leading the furious countercharges which followed my speech. He said that our atrocity charges were part of a campaign to step up war hysteria and thus justify increased expenditure for arms. (The Rochester *Post Bulletin* proclaimed: MAYO, MALIK CLASH OVER RUSS FILM, loyally giving me top billing.) On the second day of the debate that ensued, I was watching a delegate from the Middle East who was insisting excitedly that the germ warfare charges were true, when I noticed a flush on his cheeks and mentally deduced that he had a temperature of about 103. When the session ended, I approached him and said quietly, "I am now speaking in my capacity as a doctor. You have a bad cold. I suggest you go home and go to bed." I couldn't resist adding, "You are spreading germ warfare."

The Communists then produced nineteen more signed confessions, from fliers who were still in prison camps. I replied on a radio show, "It doesn't matter how many of these statements the Communists make public. Zero is still zero, even when you multiply it by nineteen or thirty-six or any other number. The Communists are just multiplying the lie."

Five days after the original speech, I made another in answer to Malik's charges that our returned fliers had repudiated their confessions of germ warfare because of vile threats brought against them by the United States government, from the Secretary of Defense on down. It was tricky to disprove, because worldly people would not find this entirely unfeasible, but I was heartened by the angry young flier who telephoned me from Wichita, Kansas, to assure me that Malik was wrong, and he had repudiated his confession freely; there had been no compulsion from the Air Force. I also cited the interesting comparison: Colonel Schwable and Major Bley had been in Communist hands for eight months before signing confessions, but were home only three weeks before detailed repudiations were released. Colonel Mahurin had signed a confession eleven months after his capture, and repudiated it three days after his release.

There was more at stake than honor, or winning a debate that was reduced to exchanges of "You lie!" The Geneva Protocol prohibiting the use of gases and toxic agents and of bacteriological agents in war had been ratified by the Soviet Union, with the reservation that the Soviet Union would not

important

regard it as binding against any country which failed to respect its restrictions. If charges that the United States used
bacteriological warfare against Korea were not totally dis-
credited, the Soviet Union was free to use germ warfare
against the United States in the event of another war, which
then could be known as World War III, And Out.

Our victory, when it came, wasn't clear-cut or dramatic.
Nations which had believed the germ warfare charges against
the United States simply became less convinced, then skeptical, and then began to say that of course they had known all
along that the U.S. wouldn't make such a strategical blunder.
Malik's ardor for the debate cooled; he began to talk of other
matters. The Political Committee voted 47 to 0 to send a
record of the debate to the Disarmament Committee, "for its
information." Thirteen countries, including the chagrined
Soviet bloc, abstained from voting. And that ended it.

The State Department arranged to show any interested
delegates the Communist propaganda film. I went along to
the special screening at the St. Regis Hotel and marveled
again that it had been taken seriously. Other delegates noted
the primitive laboratory, the so-called scientists who were
handling bacteria without wearing gloves, the strained, desperate faces of the United States prisoners making their obviously memorized speeches. It was an hour of wicked, inept
horror, but it came close to wrecking the scary balance of
Cold War alignments.

There was a sad sequel to the wretched business. The fliers
who confessed were being accused of being traitors to their
country and there were some who wanted them punished.
A special board of officers was convened in Washington to
decide what should be done, and General Nathan F. Twin-
ing, USAF Chief of Staff, asked me to appear before it. "The
presentation of your views would be of tremendous benefit
in handling the extremely difficult task of passing judgment
on fellow Americans who were caught in the meshes of this

269

painfully bizarre conflict. We are anxious to solve this problem not only with sympathy but with true justice."

It was my feeling that the fliers had suffered enough, and that further humiliation or censure was unthinkable. "I'd have hated to be in their shoes," I told the board. "Everyone has a breaking point. It takes quite a guy to be a martyr all by himself, especially when no one on the outside knows whether he is dead or alive."

The brass agreed; I think very few who read the details of the torture the men endured could be inclined to condemn them. All the fliers were given honorable discharges or else restored to full duty status. Lieutenant General Emmett O'Donnell, Jr., USAF deputy chief of staff personnel, thanked me when it was all over and wrote that my advice and guidance contributed greatly to the success of their efforts.

In the meantime, I was causing consternation and prostration among the United Nations simultaneous translators because of my affection for puns, which I think I inherited from my father. Their blackest day came when we were considering a resolution to thank a committee for work well done. Jamil M. Baroody, the flamboyant delegate from Saudi Arabia, opposed the motion on the grounds that the participants had been paid for their efforts and therefore didn't have to be thanked. I protested that gratitude was always appropriate wherever zeal and efficiency are displayed and illustrated this by adding, "We have a saying in Minnesota that an ounce of taffy is worth a pound of epitaph-y." That had to be converted into six languages and, I was reliably informed, lost everything in the translation every time.

Baroody later wrote me a silken letter, just before a trip I planned to make, asking that I not bring any taffy with me, as of all people, being a wise doctor, I should know that even tons of taffy could not serve as a cure for the ills and ailments of mankind.

I was the only doctor among the U.N. delegates, so, as

always happens when doctors are stranded among laymen at a social function, I attracted a cocktail party clientele of delegates with sore shoulders and mysterious belly pains. When I was stuck, I called for help from the Mayo Clinic. After a while I was even getting X-ray plates to diagnose. It had James Bond overtones when the ailing delegate happened to be from behind the Iron Curtain. The delegate from Yugoslavia, for instance, slipped me an envelope one day; I examined the contents, shook my head, sent them to Rochester and a few days later returned the envelope to him and we huddled for a long talk. We were discussing the X-ray plate of his hip.

I used to wonder if a subversive doctor had helped in the design of one of the murals in the United Nations Assembly. The murals were supposed to be nonpolitical, of course, but there is one wall that to me depicts red cells trying to destroy white ones. I found it disquieting, especially when Vishinski had the floor.

The United Nations is full of the tense feel of power while it is convened, but its social side is a striking contrast. Vishinski, for instance, was gruff and frightening in public, but at a cocktail party he was gentle and grandfatherly. Even the hard-faced Malik was charming away from the council chambers. One time Alice, who had a child's directness with people she liked, was thanking Malik for bringing her a martini and blurted out that she always admired him for his dimples. He was pleased, but blushed a deep scarlet. I said, "It's the first time I've seen you in your true color, red." Malik laughed, and repeated the exchange for days after.

It seemed that every country felt some sort of potlatch obligation to give huge cocktail parties, and we all grew heartily sick of them. Sometimes the State Department asked me to give a dinner, and suggested my guest list. It would result in interesting mixtures: once I asked people from the delegations of Australia, Chile, Cuba, Honduras, New Zealand, Peru, Canada, Thailand, Belgium, Sweden, Uruguay, the

United Kingdom, France, Greece and China—one from each. It was a stag dinner and I took them all to the Princeton Club.

Just before we returned to Rochester, early in December, Alice and I gave a party in the United Nations dining room and asked three hundred of the people we had liked best. We paid for it ourselves, of course. We had quite a few from the other side of the Iron Curtain, Mrs. F. A. Novikova of Byelorussia (I'd never heard of that country before going to the U.N.); Ambassador Robert Schmelz of Czechoslovakia; Abdel Hamid from Egypt and Mrs. Zena Harman from Israel; Ambassador Luc E. Fouche from Haiti; His Royal Highness Prince Wan Waithayakon of Thailand; four people from Poland, Mrs. E. N. Khokhol from the Ukrainian S.S.R. and G. F. Saksin from Yugoslavia, and dozens more.

We also asked our friends, like writer Bob Considine and his wife, and Mr. and Mrs. Bernard Gimbel, and Dag Hammarskjold, one of the most dedicated people I've ever known, and some vice admirals and the entire U.S. delegation and staff; and some Princeton classmates, like John ("Heinie") Leh, from Allentown, Pennsylvania. They loved meeting all the ambassadors and a few of them maneuvered the Poles into a corner for a half hour of what sounded like a hilarious exchange of jokes. It was a great bash.

Just before the session concluded, President Eisenhower gave one of the greatest speeches of his career. I knew about it in advance because it contained several references to medical matters and he most flatteringly sent me drafts of the speech for my comment. It generally is known as Eisenhower's Atoms for Peace speech and it marked one of few times in U.N. history when all the delegates were united wholeheartedly behind a major policy resolution.

I met Eisenhower at the United Nations for the first time since he had become President. There is no question in my mind that he is incomparable as a man. I liked his informality and homeyness, and the fact that he's a straight-shooter and you can rely on his honesty. I've known seven Presidents—Harding, Hoover, Roosevelt, Truman, Eisenhower, Kennedy and Johnson—and if I were told to sit down to dinner with one of them I wouldn't hesitate to choose Eisenhower.

The speech to the United Nations was given on December 8, 1953. Eisenhower called for a pooling of atom research on peaceful projects that would benefit all men. "Who can doubt, if the entire body of the world's scientists and engineers had adequate amounts of fissionable material with which to test and develop their ideas, that this capability would rapidly be transformed into universal, efficient and economic usage." He proposed that governments with atomic stockpiles should make contributions to an International Atomic Energy Agency, under the aegis of the United Nations.

Some were moved to tears when the U.S.S.R. supported the program and the United Nations voted for it 60 to 0. After the ugliness of the germ warfare charges, it was a welcome promise that the world was moving in the direction of trust and peaceful cohabitation.

I lost no time in appealing to medical and scientific groups to support the Atoms for Peace project. Doctors tend to be insular because there is so much to do within the profession, so much reading and working and exchanging of ideas. They have to be reminded from time to time that there is a world going on outside. The potential for atomic power to improve health intrigued me. It would mean a much more rapid solution of medical and health problems if nuclear materials were pooled and gifted scientists from all over the world, specially trained, were to work together. I could see an application in the diagnosis and treatment of cancer and hypertension, among other ailments, and a possibility that it would aid in the increase of food production. A portion of this has come to pass, but the wide vision that Eisenhower had of a community of international scientists working together selflessly for the good of all is largely unrealized.

Effie Shoholm, our secretary and loyal friend, was amassing more clippings than Alice and I could find time to read. Alice had a favorite, written by Thena Townley Perry in the Miami *Herald*, which described me in the following way: "White haired, with black, quizzical porcupine eyebrows, he has an impish twinkle in his brown eyes, a humorous quirk to his mouth and a faint deep chuckle in his soft voice." The same lady reported that Alice had perfect posture; "she walks 'tall' with her small pointed chin lifted high. . . . She has a radiant smile, the kind that makes people smile back at her." That part about Alice caught her; I can't speak for the other.

A Chicago *Daily News* Service reporter asked me a simple question: "What ails the world?" I was simple enough to try to answer. "I suppose it is fear . . . but there are nations who seem to be sick with a malignant illness, who are just suffering the processes of evaluation. If we can avoid a war, they will not die but will get well in time. . . . The United Nations will give us the time we need."

I had become a passionate advocate of the United Nations and its goals. From a state of indifference, I had progressed all the way to agreeing with something Winston Churchill once said, that if we didn't have a United Nations, we would have to build one. Henry Ford had the same experience. He had gathered from reading newspapers, he said, that an awful lot of talking went on at the United Nations but nothing much was accomplished. After his stint as an alternate delegate he declared, "My views have changed considerably. . . . Without the United Nations, our position would be much more lonely and precarious than it is now."

My close-up view had disclosed difficulties beyond the mere mistrust of intentions that I had expected. For one thing, the problems posed by language are beyond the scope of translators. Over and over, we would draft a resolution to put before the General Assembly and spend hours on its wording, to ensure that it was as simple, straightforward and logical as it could possibly be. It would seem so innocent and so obvious that it should pass in less than twenty minutes—but other nations would hear it in their own language and fret over its meaning for two weeks of irritable debate, during which tempers would rise under the suave facades and confidence in one another would be shredded.

Then too, very few of the delegates I knew had achieved a perfect family life. Most of them were having problems with their children, or disagreements with their wives. Yet it was expected that they could display harmony on an international scale. I think if we could form a United Nations from only happy husbands we might have a better chance.

I noticed this, on a much smaller stage, when I was serving in New Guinea and I sent Alice a poem I wrote about it, which I called *It Can Be Made Complex*:

> Impressed, I've been, by this one thing
> That seems to be the truth
> The things that seem to help mankind
> Are simple things, forsooth.
>
> Simplicity is based upon
> A thorough understanding
> The thing the well-trained pilot has
> That brings the happy landing.
>
> Nations have a common bond,
> Though they don't seem to know it,
> In the truths of proverbs which they have
> I wish the hell they'd show it.

When I left the United Nations in December, when the session ended, Alice and I went to Hawaii to recuperate for three weeks. It rained every day, the worst rain I'd seen since New Guinea, so we had plenty of time to stretch out in our room and read whodunits. I had some mail to treasure, such

275

as the letter I received from James J. Woodsworth, the deputy representative of the U.S. at the United Nations, who wrote, "I could not resist dropping you a note to tell you how much we all appreciate the grand work you did at this eighth assembly. As was to be expected, you did a great job for the delegation, for the United Nations and, above all, for your country."

President Eisenhower telephoned me when I got home and asked if I would be the Republican candidate for Senate in my state, running against Hubert Humphrey. He told me not to give him an answer right away, but to think it over. I gave it some thought, but it just didn't feel like the right move for me. When I called him at the White House, I got through to him right away and explained, "Politics is too far afield from my training."

Later on I was speaking at a dinner in the Cities when Humphrey came in, wearing a tuxedo. I grinned at his splendor and said, "It was lucky for you that I didn't run against you, or else I'd be in your shoes now." He was amused, and I added that I would have run if they could have guaranteed that I would be defeated.

I found that I wasn't finished with the United Nations after all. I received a letter from Clark M. Eichelberger, executive director of the American Association for the United Nations, asking me to be its president for a two-year term, succeeding Dr. William Emerson of M.I.T. The A.A.U.N., as I had discovered while in New York, is a voluntary, nonpolitical and nonpartisan organization devoted solely to the dissemination of facts about the United Nations and the educating of citizens. Most of the nations represented at the U.N. had an auxiliary U.N. association at home, informing its people and sometimes presenting resolutions on matters of public interest. They are bound together, loosely, in an organization called the World Federation of United Nations Associations.

I sent Clark a single-word telegram in answer to his invitation: OK.

I well knew that a number of my friends disliked the United Nations intensely, and many of them detested Mrs. Eleanor Roosevelt, who was chairman of the board of governors of the American Association for the United Nations, but I felt a responsibility to share the insight and perspective I had gained from the inside of its workings. Few other Americans had been provided my opportunity to discover for themselves how valuable the United Nations is to the world, so I had a duty to tell them about it.

It meant much more than my name on the A.A.U.N. letterhead, along with the honorary presidents, William Emerson, James T. Shotwell and Sumner Welles; the chairman of the board of directors, Oscar de Lima; chairman of the board of governors, Mrs. Roosevelt; and vice-presidents Joseph E. Davies, John W. Davis, Douglas Fairbanks, Jr., and Manley O. Hudson. In the years that followed my acceptance, I spent long hours in airplanes on my way to keep speaking engagements all over the country. Often Eleanor Roosevelt and I traveled together and I marveled at her unswerving courage and dedication. She was a pleasant companion, rambling a bit as older women will, but strictly avoiding any mention of her husband. She had a great talent for falling asleep anywhere, and could drop off abruptly for ten minutes in a taxi or two hours on a plane. We'd arrive with me wan and worn from the trip and Mrs. F.D.R. bright as a daisy.

The tone of the speeches that I gave was low-key, I think, but fervent. A good example of them is the one I gave on ABC during the Berlin confrontation. Speaking "as a surgeon who has spent his entire adult life practicing medicine," I said I didn't know much about the United Nations when I began as a delegate, but I had discovered that it was a great deal more than what has been called "a debating society in a glass palace."

"The United Nations is the greatest force for peace mankind has ever created," I stated, and pointed to the record of disputes that it had settled, the one between the Netherlands and Indonesia, the clash between the Arab states and Israel, the problems of Pakistan and India over Kashmir, the war in Korea. "Government begins at home—with the people. Good world government or collective security from aggression must also begin with the people. The United Nations battled war, hunger, disease and discrimination."

The problem, as I saw it, was one of education. The world needed citizenry which understood the United Nation's charter and purpose. "If we are to avoid global war and prevent aggression, no matter how small, we must think in terms of the world, not just ourselves. This thinking, condemned not so many years ago, is now a policy of the United States government."

What I asked, wherever I went, was that my fellow citizens take the time to study the United Nations seriously and learn something about it. "Take time out for adventure," I begged.

Occasionally my approach was the practical one of money. I addressed the American Veterinary Medical Association in Minneapolis in 1955, and pointed out that the U.S. contribution to the United Nations that year amounted to $93,000,-000, which worked out to about fifty-six cents for every citizen; at the same time the U.S. military budget was about four dollars for every man, woman and child in the country. The U.N. therefore was a bargain as a defense weapon and, in addition, provided the treasury with revenue from the $37,000,000 that delegates annually spent in the United States and the $2,000,000 income tax paid by U.S. citizens who worked at the United Nations.

I always mentioned isolationism in my Midwest speeches: "In my opinion, isolationism in this day and age of fast transportation, faster communication and economic interdependence is fantastically unrealistic."

Mostly I hammered at one blunt point: "The United Nations might not be a sure ticket to heaven, but at least it's a sure ticket that we won't go to hell."

I was also taking what some thought were daring stands against the mindless panic of those years induced by Senator Joseph McCarthy's irresponsible and largely baseless attacks on the Army and State Department as shelters for Communists. I said on radio one evening, "The Army-McCarthy hearings are so far below the dignity of this country that it is almost not understandable," and repeated denunciations of the hearings everywhere I spoke. When J. Robert Oppenheimer, the physicist who helped develop the atom bomb, was vilified by McCarthy, I spoke angrily in defense of the individual's right to differ.

I was active in more and more events of international significance. I once wrote President Eisenhower respectfully asking him to make more use of the United Nations in dealing with world tensions. The A.A.U.N. was concerned that the United Nations frequently was being bypassed by backroom deals and we felt, as I once said in a speech, that "the surest way to weaken or destroy the United Nations is not to use it." I said to Eisenhower, "The struggle [for peace] must be waged where the greatest number of nations, bound together by common obligations, can participate. That place is the United Nations."

As A.A.U.N. president, I protested a move to seat Communist China in the United Nations. I issued a statement that "the United States must continue to oppose the seating of the Chinese Communist delegates until they have given positive and acceptable evidence of their willingness to abide by the provisions of the Charter."

Cabot Lodge was almost frantic at that time that I made such a clear-cut statement. The World Federation of United Nations Associations had just met in Geneva and approved seating "the actual government of China, established since 1949 at Peking." The A.A.U.N. promptly disagreed with the motion, pointing out that the Chinese had been in defiance of the United Nations in Korea and were aiding in the aggression against Indochina.

We had a rally-around-Lodge week early in 1955, when a few newspaper editorials were unkind to him. Along with many others who were asked to do so, I wrote some letters to the editors stoutly supporting him.

The State Department had asked my help in obtaining a half million dollars from Washington to assist the United Nations Refugee Committee. Accordingly I wrote to my state's representative, Dr. Walter Judd, who had been at the Clinic, and my state's senator, Hubert Humphrey. As it happened, they were chairmen of their respective Foreign Affairs Committees. I urged them to provide funds for the humane work of the U.N. Refugee Committee, but we were turned down. I sent a note to G. J. van Heuvan Goldhart of the Netherlands, who was U.N. High Commissioner for Refugees, commiserating with him and adding philosophically, "If we become overwhelmed by the things we do not like, life becomes a most difficult proposition." Eventually, as I recall it, the money was given for work with the refugees.

My activities were not admired universally. On one occasion all the A.A.U.N. executives were asked to send out letters to everyone we could think of, setting out the purpose of the A.A.U.N. and requesting financial support. It was suggested that the letters begin with the salutation "Dear Friend," but I changed mine to "To Whom It May Concern." I reasoned that the recipient of the letter might not be my friend, but the contents of it should be of concern to all.

A former Princeton classmate wrote me furiously that he didn't appreciate getting such a letter from me, and had no use for such overselling of the United Nations, and particularly since Mrs. Roosevelt favored it. I ignored the latter crack, and answered moderately, "I do not think the United Nations should be oversold or undersold, but that it should be looked on simply as the best instrument we have at present for keeping at least the major wars on a talking basis, rather than a shooting basis." I was gratified to receive a donation from him in the next mail.

Such conversions were uncommon, the adult mind so often being the inflexible thing it is. Whenever I spoke, I waded through picket lines, with signs that usually proclaimed U.S. GET OUT OF U.N. and U.N. GET OUT OF U.S. There was a substantial body of opinion that the United Nations was a Communist organization, an attitude that was inflamed by the continuous, deadening use of the power of veto at the Security Council by the U.S.S.R. When the seating of Communist China seemed imminent in 1954 and 1955, there was a crescendo of voices insisting that the United States should quit the United Nations.

The A.A.U.N. already was considered a "Commie front" organization by people with a low threshold for mistrust, and our reputation with them wasn't enhanced by my statement that the United States should not consider withdrawal from the U.N., even if Peking China was admitted. "It would mean the throwing away of our moral influence and leadership in the world community. . . . Nothing could be more advantageous to the totalitarian cause or more weakening to our friends."

Enemies of the United Nations were also outraged when I declared, "We have justifiably berated the U.S.S.R. for unwillingness to conform to the resolutions of the majority of the U.N. It is highly inconsistent that we should threaten to withdraw from the U.N. if, perchance, at some future time the majority viewpoint is different from ours."

I'll stick to that, though I don't always like the consequences. The United Nations isn't perfect, but it is our only hope for world peace.

Mrs. Roosevelt was seventy years old on October 11, 1954, and consented to have the occasion turned into a mild fund-raising campaign for the A.A.U.N.'s education budget. With a blinding flash of ingenuity, we decided to name the committee heading the drive the Eleanor Roosevelt 70th Birthday Committee, and it had one of the most distinguished rosters the country could assemble: Marian Anderson, Ralph J. Bunche, Norman Cousins, Albert Einstein, Douglas Fairbanks, Jr., Felix Frankfurter, Oscar Hammerstein II, W. Averell Harriman, Archibald MacLeish, George C. Marshall, George Meany, Chester W. Nimitz, Walter Reuther, John Rockefeller III, Dore Schary, Cornelia Otis Skinner and Adlai Stevenson. It raised a modest sum of money, I recall, which we needed desperately.

I sent Mrs. Roosevelt a telegram on her birthday, deeply meant: "I thank you for the years you have unselfishly expended in thought and work on behalf of others, while with strength and no malice you have moved serenely among commenders and detractors, smiling on both. Chuck Mayo."

When my term as president of the A.A.U.N. expired in 1956, the post was offered to Nelson Rockefeller, who turned it down with regrets and thanks. They asked me then if I would continue for another two-year term, which I felt obliged to do because the United Nations was having a heavy time of it in those days of acute cold war.

I stepped down finally late in 1957 and remained as honorary president. Mrs. Roosevelt sent a simple telegram, expressing her "deepest thanks" and Clark Eichelberger wrote, "You were always friendly and understanding; you stood for liberal policies; you were democratic with the staff." I was deeply moved by what he said, and particularly the last part. Boors who cannot be bothered knowing anyone not of what they imagine to be their own social class infuriate me. At the Clinic, I know the names of hundreds and hundreds of secretaries, nurses, maintenance men, lab assistants, receptionists, elevator operators and technicians, and I generally can remember something about their families. I wouldn't call it democratic of me—there's something slightly patronizing about that—but it's a good sensation to feel you're among friends.

THIRTEEN

The mood of international cooperation which spawned the United Nations also, in 1946, led to the establishing of what is called the World Health Organization. Its function is to coordinate medicine's fight against such diseases as malaria, which don't observe national borders. In May, 1955, I was named chief delegate of the United States delegation to the Eighth World Health Assembly, meeting for the first time on this side of the Atlantic, in Mexico City.

The other delegate was Dr. Frederick J. Brady, assistant chief, Division of International Health, U.S. Public Health Service, and we were flanked by learned alternates, Dr. Leroy E. Burney, deputy chief, Bureau of State Services, Public Health Service; Howard B. Calderwood, from the State Department's Office of Economic and Social Affairs, and Dr. Martha Eliot, chief of the Children's Bureau, Department of Health, Education, and Welfare, and thirteen advisers, two from Congress and the rest deans of medical schools, heads of dentists' and nurses' organizations, quarantine experts, and a Latin American specialist.

All of us had an abiding concern for the main items on the agenda, the launching of President Eisenhower's Atoms for Peace proposal as it affected medicine; some indent in the incidence of malaria, which devitalizes some 350,000,000 people annually; world distribution for Salk vaccine for the prevention of polio, just introduced in the United States; an updating of international quarantine techniques. But the commanding problem was money.

The World Health Organization then was supposed to be financed by its eighty-four member nations, but nine of these, including Russia, were supplying no money at all. The arrangement in the beginning was that no single nation could be required to pay more than a third of WHO's annual budget and the United States was assessed to the cent of this. But the U.S. government had put a three-million-dollar ceiling on its contribution to WHO and, in 1955, these decrees were on a collision course: the U.S. assessment would exceed the three million dollars allowed.

It was our task to appeal to the World Health Organization to make the reasonable adjustment that the one-third allotment should be computed on the basis of *paying* members only. Nations deadheading were throwing out the balance, and the U.S. actually was paying more than its one-third obligation. Simultaneously, we had to hope that the government would pass special legislation so the extra assessment above the three-million-dollar mark could be paid.

To the relief of all, the WHO agreed to phase out the apportioning of assessment by including nonpaying nations; the U.S.S.R. decided to contribute to WHO; and Congress and Senate voted to extend U.S. financing for that year. It wasn't a thunderous success, since the phasing out would be stretched over the next four years, but failure and ill will at that stage of WHO's history might have mutilated its potential. We were grateful to be able to turn our attention to our better function, the service of health on a world-wide basis.

"Humanity can be proud that this organization continues to develop along lines that are influential and sound," I said in my address, "and fosters both public health and good will among nations." We drove the lesson of international cooperation home by arranging for seminars after the Assembly ended, in which doctors and scientists from some fifty countries toured hospitals and medical facilities in the United States and were briefed by leading figures in such related specialties as hospital design, parasitology, insecticides, medical statistics, poliomyelitis, pandemic influenza, tuberculosis control, blood banks and mental health.

I returned to my surgery, and the laborious preparation of medical papers to demonstrate the effectiveness of the anus-saving operation that was still regarded by many as dangerous pioneering. In addition, I had risen rather majestically to become chairman of the Mayo Properties Association, which controlled all the physical assets of the Clinic and determined expansion policies. I was in favor of stretching out, even of overbuilding; I reasoned that it would be more economical in the long run, in view of the tendency that building costs have of mounting steeply every few minutes.

We had built a Medical Sciences Building in 1941, which at that time I complained was far too small to be adequate for long. It was enlarged once in 1949 and again in 1952. By then we had begun the most ambitious building of all, a new Clinic. The Plummer Building on which Father and Uncle Will had lavished such luxurious care, with its carved oak doors, marble floors, scrolled bronze around the elevators and stone gargoyles glaring from the tower, could no longer meet the needs of a case load of patients that had grown from 130,000 patients a year in 1940 to 150,000 patients a year in 1950.

The proposed new building, to be called the Mayo Building, took years of planning, with the best medical architects and our own staff doctors pooling their ideas and complaints. It was to be ten stories high and would contain all the diagnostic offices, examining rooms, dressing rooms, consultation rooms and doctors' offices, leaving the Plummer Building free for the Mayo Clinic Library, a museum, research laboratories, offices for retired doctors and other facilities.

It was decided to group related specialties together for greater efficiency, one floor for eyes and neurologic examinations, one for proctoscopic and urological tests, and so on. Patients were to wait for their names to be called in large areas seating about two hundred comfortably, with a handsome abstract mural to distract them and a different color scheme on every floor keyed to it.

I discovered that the Board had asked artists from all over the country to submit designs for these murals, but had overlooked Bill Saltzman, director of the art center in Rochester. I suggested to the Board that this was somewhat odd so Saltzman was invited to take part in the contest. His mural was one of the winners and now adorns the third floor X-ray department waiting room.

The Plummer Building in its time had been a model of contemporary design and the same is true of the Mayo Building. It is paneled with a different wood on every floor with good bright colors everywhere, and the north wall is a solid sheet of white marble. This forms the background to a two-story-high sculpture in copper, of a nude male with an uplifted arm that always reminds me of a basketball player making a shot.

I insisted that the Mayo Building be planned so that additional floors could be added easily. This meant some extra expense and there was a good deal of disagreement among Board members, but finally it was done. We found ourselves overcrowded again not ten years later, and began adding eight more floors on top of the original eleven. I protested that the circular ramp parking garage should also be built so that it could take a new topping, and this debate had some exciting moments but I lost. I take no satisfaction in having been right about that, since I'm one of the many people who can't find a place to park near the Clinic in recent years. I think the Board strangles itself by having too many committees to see problems clearly. We started the committee system back in the 1930's—I think it was Father's and Uncle Will's idea because they wanted the Clinic doctors to learn how to govern themselves in the greatest possible numbers—but I think it is a mistake. And I have said so, many times.

The Mayo Building was rising behind its construction wall when I tangled with my friend Dr. Howard Gray over a trivial matter. The contractors and electricians and those concerned with the new building wanted a large sign erected to state what was being built and who was doing it. Many of the Board thought this was ostentatious and Howdie was among them. Howdie was a devoted Baptist and as fixed in his ideas as I am in mine, so I thought to break the tension with a light recommendation. "We'll take the sign off the Baptist church that says 'Jesus Saves,'" I told him, "and we'll put it on one side of the construction and then we'll get a picture of me and put it on the other side, with the words 'So Does Mayo.'" Howdie thought that was unpardonably irreverent, and didn't speak to me for three weeks.

When I finally did move into my new office on the sixth floor of the Mayo Building, I found that the architects had put panes of clear glass in all the doors, giving doctors no privacy to do their paper work. I complained about this but nothing was done. One day I obtained a large picture of the stripper Lili St. Cyr in the nude and covered over the window in my door. It was only there a few days before I was informed that I could have a solid wood door if I promised to remove the picture of Miss St. Cyr's well-endowed frame. Some people will accept anything architects give them, no matter how dumb.

I used to find that our staff conferences bogged down in long boring discussions about tedious details, so I once attempted to enliven one of them by announcing with a grave face that I had an unusual problem to present to my colleagues: a patient of mine seemed to have swallowed an octopus. I illustrated this by showing them a stomach X ray, on which I had superimposed the shadow of an octopus. There was a shocked silence before someone finally started to laugh.

287

In and around all of this, I still gave speeches to inform people about the United Nations. My presidential address to the Interstate Postgraduate Medical Association in 1955 was titled "The Role of Medicine and Physicians in International Affairs." It was widely reprinted. In it I reminded my fellow physicians, some of whom I knew were grumbling that the United Nations was supported entirely by U.S. taxpayers, that eleven member nations contributed more per capita to the U.N. than did the United States, and that the second largest contributor to the United Nations was the U.S.S.R., close behind the States. The surest bond between nations, I told them, was the common interest in improving health, which meant that physicians had a special obligation to take an interest in international affairs.

"Because of the limitations of time, the great majority of us are not able to do justice to our own patients and at the same time take an active part in international affairs, but we should be informed on these matters and we should be aware of the fact that support of health programs beyond the confines of our country serves as an element of great strength in the foreign policy of our Department of State and in the protection of our own domestic health."

When I was asked to give the 1955 Jerome Cochran Lecture before the Alabama Medical Association, I gave approximately the same speech, just changing the words around. I called it "The Role of Medicine and Doctors in International Relations" to give it a look of freshness.

President Eisenhower had asked me to be a U.S. delegate again at the next meeting of the World Health Organization, the Ninth World Assembly to be held in Geneva in May, and I had accepted. Alice was planning delightedly to come with me (at our expense) in order to see Muff again. Our oldest child was still married to that Swiss I disliked so much, and wandering around Europe or the Mediterranean. When friends inquired about her I told them as little as possible, only that she had picked out a Swiss movement.

On April 2, a month before we were to leave for Geneva, I received a call from George Allen, the Under Secretary of State, asking me if I would be President Eisenhower's personal representative at the coronation of the King of Nepal. It would be required that I leave Rochester in seventeen days. I told him I would be pleased to attend, though I hadn't the faintest idea where Nepal was and I knew my own schedule would be in a shambles. Alice would come with me, at our expense.

In the hectic days that followed, I boned up on Nepal. I discovered that it is a tiny kingdom between India and Tibet, cut off from the rest of the world throughout history by the Himalayan Mountains in which it perches. It is about two-thirds the size of Minnesota but has a population of close to four million, mostly Mongolians and Indo-Aryans. The people resulting from intermarriage between those races are called Gurkhas. The people are Hindus or Buddhists. Nepal had always been remote and mysterious, rarely visited by strangers, but its new young monarch Mahendra Bir Bikram Shah Deva wanted to change all that and was planning to have his country join the United Nations and accept aid from both the United States and Russia. He was proclaiming his new internationalism by making a public ceremony of the ancient, secret ritual of Nepalese coronations and had invited heads of state to attend. Most sent ambassadors, or, like me, special representatives.

I was committed to make a ten-day trip around the United States, attending a Surgeons Club meeting in New Orleans, an American Surgical Association meeting in White Sulphur Springs, a hustled day in Washington to pick up passports and suggestions as to our wardrobe, a Nu Sigma Nu lecture in Detroit and, finally, a talk on the United Nations and the World Health Organization in Aberdeen, South Dakota. When I arrived back in Rochester on April 18, I hadn't been out of my clothes in twenty-six hours. Nonetheless, I managed to be on a plane the next day, bound for the adventure of Nepal.

We flew day and night and through the international date line, from Rochester to Minneapolis, to Seattle, to Anchorage, to Tokyo, to Okinawa and Formosa, to Hong Kong, where we rested for two days and partied with the consul general Everett Drumright and Dr. Li Shu-Fan.

We were to stay in New Delhi at the home of the U.S. ambassador, George Cooper from Kentucky. He and his wife had left the day before—he was returning to the States for some surgery—so we had the luxurious place and the four or five polite, white-clad servants to ourselves. Alice decided that a massage would help her relax from the journey, so she inquired if it could be arranged. I can't do justice to the story—she told it very well—but a huge, bearded, turbaned, tattooed Sikh appeared in her bedroom and proceeded to give her an excellent massage. She was thanking him when it was over, assuming that he would be leaving, when he startled her by picking her up, putting her under the shower and—deaf to her protests—soaping her thoroughly. When he was satisfied she was clean, he dried her and withdrew, leaving the former Alice Plank of Philadelphia halfway between hysteria and laughter.

The embassy thoughtfully had arranged for me to tour hospitals in New Delhi and give my two best speeches, one on medicine and world peace and the other on diseases of the colon and rectum, and there were cocktail parties and receptions laid on, and a moonlight look at the Taj Mahal, which is all that it is cracked up to be. We took off in an Air Force DC-3, loaded heavily with the food and drink for the party we would give as our share of the festivities, and with ambassadors from Burma, Japan and France who were hitching a ride.

We flew to the capital, Katmandu, which is in a valley between the highest mountains on earth, and were welcomed by a shrieking crowd who loaded us with garlands of flowers and words of welcome we couldn't understand. We were escorted through narrow streets lined with jubilant people to the Royal Hotel, the former palace of a prince, with enormous rhinoceros heads flanking the entrance and tiger skins everywhere.

The crowds chanting "Hi Hi Hi America!" brought out the hotel manager to greet us. He was a Russian, Boris Lisovitch, a lusty, swashbuckling character who had run the 400 Club in Calcutta. He had been arrested in Katmandu for operating a distillery, we were told, and spent three months in jail, during which he rented the jailor's home, lived regally and was saluted by the guards. Boris ushered us to our suite, a huge reception room and a bedroom that were linked by a marble bathroom of equal size.

We explored Katmandu the next morning, a city whose normal population of a half million was already tripled with coronation visitors in gala clothes, ecstatic amongst the streamers and freshly painted buildings. The king had built a new road from India, in order to bear the weight of the forty elephants he wanted for the coronation parade. They had just arrived, complete with mahouts, further exciting citizens who never before had seen elephants. The king's new airstrip was receiving air-borne guests from all over the world, each one—even the somber Communist Chinese, dressed in black peasant working clothes—received with flowers and screams of joy, for they were establishing an embassy. We were told that for centuries this part of the world had been called "the Forbidden Land"; we were witnessing a nation's coming-out party.

Lowell Thomas was also in Katmandu to make a film of the coronation for that travelogue series he does. He told me that until a few years ago cars were carried into Katmandu on platforms borne by eighty to a hundred walking men.

I presented my credentials to the king that evening. He was only thirty-six, a handsome, serious young monarch who wears prescription sunglasses most of the time and nervously chews gum. His shy, silent queen was with him, also wearing glasses. I was arrayed in a top hat, striped trousers and cutaway coat, the Communist Chinese were in unrelieved black tunics as before, the Tibet, Sikkim and Bhutan delegates were glorious in gold and jewel-embroidered formal dress, and the British were covered in medals. Afterward there was a cocktail party in the palace garden and then we drove back to the hotel through narrow streets, where people were still hanging bunting and cheering every passing vehicle. Ours, a limousine chauffeured by a Sikh, was identified by the Stars and Stripes on the hood ornament and drew such a continuous clamor that my right arm began to ache from waving acknowledgment.

The temperature was 114 in the midday of the coronation. The royal astrologers had fixed the exact moment when it was favored by the heavens that the king should be crowned, at 10:43 in the morning. We sat in the courtyard, sweltering, as the strange, dignified and beautiful ceremonial was completed. The king wore a crown of pearls, emeralds and diamonds, with the tall plume of a rare white bird-of-paradise rising from it. He was the ninth ruler of the Shah dynasty to be crowned according to ancient Vedic rites, and we foreigners from fifteen countries watched the priests lighting sacred fires, the throne covered with leopard skins, the canopy adorned with the design of eleven gold-headed cobras and marveled at the will and courage of the stern young king who had vowed to bring his nation into the twentieth century almost overnight.

The procession, featuring the elephants, followed. We dignitaries were to ride on their backs, in red and gold howdahs that held six men. I ascended by means of a ladder placed against the elephant's stern and was joined by Nepalese government officials and the ambassadors from France, Switzerland and Japan. When the elephant began to urinate a thundering stream, I explained that it was caused by too much pressure on her bladder. The Japanese ambassador considerately moved over a few inches.

When the elephant began to move, I took pains not to look at the distant swaying ground. The effect on the passengers of a strolling elephant is pretty interesting: it's an induced hula. I found that our high perch enabled us to look into the second floors of buildings we passed, and put us eye-level with the beautiful people waving from balconies. Up ahead, the driver of the lead elephant had discovered that the city's electrical and telephone wires were too low for the howdahs. He solved the difficulty coolly, by slashing them with his sword.

The coronation ceremony and parade were only the beginning of the festivities. The schedule was filled with athletic demonstrations, military drills and wall-to-wall cocktail parties. The Communist Chinese gave one in our hotel and I happened to pass through it, though I didn't pause because I hadn't been invited. The band was playing "Red River Valley," which I thought an inspired choice. We had learned that the head of the Red Chinese group was no less than a deputy premier, a Mongolian named Ulan Fu. The State Department had advised the Americans not to speak to the Chinese, but it makes a man feel silly not to speak to someone he encounters every day, so I always nodded cordially to him and I detected a slight bob of his head in return. I suppose he had his own instructions from some Chinese version of the State Department.

When the king and queen gave a state dinner in the palace, Alice was seated in the place of honor at his right. The meal had seven courses, each with a different wine, and lasted until one thirty in the morning. During this time Alice, in her natural way, invited the king and queen to visit us at Mayowood, and he seemed interested in the prospect.

The United States reception was planned for almost the end of the celebration week, so I was gathering tips while attending all the rest. The British party seemed the best to me, partly because of the exciting and handsome kilted Gurkha pipe band. I learned I could secure them for our affair by paying each man a bottle of beer, so we made the deal on the spot. Some of the Americans planning the party were annoyed at me, since they already had hired a police band and a 75-piece military band; I maintained that the fifty Gurkhas would just round out the entertainment nicely.

When we returned from the British reception, the hotel manager Boris was waiting for us. He had noticed the gap in our schedule, between the British reception and dawn, and to fill it came up to our room with a washtub packed with ice and champagne. We had a private party with him that was by far the finest social event in Katmandu. We learned the champagne was from the British party.

But the U.S. party came off quite splendidly, I thought, despite the stark horror that I caused in our protocol department. It was the custom at these affairs for the king to take the salute as the bands marched in, while the queen stood aside and watched. After the king had saluted the military band and the police band, I stepped to his side and asked if he would allow the queen to have a turn. He was becoming more relaxed and approachable every time we met, so I wasn't surprised when he smiled and agreed. When my borrowed Gurkhas swung onto the lawn, all fifty of them, the queen stepped forward and gave a small, flustered bow. When I escorted the royal couple to their car after the affair, the king put his head out of the window and said with a breezy grin, "I'll be seeing you."

The final event on the coronation program was a stunning military tattoo, with a concert from the massed bands, that lasted until three in the morning. Alice wearily packed until five thirty and fell exhausted into bed. We were wakened a half hour later in order to catch our plane for New Delhi, and were a decidedly unmerry lot of passengers during the flight. We got off the plane, in 111-degree heat, to be informed that we were to be hosts that night at a formal dinner. I don't know how we did it, but we did.

We flew the beautiful and exotic route from New Delhi to Karachi and Beirut and Rome, and then caught a train for Geneva. When we arrived in our hotel suite, Muff was waiting for us. We hadn't seen her for two years, so we all wept a bit. The next morning, the Ninth World Health Assembly convened and I got down to the business of fighting malaria and yellow fever again.

I gave another in my long series of addresses defending the United Nations and especially its good sane arm, the World Health Organization: it was becoming almost a reflex with me. "Science as related to health should eventually know no geographic, racial or religious boundaries," I said. "The work of the World Health Organization is limitless. . . . I know of no greater or more potent ingredient or part in the United Nations by which to achieve that state of international health we all seek—peace."

I was interested in the development of WHO's Central Technical Services Department, which was providing information about such matters as epidemiology, statistics, drug standardization and medical publications to all the member nations, helping them to keep their health administration up-to-date.

My devotion to the cause of health on an international basis hasn't waned in the years since the mid-fifties, when I gave so much time to it, but I gradually had to restrict my activities when they threatened to crowd my role as a surgeon out of my life. I was a delegate to the Eleventh World Health Assembly in 1958, because it was held in Minneapolis, only eighty miles from the Clinic, and I consented to serve on the Board of Directors in 1958 of the World Rehabilitation Fund, because I was touched by its goal: to bring some seventy doctors and physical therapists from thirty-five different nations to the United States for training at such centers as the Kessler Institute for Rehabilitation,

Newington Hospital for Crippled Children and the Veterans Administration Prosthetic Service. It was a great scheme, one that benefited handicapped people all over the world. Industry contributed too: General Foods helped start the San Pablo Rehabilitation Center in the Philippines, fifty miles south of Manila, which provides an out-patient service together with social work and prosthetics and brace manufacturing.

I was also on the National Committee for the Tenth Anniversary of the Universal Declaration of Human Rights, which seemed a significant occasion worthy of wide attention, and generally threw my small weight in with others whenever the United Nations or World Health Organization was threatened by the tides. As emerging nations came into the United Nations, I was one of many who worried about the strengths and weaknesses of a system which permits an insignificant, indigent nation the same vote as the powerful contributing countries. There's something beautiful about that kind of equality, but it doesn't lend itself to a mood of collective responsibility. I just don't know how it can be solved; maybe representation by population would be more fair. I still fret that the United Nations is being bypassed where it could be doing the most good: in the Vietnam war, for instance. We juggled around diplomatically so that the United Nations could enter the Korean war, and we could do the same to permit the United Nations to solve that appalling war in Vietnam.

Of all the speeches I gave in support of internationalism, and all the papers I wrote—mostly in medical journals—fighting the mood of the time to swing to isolationism, I think I put my feelings best in a brief editorial that appeared first in *The American Surgeon* in December, 1956. It was called "Not for Ourselves Alone" and I will quote all of it:

"The good Lord gives specific gifts to each and every person at birth. We would learn that this is also true of every living thing if only we had an intelligent interpreter for each form of life. Such gifts signify that there is a purpose for the existence of living things. There is also a purpose for the existence of inanimate or material things, for without them, there could be no life.

"We who delight in calling ourselves 'mankind'—at times with tongue in cheek and often, in this country, with the feeling that the term includes only those who speak the English language—have much to learn about the purpose of our existence. We first must learn about ourselves. Socrates put it in two words, 'Know thyself.' To this some might reply, 'That is a lifetime study in itself and leaves no time for action.' My reply, however, is that knowledge of ourselves leads eventually to but one conclusion, namely that we do not exist for ourselves alone and that, consequently, we should lead a devoted, purposeful life in a chosen field of worth-while human endeavor.

"We must know something about other people's problems. A person must be mentally sick if he can exist on earth but live so high in the clouds that he is unaware of what is going on about him. We are in no Utopia; rather, we are in a world of many faults, and not all of them belong to the other person.

"In the United States, we are blessed with more of the material things of life than are the people of any other country. We as a group, as well as individuals, are gradually coming to the idea that our concept of life in terms of the freedoms as we know them should be the right and privilege of all mankind. We would not, however, thrust this concept upon other peoples who are separated geographically from us and have different creeds, any more than we would want their concepts thrust upon us.

"The path of true progress in international affairs must be trod in an orderly manner, step by step, both at home and abroad. Progress stems not primarily from huge monetary gifts but from the education of native persons as teachers who in turn may educate their own peoples in the true values of life and living as they may be adapted to their own souls and soil. I would pick medicine, agriculture and engineering as the three principal fields for education and endeavor in those countries less fortunate than ours. These fields could contribute best to international co-operation and understanding, which are the watchwords of peace.

"The day of the individual isolationist will never be over, but the day of group isolationism is past."

When I returned home from that round-the-world trip to Nepal and Geneva, I wrote President Eisenhower an informal report on my stewardship of the duties entrusted to me. I advised him that in Nepal "I caught every disease that you would have got if you had gone." He later told me that he had enjoyed the letter hugely, "and so did Mamie."

I dropped by the White House not long after that, in part to ask President Eisenhower to sign a picture of himself for my friend Heinie Leh, the secretary of my Princeton class. I explained that I was on my way to a Princeton reunion. Eisenhower asked, "Is he one of our boys?" I said, "No," although knowing that Heinie was a Republican, "but he will be, as soon as he gets this picture."

I learned the next day that Eisenhower had undergone surgery for ileitis on the same day that I saw him. People were amazed that I didn't know, and asked me how he looked. I could only report that he seemed in wonderful health and spirits, and I marveled at the modesty of the man in not mentioning it to me. He is a truly great man, as I have said.

He helped me out one day when I wanted to teach a lesson to a self-inflated patient of mine, who had irritated everyone with his constant name-dropping of famous and near-famous people he claimed as friends. On my rounds one morning I told this patient that I would be dropping in to see him later with some friends of mine, and he nodded condescendingly. It was during the election year, and Adlai Stevenson and President Eisenhower happened to be in Rochester at the same time, so first I took Adlai in to see the patient, introducing him casually, and then an hour later I brought in President Eisenhower. Maybe it was too subtle: after that, the patient had two more names to drop.

As a postscript to our Nepal visit, Mahendra Bir Bikram Shah Deva and his queen actually did come to Rochester to visit us. I had been nagging the State Department to bring them to the United States and when the invitation was accepted in Katmandu the king requested that there be time on his agenda for a day in Rochester. They toured the city and the Clinic, and then came out to Mayowood for dinner. I couldn't pronounce his name too easily, so I called him Butch, and he called me Chuck.

Seventeen years after I had met him in the jungle of New Guinea, Jack Benny called me on the telephone. It was about three in the morning, because he had forgotten to allow for the time difference, and when he identified himself I said, "Oh, you again."

He wanted to ask me to help make arrangements for his friend Danny Kaye to come to the Clinic for an examination, and I promised to oblige. Danny and I struck up a good friendship, based on our mutual interest in medicine and humor, and his regular visits to the Clinic after that led to many exchanges of anecdotes about our activities. In this way he learned of my abiding distaste for Muff's first husband, the French-speaking Swiss. One afternoon my telephone rang and it was a man with a thick French accent, saying that he was my son-in-law and was in New York, on his way to California. If I would give him directions, he would like to visit me.

I was dismayed, but I politely explained what plane connections he should make. He disagreed, feeling that another route was preferable, and I hung on to my temper and continued to point out the greater directness of the route I always used. He said it didn't sound very sensible to him, and how about if he came by way of Memphis. I was getting madder and madder and finally, as he kept suggesting other wildly implausible routes, I uttered a loud unprintable oath and hung up on him. Alex, our youngest, was nearby watching television and he looked up in amazement. "Daddy," he rebuked me, "if I said that you would whip me."

Later that evening Danny Kaye phoned to inform me that the man with the French accent had been he all along. "I thought I'd better set it straight, so you can sleep tonight," he told me kindly.

Jack Benny often comes to Rochester too. One time when he was here to give a concert with the Rochester Symphony, we had a splendid party for him. I arranged for a violinist friend of mine to stand behind a screen, playing an expert version of "Love in Bloom," while I stood in front going through the motions. Jack is the world's best audience for a joke and I thought he would have to be carried off in a stretcher.

The Mayo Clinic has a tradition of protecting the privacy of its many famous patients to a degree that used to verge on the fanatical. The Chicago *Tribune*, in a magazine supplement article about the Clinic in 1967, commented, "Next to the Hippocratic oath, the most sacred concept at the Mayo's is the patient's privacy. No cameras. No interviews. No nothing."

It arose in part from the usual disinclination shared by all doctors to expose the secrets of the examining room to anyone outside the patient's immediate family, but was exacerbated by the shrill criticism a half century ago that Father and Uncle Will used their personal fame to advertise the Mayo Clinic. They were so sensitive to charges that they were exploiting the celebrated people who came to Rochester for treatment that they attempted to impose a press blackout that was total.

Thus, though Eddie Cantor could be seen every evening playing cards in the lobby of the Kahler Hotel, the Clinic would insist that it didn't know that he was in Rochester. Movie stars discreet enough to stay in their rooms can almost be guaranteed that they can remain incognito, a great comfort to those such as Johnny Carson and Ed Sullivan who prefer to slip in quietly for their regular checkups, and no doubt a great relief for the glamorous movie queen of the twenties who came to the Clinic with a nasty case of gonorrhea.

The Clinic did its level best to maintain secrecy requested by Admiral Richard Evelyn Byrd, the polar explorer, who advised us ahead of his arrival that he wanted no fuss and would like to be registered at the hotel under the name of Smith. We did as he requested, but the admiral arrived in full uniform, despite the niggardly detail that he was retired at the time; he entered the lobby with everything to identify him but the sled dogs.

We had some difficulty in keeping secret the presence of John North, the circus man. In his entourage was a lion cub.

The Clinic was so strict about the prohibition against cameras that it wouldn't relent when *Life* magazine wanted to publish an article about it, and an artist made drawings of the interiors in order to furnish the necessary illustration. Nevertheless, we were deluged with protests from angry doctors, who accused the Clinic of advertising, of soliciting business, of exploitation. In defense, the Clinic published its files of correspondence with publications all over the world seeking to write articles about the Clinic, and our letters of refusal.

Our rigid devotion to total secrecy has eased. In the glare of modern communication, it is no longer feasible to conceal outstanding patients. If asked, we now admit that the person is undergoing examination at the Clinic; naturally, we give no further details. I think we abandoned our former practice of issuing flat denials when Ernest Hemingway was being treated in St. Marys Hospital for depression. He had registered under a Spanish pseudonym, but everyone in town knew that he was in Rochester and there was almost a parade of curious staff in the corridor outside his room, hoping to find his door ajar and catch a glimpse of him. Kenneth McCracken, a distinguished reporter on the Rochester *Post-Bulletin*, enterprisingly confirmed for himself that Hemingway was there, despite our denials, and published a story to that effect. It was pretty well unheard of for a Rochester reporter to clash with a position taken by the Clinic, but McCracken maintained, with some justification, that we were unrealistic in thinking that a giant figure such as Hemingway could be hidden in a busy, modern hospital. The news was bound to leak out anyway, he claimed, and past experience has demonstrated to us that he was right. Victor Cohn, the great science writer now on the Washington *Post*, but then on the Minneapolis *Tribune* and a devoted friend of the Clinic, had been complaining for years that our press relations were appalling.

Many famous people now come to the Clinic under assumed names, and we protect their identity so far as is practicable. Others, like Roy Rogers, try to hide under their real names—in his case, it is Leonard Slye. But most accept the inevitable and go through their two, three or four days of tests with no attempt at concealment. Some of our regulars were guided through their appointments by Dr. Jan Tillisch, a large, witty and warmly kind physician now retired from our medical staff. He claims that Ed Sullivan is one of the most thoughtful and engaging patients we have ever had, and that Leo Durocher is a model of cooperation and consideration. "He's a good guy who finishes first with us," Dr. Tillisch says.

Some celebrities don't enjoy such popularity with the staff, but our major headaches come with royalty, or people with unusual requirements because of their religions. A queen of Egypt immediately springs to mind as an example. She announced that she would not use a toilet that had ever been used by a Christian, which posed quite a problem for the

Clinic. A minister of the Norwegian Lutheran Church found her one, a souvenir brought home by missionaries I think, and she was satisfied.

That same lady established a checking account in a Rochester bank of $300,000, for "incidental expenses." When she departed, she left thousands of it as gifts to Rochester churches, most of it, of course, to the Lutherans. During her stay in Rochester she dressed in astonishingly inexpensive cotton dresses, but behaved in an unmistakably regal manner. One Mayo doctor arrived in her suite for an appointment and was told that the queen was saying her prayers. He waited with growing impatience for a half hour and then declared that he was going to leave. Her servants were aghast. "You can't!" they cried. "It's royalty!" He controlled himself, and left. It was I.

Another Mayo doctor who was caring for the queen was roused from sleep several times one night by summonses from his patient, who was fussing that she was uncomfortable. He complained furiously about it to his wife as he was undressing to get back into bed for the third time, and she said coldly, "You're complaining to the wrong woman." He considered this, got back into his clothes and returned to the amazed queen and crisply told her to stop being a nuisance.

I hold firm to the belief that what passes between a doctor and his patient is privileged information, just as that of the confessional or a lawyer with his client, but increasingly patients in very important positions agree that it is in the public interest to reveal the details of their illnesses. This improved situation is nowhere illustrated more dramatically than in the cases of Presidents of the United States.

When Grover Cleveland underwent surgery in 1893 for the removal of a cancerous tumor in his upper jaw, secrecy was considered so imperative that the operation was carried out on a yacht which steamed slowly up the East River off New York City. A second operation was performed a few days later, also on the yacht. The press was informed that the President had an attack of rheumatism in the legs.

The true account of the first operation didn't reach the public until 1917, and the story of the second operation wasn't published until 1928. The man who had been confidential secretary to the President at the time of the surgery later remarked, "It seems wonderful how many people were thrown off the scent, when so many incidents connected with the affair were calculated to arouse suspicion."

In contrast, President Eisenhower's heart attack in 1955 was made public immediately and bulletins about his condition were issued every few hours. President Lyndon Johnson's abdominal operation was also described in detail, complete with photographs of the neat scar that resulted.

There are several reasons for the remarkable progress demonstrated by these incidents, as I once wrote in *Postgraduate Medicine*. One undoubtedly is the increased sophistication of the public in matters concerned with medicine, and the consequent sharpening of curiosity toward science generally. Then too there is the increased ingenuity and training of newspapermen. The third, and perhaps largest contributing factor, is the acceptance on the part of the medical profession of its own responsibilities in the enlightenment of the public in questions of health and disease.

In my lifetime, newspapermen have gained and earned access to professional meetings of physicians and surgeons, previously barred to them. Interviews are arranged with distinguished speakers, who answer questions on medical and other matters—which would have caused a scandal twenty years ago. Medical writers have their own professional group, the National Association of Science Writers, with very high standards for admission.

Doctors are justified to a great extent in being wary of the press. It is ingrained in us to be skeptical of what enthusiastic colleagues may describe as wonder drugs, or breakthroughs; the press, however, has no tradition of waiting for develop-

32. Alice in 1955

33. Me on a visit to Hospital del Torax, Santiago, Chile

34. General James Doolittle; my son, C. H. Mayo II; and me

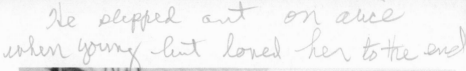
He stepped out on alice
when young but loved her to the end

35. Alice and me (Copyright © Nordisk Pressefoto)

ments over a five-year period and often has plunged ahead to make wild claims and raise cruelly the hopes of the afflicted. The new breed of science reporters now pays close attention to such phrases as "preliminary report" or "now under investigation" or "too early to decide" and gives guarded reports accordingly. It makes for easier relationships, marked by trust on both sides for the first time in medical history.

The last bastion, still almost undented by the new camaraderie which prevails with the press, is the reticence of the individual doctor to provide information that a reporter seeks. It is almost instinctive for a doctor to flinch from such interrogation. He feels it is unfair to his colleagues, possibly misleading to the public, unbecoming to his modesty and encouraging to quacks if he puts himself forward as an expert, even inadvertently. To avoid a suspicion of this, many doctors still behave with reporters in a manner that can only be described as rude.

But even this is giving way. The American Medical Association has issued a proviso to all its members that when it is apparent that illustrations or photographs will contribute to the public's understanding in a medical problem, they may be furnished freely to the press. It is by no means an open-door policy, and has been interpreted on the cautious side, but it illustrates the mood of identical aims which is growing steadily.

For my own part, reporters have never pressed too close in professional matters. Once they learned that my chief surgical concern was the rectum, they showed an eagerness to discuss the United Nations with me instead. It was an arrangement that suited me perfectly.

I haven't escaped the censure and scorn that used to be plentiful when my father and Uncle Will were reported in newspapers, but it has been slight in contrast. Resentment of them reached peaks several times, but one of the most memorable occasions involved an operation they performed jointly in 1909 on John A. Johnson, then the much admired Democratic governor of Minnesota and frequently mentioned as the next candidate for the U.S. presidency. He had just embarked on a bitter exchange with President William Howard Taft over a tariff problem when he was stricken with severe abdominal pains.

Father and Uncle Will performed an operation in St. Marys Hospital which one observer, Dr. Raffaele Bastianelli, personal physician to the king of Italy, described as "one of the most difficult and dangerous operations I have ever seen . . . a brilliant success, but I did not believe that the patient would recover." For days, while the patient's life hung in the balance, newspapermen from all over the country hurried to Rochester. Hungry for news, they hid in the trees around Mayowood, alarming my mother, and wrote about everything that moved. The Mayo brothers intrigued them, and the unique group practice of medicine in Rochester, so they filled in the time waiting for news of the governor by describing the Mayo Clinic. After four agonizing days, Governor Johnson died, but doctors across the nation were inflamed at the publicity the Clinic had received in the meantime and blamed Father and Uncle Will for it. I think they would have been even angrier if Governor Johnson had lived.

From the fifties until my retirement in 1963, my face turned up frequently in newspapers here and there, as I began to accumulate some odds and ends of honorary degrees and that sort of thing. Awards of any kind always make me feel bashful; I attempt to demonstrate aplomb by telling some of the innocent, chuckly jokes that I keep in a file, but it isn't much of a disguise among the knowing.

I was proud to be given the Princeton University Class of 1921 Meritorious Achievement Award in 1954, and the first annual award of the Pittsburgh Surgical Society in 1955, and some other distinguished-achievement awards from *Modern Medicine*, the Masons, *Wisdom* magazine, the Boy Scouts of

America, my fraternity Nu Sigma Nu, the Public Relations Society of America, and a surprising number of other good people.

I also received honorary degrees from St. Lawrence University in Canton, New York; Franklin and Marshall College in Lancaster, Pennsylvania; Drake University in Des Moines, Iowa; Nasson College, Springvale, Maine; Gonzaga University in Spokane, Washington; and Nebraska Wesleyan University in Lincoln, Nebraska. They are a minor extension of the family tradition: in his lifetime Father received twenty-five honorary doctorates and fellowships, and Uncle Will, thirty-one. People who tour the Mayo Clinic are taken down a long, silent corridor lined on either side with their gowns, the colors of the satin facings dull with age behind glass doors, the mortarboards and fur-edged hats at jaunty angles on the dusty hooks.

I tried to avoid accepting any appointment that I suspected was offered solely because of my name, but it isn't easy to tell about these things. I felt safer, knowing that I would serve to the limit of my ability, in agreeing to such duties as being the honorary civilian consultant to the Surgeon General of the U.S. Navy, which hasn't been onerous; a member of the advisory council of the Student American Medical Association and the policy committee of the National Citizens Committee for the World Health Organization, which no one hears much about, but which tries to do the same job of educating Americans on the value of WHO as the A.A.U.N. does for the United Nations.

One of the most treasured distinctions that came my way was an honorary fellowship in the Royal College of Surgeons of England, a group renowned for chariness in dispensing fellowships of any kind. It was given in 1958 and Alice went with me for the dignified and impressive ceremony and afterward we made a swing through Europe, looking at surgery and hospitals as far east as Moscow.

I was impressed by what the Russians were doing, as most

307

visitors are. At that time they were making extensive use of blood collected from cadavers, something unknown on this side of the Atlantic. Close to 70 per cent of blood donations is collected from recently dead people, victims of sudden heart failure, stroke or shock. Accident victims can furnish little blood, since in most circumstances it is lost through wounds. The Russians used living donors only when it was impossible to match blood from the morgue compatibly. They would remove the blood within six hours of death and store it for as long as six weeks, which is twice as long as blood generally is stored in the United States. We are not trained to do this in our country, but I believe it merits close attention. There was a time when it had a ghoulish aspect, but the wide use of such parts as hearts, kidneys and eyes taken from the recently dead and transplanted into the living is breaking down this prejudice.

I noticed in Russia too that the top surgery was matched by concern for the individual patient, which is my idea of how medicine should be practiced.

FOURTEEN

My son Charlie started his fellowship at the Mayo Clinic in 1960 and I cannot conceal that it moved me deeply. It made four generations of Mayo doctors practicing in Rochester, from William Worrall who had owned the first microscope in his part of the country and thundered incessantly that good medicine was the result of hard work and constant study; to my charming, dedicated father Charles Horace and his severe, dedicated brother William James, who helped found one of the world's leading medical centers and gave it away, free of charge; and myself, Charles William, about whom I can speak with less detachment: I know that my life has been honest and that I always gave my best. My son, Charles Horace II, seemed to me a type like my brother Joe, instinctively a great doctor, and relaxed and amused in the face of pomposity or confusion. I kept an eye on him, without being too obvious about it, and rejoiced that he was there.

When it came time, I chose him to be my first assistant and I can say truthfully that I would have picked him if he hadn't been my son. I think he is one of the best surgeons I ever trained, and he has that other quality you can't be without as a doctor, which is concern for the individual patient. He could feel fear or pain in another person and react to it with sympathy. His presence seemed to cheer people up— he always seemed to be in a good mood, but you felt his toughness.

One day I found one of my grandfather's prescriptions, which I always had been told went heavy on the brandy, and I showed it to Charlie. He was intrigued and decided to have it made up. I think it took him about three weeks to get all the ingredients but when finally it was prepared we both had a sip. We agreed that it tasted like a Manhattan. They really knew how to make a man feel better in Grandfather's day.

Muff was getting her divorce in Mexico about that time, and met a Mexican engineer, Hugo Torres, whom I liked very much. Hugo is a laughing man and we got along fine from our first meeting. Alice and I were delighted when Muff and he decided to marry. Ned, meanwhile, was having a difficult time getting settled. He had gone from learning about documentary films in Mexico to California, where he thought he would study film technique in Hollywood, but he hated the film colony that he met there. He telephoned home one night and said he had decided to study medicine. He had just married an English nurse at the Clinic, a steady, loyal and perceptive girl named Rita; she worked while he attended university in Minnesota.

They came to Mayowood one evening and Ned made the despairing confession that he didn't want to be a doctor either, so he switched to law—this also failed to interest him. What appealed to him? we asked. Well, he would like to run the farm and he and Rita had thought of going into the antique business. We told him to give it a try, and it turned out to be the answer. He's raising Arab horses and a good dairy herd and corn, and three small children, and the antique business that he and Rita established tastefully in the former greenhouse is known to collectors across the country. Rita and Ned make buying trips to Europe twice a year and I realized the dimension of their nerve and discernment when they returned from England one autumn with two small, simple leather armchairs, and sold them at $1600 each. Lately they have been dealing with tiny, exquisite paintings, about which they are impressively knowledgeable. Best of all, Ned is doing something he wholeheartedly enjoys, which is the important thing.

Joe also wandered a bit. He left the Topeka zoo to become curator of the zoo in Duluth, but longed to be in research. He married again and they were getting established when he made up his mind to leave the zoo. He once had some bad luck on an animal research project, when he got a grant and went to Nepal to hunt miniature wild pigs. The pig anatomically is the closest animal to man, very useful to scientists. Unfortunately all the pigs died on the return trip, which discouraged Joe for a time. Eventually he joined the animal research branch of the Veterans Administration in Minneapolis, where he is very well pleased. Unhappily, his second marriage also ended in divorce.

Maria, the next child, had been a brilliant student at Sarah Lawrence when she married a young doctor at the Clinic,

Donald A. Sones. She later commented wryly that there must be a jinx about weddings that take place at Mayowood. Hers, like a few others we held in the Big House, ended sadly. The Soneses had two small children when Maria returned to a house on the farm and obtained a separation.

The youngest, Alex, is a turbulent young man. In his early teens, he talked of running away with a circus. He was indifferent to school and stayed in Rochester's public school system until he was ready for the University of Minnesota, which didn't appeal much, so he transferred to Parsons College in Iowa. One day he joined the Navy, without telling us about it, and served the next four years, some of it in Vietnam. He tried the University of Minnesota when he got his discharge, but it didn't take. He's newly married and still finding his way; I sympathize with him.

As I said, every family has to go through a lot of things. If you have a big enough family, you'll get every problem there is.

All our children, it will be noted, are determined to march to their own drum. Not one of the six cares about conforming, or being accepted by the kind of people who value appearances. Muff's life story is out of the Perils of Pauline, Charlie is prone to such original notions as going out to ski at night in the privacy of his own grounds, Ned turns up in downtown Rochester in rumpled riding clothes, with a candelabra under one arm and a small, solemn son by the hand, Joe amiably ricochets about the country, Maria rides around the farm like a Cossack and Alex for a while resembled a hippie. In addition, the girls share my mother's fascination for the occult. They claim to have made contact with my brother Joe, whom they never knew, and receive from this alleged spirit comments in the blunt earthy language that Joe would have used.

Like my father, who served eight years on the Rochester Board of Education and spearheaded a school building campaign—he and Uncle Will even paid the salaries of a few good teachers for a while—I have a lifelong interest in education. The trend has been reversed in recent years, ever since the Russians beat us into space, but Americans still tend to skimp on education costs in favor of expenditures that matter a ton less. The eccentric path traveled by my children in and out of the halls of learning only increased my conviction that there is something basically at fault in our schools.

I put my argument in a *Bulletin of the Medical Library Association* in 1959, pointing out that the United States was then spending only 1 per cent of its gross national income on universities and colleges. We have only 6 per cent of the world's land and 7 per cent of the world's population, and yet we publish 27 per cent of the world's newspapers, own 31 per cent of the world's radios and television sets, produce 40 per cent of all electric power, use 58 per cent of the world's telephones and drive 76 per cent of the world's automobiles.

If we are to keep leadership in a world which so greatly outnumbers us, I insist that we must make it possible for all able students to attend universities and colleges, which means government scholarships. In Britain, 74 per cent of full-time students are on government scholarships. But only 14 per cent go to college. I think it is a scandalous waste that one-quarter of all our high-school graduates are capable of handling a college education, but only half of these go on to post-secondary school education, largely for economic reasons.

Also, I can't approve of stuffing young people full of math, physics, chemistry and engineering without teaching them a good deal about literature as well, and psychology and philosophy. The heart of the future lies in the hearts of people, and we need to develop compassion and understanding if we are to matter to ourselves or anyone else.

I often quote Woodrow Wilson's inaugural address at Princeton in 1902, when he said: "The college should seek to make the man whom it receives something more than an excellent servant of a trade or a skilled practitioner of a profession. It should give him elasticity of faculty and a breadth of vision, so that he will have a surplus of mind to expend, not upon his profession only, but on the broader interests which lie about him."

The move toward individualized education interested me then, though it was but a gleam in the eye of progressive educators at that time. I thought the mass type of education flattened initiative and curiosity, which I regard as a fatal flaw in the learning process. Without the spark of motivation, as I wrote then, "No one can expect success, nor should success be expected of him." I know in my own life, motivation has been the fuel.

Once I was giving a speech at some graduation ceremony, and making some of these points, when I became aware that what I was reading was something I had just finished saying. I stared at the typewritten words on the cards that I use in making speeches and discovered that my secretary inadvertently had typed the same sentence twice. I'm rather proud of my ingenuity: I finished to the end of the sentence, looked up and said calmly, "That was such an important point that I felt it deserved to be made twice."

My surgical career was drawing to a close and I was much encouraged by the acceptance that was growing for the sphincter-preserving operation that I had helped to pioneer. Young surgeons in particular tended to prefer it to a colostomy when the cancer was located in the controversial part of the rectum, and even older doctors no longer reacted coolly when I presented papers dealing with my statistics at various medical meetings and conventions.

By the summer of 1960, my figures had an unusual depth of detail, thanks to my own anxiety to have thorough records and the help of the Clinic's Section of Biometry and Medical Statistics. I had done the one-stage low anterior resection on 362 patients living in the United States at that time and followed up 99.4 per cent of them. In 58 cases, the operation was hopeless because the cancer had spread; but in the remaining cases, the five-year survival rate was a respectable 61.3 per cent. In addition I could report that the average hospital stay was 15.3 days, a remarkably brief time for such major surgery, and that 82.2 per cent of patients returned to normal bowel habits—13.6 per cent suffered from some degree of constipation and a statistically near-invisible proportion had diarrhea. The ten-year survival rate was 52.6 per cent, which wasn't too discouraging since most of my patients were close to sixty at the time of the operation and one was ninety-two.

I put in more than thirty years as a surgeon, refining a few techniques here and there, designing some instruments, pressing for simplicity, performing thousands of operations —but the outstanding achievements of my career were the two abdominal operations that I advanced as being better than what was being done, and stuck with until my judgment was vindicated. One was the low anterior resection to save the sphincter and the other was the combined abdominoperineal section in one operation instead of the previous two. Both of these represented hard-made decision and a measure of nerve, because the opposition to both was fierce, but both turned out to be the right things to do. The two have something in common: they reflect my aversion to waste, my stubbornness when I believe in what I am doing, and my disinclination to believe that traditional techniques are immutable.

Although my medical papers frequently described the progress of these two techniques and quite often dealt with diverticulosis, I had occasion from time to time to report on medical oddities that came my way. One of these was a hair cyst, a rarity first reported in 1833 in England by a Herbert Mayo, who possibly was a distant relative. These hair cysts are found most often in the navel, but also in the horizontal fold of the buttocks, or the clitoris, or even the sole of the foot. Barbers sometimes get them between their fingers, from hair that penetrates the skin and then grows inward in a ball.

The single hair cyst in my practice appeared in a twenty-one-year-old man who came to the Clinic complaining that his duodenal ulcer had been acting up. He also said that he had a sore navel, which for two months had been discharging pus and blood. We tried antibiotics and hot packs for three days with no effect, so I decided to remove the lesion. When I cut into it, I found what seemed to be a pilonidal sinus, with free hairs growing in it. There was no follicle, just hair lying there growing.

A number of my medical papers presented statistics that the Mayo Clinic is particularly well advantaged to collect because of the huge number of patients we serve and the respect we always have shown for keeping records. In May of 1961, I assembled 7132 cases of cancer of the colon or rectum in order to emphasize where the carcinoma most frequently locates. The incidence in the rectum proved to be 41 per cent, even though the rectum is a small part of the large intestine; in the rectosigmoid, which also is short, the incidence was 18 per cent; the sigmoid accounted for another 18 per cent—illustrating that 77 per cent of colon cancer is within inches of the anus. The cecum, ascending colon, transverse colon and descending colon, long as they are, account for only 23 per cent of cancerous tumors.

We were beginning to gather some helpful statistics about diverticulitis which demonstrated that the ailment is a grave threat to a considerable proportion of adults. From 3 to 10 per cent of all Mayo Clinic patients have diverticulosis in their colons, we estimate: those patients who underwent colonic roentgenograms had diverticulosis pouches in their colons in 7 per cent of cases. We continued to find reassuring evidence that the condition doesn't lead to cancer, except rarely; and that it is part of the degenerative processes, turning up commonly in people more than fifty and sixty years of age and almost never in thirty-year-olds.

Our surgical meetings at the Clinic sometimes were presented with especially difficult cases and we were asked to outline how we would handle them. One such, which demonstrates the maze of alternatives that surgeons face, concerned a sixty-year-old man with a gastrojejunocolic fistula of six weeks' duration, an opening between his small and large intestine near his stomach. Some eight years before, the man had a gastroenterostomy without resection, creating a bypass between his stomach and intestine. When he presented himself for treatment he was seriously sick, with a weak heart and a loss of twenty-three pounds.

One possibility was to resect about two-thirds of his stomach, taking it out, perform a posterior or anterior gastroenterostomy at the same time, making a new bypass, and then sewing up the hole in the transverse colon. Some surgeons also would cut out the right and left vagus nerves that flank the stomach and stimulate gastric juices, and might also perform a colostomy in the transverse colon nearby, allowing for the discharge of feces outside the abdomen.

Or others might take down the gastroenteric anastomosis, close the stomach and the colon, make a new gastroenterostomy and cut the vagus nerves—which means cleaning out the untidyness and everything near it and making a new bypass.

I would choose to do none of these. I would eliminate the fistula by pulling the colon away from the jejunum and disconnecting the old bypass, removing it. If I found that the gastric juices in the stomach were high, it would be necessary to remove part of the stomach, but if the gastric juices were not high I would put in a new bypass, performing a gastrojejunostomy, and cut the vagus nerves. Then I would freshen the edges of the colon and close the hole. I would not perform the colostomy, but would dilate the anus manually after closing the abdomen, without drainage.

316

My response to this problem reflects my avowed purpose to do always the operation which is the simplest and the least radical, consistent with the patient's safety. Really radical operations, in some cases, approach butchery. I don't remember the circumstances, and maybe they justified the procedure, but I was disturbed when I heard of some surgeons in California who successfully cut a fellow in half, just below his navel. A colleague of mine, George Hallenbeck, remarked, "I wonder which part they threw away?" and I concur with his implicit sentiment.

My career spanned a time when abdominal surgery had brought itself close to perfection, and the Clinic's graphs tracing mortality had the cheering downward slant of ski jumps. The procedures usually were not new: the great surgeons who were liberated by the discovery of ether had attempted almost everything done today during surgery's renaissance of the late nineteenth and early twentieth centuries, but they had a frightfully high mortality because of shock, infection and poor comprehension of the importance of maintaining fluid balance throughout the operation.

I observed in a 1959 edition of the *American Journal of Digestive Diseases* that the reasons for the great strides made in the previous quarter century were safe blood transfusions, antibiotics, understanding of fluid and electrolyte balance and better anesthesia. We now were in a protected position to revive the daring, brilliant surgery techniques of men like my grandfather, father and uncle, with remarkable results.

These new and sophisticated aids had also benefited patients with bowel obstructions, who frequently used to suffer agony and death. I investigated for a long time by putting a tube inside the intestines to decompress the obstruction before the operation, making surgery safer. It was a fascinating procedure, trying to snake a tube through the small intestines, where about 80 per cent of safety pins, gallstones and suchlike lodge. We threaded a tube, generously lubricated with a creamy local analgesic at the tip, into the patient's nose for a distance of about four inches. Then the patient would sip water while the tube worked gently into the esophagus and he continued to sip water until the tube entered the stomach.

We then pumped up some of the gastric content of the stomach to make certain that the tube had arrived at its destination, after which we forced 50 cc. of air into the tube to distend a balloon we had secured at the tip. By pulling on the tube, the balloon wedged itself at the cardia of the stomach. We put a marker on the tube at the nostril, let the air out of the balloon and replaced it with 3 cc. of mercury, for weight. Then we elevated the head of the bed and commenced to push the tube into the patient at the rate of an inch every half hour, assisted by the patient's swallowing movements.

In three or four hours, the tube reached the duodenum, which was checked by spotting the mercury on a scout film. If it wasn't there, we started over from the cardia again, helped by the marker when it appeared at the patient's nostril. If it was in the duodenum, we put a small amount of air or water into the balloon and began to move faster, at the rate of two inches an hour. It was necessary to have continuous suction of the mercury and irrigation of the tube with water, and we took a scout film every day to trace the progress of the tube. A few times the tube appeared in the rectum, in which case we cut it off at the nose and gently pulled it through.

It was a tricky thing to do: the patient had to be checked constantly to make sure the suction and intravenous needle were operating properly and the tube wasn't coiling in the throat or stomach. But it was worth it because it kept the intestine open around the blockage and meant there was less damage being done.

I found I was winding up my medical career, but keeping busy in my role as a citizen. I did some varied projects, like heading the 1959 Easter Seal Sale for crippled children and adults in Minnesota, and serving on the National Council of Boy Scouts of America in 1960, and being one of the committee members of the Eleanor Roosevelt Foundation, which President John F. Kennedy established in 1962. Eighteen of us were named to that committee, and we were invited to the White House for the signing of the bill that launched the Foundation. President Kennedy used eighteen pens to make his signature, so we could each have one; I've always thought that was a strange ritual, but some people like it.

President Kennedy was an attractive man, though not my favorite President. You could sense his ambition, but he was likable and friendly to talk with. I knew President Lyndon Johnson better, first when he was a senator and had a kidney stone operation at the Clinic and later when I used to call on him as minority leader. He named me to his President's Commission on Heart Disease, Cancer and Stroke just after I retired, and invited all the members to attend a cocktail party at the White House.

I was staying at the Hay Adams across the park from the White House so I walked over, forgetting my identification. I was stopped at the gate and stood there, feeling a fool and fumbling through my pockets for the invitation, when Walter Reuther, the labor man, came along and asked what was the matter. I knew he was on the same Commission, so I asked if he could help get me past the guards. He managed it without difficulty, which amused us both—we are intractable opponents on the subject of Medicare, though we have always been polite enough to keep our differences on the level of social jokes. I like Reuther; no man could get where he is, and stay there, without having a lot of ability.

That reception at the White House was a congenial one. A Marine band kept playing softly and there was plenty of Scotch and canapés and Mrs. Johnson kept circulating most ingratiatingly. When I thought it time for me to leave, she was surrounded by a group of women so I just caught her eye and waved my hand. She rushed out and kissed me, which is the way women should behave; I figured she was grateful for the excuse to get away from the encirclement. I bid her good-bye, telling her that I had had enough to drink and therefore was ready to go home.

The Eleanor Roosevelt Foundation hasn't been heard much of, but it is supposed to forward human rights causes and it established a library and helps to support a school somewhere.

Dwight Eisenhower was the greatest President of the five I knew, but I have a fondness for Harry Truman as well. He took no pains to control his temper, if he was interrupted unjustifiably when he was developing a train of thought, and his language on such occasions was pungently male. I enjoyed him, and I think he is a better man than most Americans give him credit for being.

During the summer of 1962, I received word that I had been given one of the two Distinguished Visitor Awards to Australia, offered under the Fulbright Educational Exchange Program. I was to spend eight weeks in Australia and New Zealand, delivering medical papers in the major centers, while an outstanding Australian would be doing the same in the United States. The terms included round-trip transportation and a per diem allowance for me; I took Alice along and got a small extra per diem for her, since she operated full-time as social secretary and Keeper of the Wardrobe.

The papers I chose to give were on my low anterior resection, ulcerative colitis, diverticulosis and diverticulitis, changing concepts in medical research, and the Mayo Clinic relationship with the University of Minnesota. I also took slides and films of operations and some of the Mayo Clinic facilities.

One of the pleasurable hazards of the trip was that Australia is crammed to the coasts with ex-Mayo Clinic doctors, who felt my presence urgently required Mayo alumni reunions; I attended about a dozen of those, with the attendant digestive distress that might be imagined. At one point during the tour I not only was lecturing on diverticulitis but was nursing an exemplary case of it in my personal interior.

In keeping with her duties as official secretary, Alice kept a rough diary of our frenetic activities. I was spending the mornings visiting hospitals, then we would both have luncheon appointments—me with a medical group and Alice with their wives—and then organized sight-seeing or television, radio or press interviews until cocktail time, banquet time, speeches time, reception time and, of course, nightcap time. An evening to ourselves became an event to celebrate, by dining wanly alone and getting to bed as early as possible.

The circuit began in Auckland, New Zealand, with dinner parties, luncheon parties, trips to the races, museums, stud farms and some caves; then to Hamilton, where we stayed in the same rooms that had been occupied nine years before by Queen Elizabeth and her husband, who had left a picture of their children on the coffee table as a parting gift. I have a blurred recollection of visiting steam geysers and boiling mud pools, an experimental farm, a man-planted forest of sixty-foot pines and taking some time for trout fishing. Alice noted with horror that New Zealand doctors are so poorly paid that their homes are very modest and they have no help; wives of titled surgeons there scrub their own floors.

Alice, who was always punctilious about the social amenities such as thank-you notes for hospitality and flowers, was complaining that she would never catch it all up even before we arrived in Australia. We started in Sydney, where a charming apartment overlooking the harbor had been arranged for us, with a housekeeper to care for us and a chauffeur-driven Rolls Royce at our disposal, a donation from Ray Purves, a good friend. Doctors who had served with me in New Guinea held a reception for us but, to my great dismay, I could recognize only one of them. Twenty years puts its mark on a man—lots of marks, in fact.

Alice was captivated by the tame gorillas at the Sydney zoo and the duck-billed platypus. Later in Canberra we saw hundreds of kangaroos, which established officially that we were in Australia. We watched Parliament in session in Canberra, a most interesting and formal occasion full of eighteenth-century significance. The highlight of our visit to Adelaide was meeting with Sir Herbert Mayo, a judge and leading citizen there. We assume that we are related, though it is difficult to trace; I freely accepted him because of his title.

Nineteen Mayos sat down to a family dinner that Sir Herbert arranged, with the table decorated in gold and black, which we regard as the Mayo colors, and many toasts to ourselves, our forefathers, our children, our countries, and future happiness. Alice, the articulate member of my household, tried to express our gratitude and became so overcome with emotion that she was in tears before she finished.

We had another memorable meal at a sheep station, where Mr. and Mrs. Ronald Angus served us such unusual delicacies as kangaroo tail soup and pigeon in wine sauce, washed down with a burgundy from their own winery. The Lord Mayor gave us a reception at the Town Hall and then we moved on to Melbourne, and to Shepparton where there were a hundred guests at a barbecue one evening. I was touring a hospital there, and found that they take inspections seriously. The nurses in identical red coats lined up at parade attention and I was obliged to walk along the serious rows of them like a visiting monarch.

We awakened one morning to the news of the crisis over the missile sites that had been discovered in Cuba, with the Soviet Union and the United States eyeball to eyeball and world-wide nuclear destruction hanging on the outcome. I continued wretchedly with the papers I was to give that day and the people I was to meet and found subdued spirits everywhere. We were to attend a cocktail party and dinner that night at the residence of the U.S. Consul General, Norman L. Smith. The event went off as scheduled, but we were a worried lot of guests.

The next day in Melbourne I was conferred as an honorary member of the Royal Australian College of Surgeons, a humbling honor, and the investment was an impressive ceremony. I was given a black gown with gold satin facings. We could not avoid discussing the world situation: Cuba was almost matched by tension in Berlin, a bad situation on the Indochinese border near Nepal and some minor struggle in Vietnam that probably wouldn't last much longer; we moved everywhere with a sense of dread that seemed to be universal.

The World Health Organization people planned a big reception for us on October 23, with 150 guests. I was surprised by a request for a speech and made my way to the microphone wondering what I would say. It came out surprisingly easily: I talked of President Kennedy's difficult decision and the breath-holding that was going on all over the world, and ended by proposing a toast to the President of the United States. The applause went on and on, making my eyes sting.

The Kennedy gamble to confront the Soviet Union over Cuba won, and we went on to Brisbane in an easier frame of mind. The Australian part of the Fulbright tour ended then, but I wanted another look at the New Guinea rain forest where I had spent the war, so Alice and I arranged for a side trip. The district commissioner, Tom Ellis, met us at Mount Hagen and conducted us to a native council meeting, where he introduced me solemnly as Great White Doctor Number One from America. He indicated Alice and added, "and his wife."

There were about fifty native leaders seated at a long table. They had just secured relief from a government restriction prohibiting them from drinking alcohol and Ellis endeavored to explain that they would have to wait one more day before they could legally drink. They accepted that, and one very elderly leader then suggested that whatever spirits were available should be rationed only to old men, and kept from the young. Ellis handled this smoothly, a striking figure in an open-necked white shirt, black trousers, a satin cummerbund and black flying boots.

The next day hundreds of natives painted their bodies and wore ceremonial clothes in order to dance for Great White Doctor Number One. The sun beat down on us mercilessly as they danced hour after hour, to chants and drums. When it ended and we were preparing to leave, Ellis gave me as a souvenir a small ax used to cut through jungle. It was unexpected, but I rose ceremoniously to the occasion and presented him with a shirt and my umbrella.

We drove to Finschaffen in a Land Rover and I found the area where the hospital buildings had stood. There were only remnants left, a few cement slabs where floors had been. A small native school was operating nearby and I met a man there who said he remembered the hospital and was pleased to see me. From him I learned for the first time that the river where we used to swim so gratefully was crocodile-infested. Only a week before, a native had been attacked. No one ever told the United States Army about it, which was probably an oversight.

The next day we drove to Nadzab and found that the kunai grass and the jungle had reclaimed what had been our base. I found the place where my quarters had been and stood there awhile, feeling desolate among the ghosts.

Alice and I had noticed that New Guinea had made enterprising use of the refuse left behind by the long war fought there. We noted Australian naval shells serving as flower vases and Japanese helmets as flower pots. They told us that a U.S. fighter plane was a fairway hazard on a golf course near Ainantu, that sawmills were using light tanks to haul logs, and that some communities used Japanese and United States bomb cases for street markers. A bomb crater in the Solomons was filled with water and converted to a swimming pool, with kids diving from a half-sunken Japanese troop carrier in the middle of it. The fighter bomber strip in Nadzab was then a go-cart racetrack.

We stopped at Port Moresby on the way home and had tea on an island occupied only by patients with tuberculosis and leprosy. The nurses and doctors who showed us around will share the short life span of their patients. We were amazed at the normalcy of the community; women with active cases of leprosy were still bearing children. We were offered cakes and sandwiches with our tea, but our appetites were poor.

We got back to Rochester in mid-November, to the news that Alex had joined the Navy. Alice always thought it was because he was lonely, and she mourned for her youngest. His letters home were comical and confident, so she soon relaxed; we put it down to another Mayo with a questing spirit, like Grandfather.

I returned to my surgery, heavy with the awareness that this would be my final year. My father and Uncle Will had decided that Mayo staff doctors should be retired at sixty-five, and the rule has been observed ever since. It is unfair to some who are capable, steady men well into their seventies, able to give good service, but it is a reasonable rule and I knew I could not ask to be an exception.

My son Charlie was my first assistant, which I found a good and easy association. I liked working across the table from him and it gave me a sense of the continuity of Mayos at the Clinic: I would be retiring just as he came on the staff. He was quick to learn and retentive of everything he observed and I was pleased to note that he was unflappable in all circumstances, which is essential for a surgeon. When what we were doing was routine, I would tell him about other similar operations that I had done or some of the funny things that have happened in operating rooms. I related the story about the patient who had a hernia operation under a local anesthetic, which enabled me to chat with him during the process. When it was finished, I said, "Oops, sorry, but I'm afraid I'll have to open you up again. I think I left my scissors in there." The patient thought that was hilarious even at the time, and was still laughing about it twenty years later.

The retirement procedure at the Clinic is that you go out at the end of the quarter year which contains your sixty-fifth birthday—everyone does, doctors, stenographers, janitors, the lot. Since I was born on July 28, it meant that my final day as an active surgeon would be September 30. As the time grew closer, I began to feel depressed about it but I kept my feelings concealed. They were talking of a big farewell fuss, but I wouldn't hear of it. They always seem to present people with watches at a time in their lives when they don't need one.

To avoid the scene I dreaded, I decided that I would not appear on my final day as a surgeon. On the second last day, I pulled off my gloves and said quietly that I was finished. I had coffee with the others of my surgical teams and a few friends, went to my office and worked my usual stint and then told them that I wouldn't be back. The secretaries had coffee with me and then it was over. I walked out of the Mayo Clinic for the last time as an active doctor, one day before I had to.

I wrote an editorial in *Postgraduate Medicine* a few months later, putting down my experiences as a newly retired man. "It is difficult to bring yourself to the realization that after all the years that have unrolled, the next day, when you wake up, you will no longer be an active member of the staff of the hospital, institution or group of colleagues you have known intimately for so many years. On the morrow, when you do awaken at the usual hour because you have trained yourself to do so for most of your life, you rub your eyes in the sudden realization that: 'I don't have to get up and meet any deadline.' Therefore you lie back and think.

"All my medical life there never seemed to be enough time

326

to do the things I wished to do in addition to what I was doing. Even when I went on vacation, by the time it got to the point where I could sleep beyond the time I usually arose at home—in other words to persuade the physiologic time regulator to become unwound—it was time to get back home and start getting wound up again. It was nauseating to think of the correspondence that was accumulating on my desk as each day away from home passed. . . ."

I explained that I had assumed innocently that my retirement would provide me with time to read books that had nothing to do with medicine or surgery, to come and go as I pleased, accepting and rejecting invitations to speak without the nagging of a sense of responsibility and obligation, traveling with Alice to exotic places without ever going near the clinics and hospitals there.

It was an iridescent dream with a short life. I hadn't realized how deeply ingrained in me were the habits of work and commitment, a preference like my father's to "wear out rather than rust out," as George Bernard Shaw put it. I also had overlooked that I had accepted countless invitations to speak, stretching for months into the distance. I always suffer from the delusion that an arrangement to appear somewhere in six months' time is not binding, since the day will never come. As the time approaches, I am horrified that I ever agreed to such madness. If I had been born a girl, I would have been married at a very young age because I never learned to say "No."

In the editorial, I wrote, "If the pace of AR (after retirement) continues at its current rate, it will not mean a cessation of activity for me, but rather, I might even say, an augmentation of my sphere of interest and an increase in my responsibilities. Many of them will be endeavors for which, previously, I never could find adequate time. I do not regret any of the many ventures which claimed my interest and energies BR (before retirement) and I certainly do not look with gloom on the different and spreading vista before me. Quite to the contrary: the prospect is provocative because so much of it promises new adventures and widespread experiences.

"Included is my association as Editor of *Postgraduate Medicine*; I am also Chairman of the Board of Regents of the University of Minnesota. I shall continue to serve as trustee of Carleton College, and my duties with Mutual of Omaha in the medical aspects of insurance have broadened. There is much to be done after one reaches the age of sixty-five years that can be vital and productive. Everything is looking up.

"What my father and uncle, as surgeons, used to say is right. 'We want to retire before surgeons who observe our work say or think we should.'"

Staunch words, with a measure of truth; but in my heart I know that everything has been downgrade for me since I retired as a surgeon. I have been busy, and hold important posts, but they don't compare.

I retired from the Board of Governors of the Clinic at the same time as I left the staff. My tenure was supposed to be lifelong, but I didn't think I should be hanging around when I was no longer on the active staff. I tendered my resignation and told the Board that I didn't want anyone to cry about it, and no one did.

They offered me office space in the Clinic, apart from the secretarial pool and suite of offices kept for staff doctors who have gone over to an emeritus status. I accepted gratefully, especially as the office given me was my father's. Visitors shown through the Plummer Building are taken to the third floor and shown past Uncle Will's office, roped off with red velvet across the doorway, and an office opposite it is said to be Father's, containing his desk and chair and books, with his spectacles lying on an opened book. Then they proceed into the old Board Room, the walls there jammed with pictures of the Mayos, early Mayo buildings, scrolls and honors, and that part of the tour is over.

328

In fact, Father's office was located beyond the Board Room, a tiny corner room with high casement windows. I have hung the walls with my memorabilia, some of it irreverent, and I have no idea what the Clinic plans for it when I no longer require it. I work there on my correspondence with my present secretary, Zita Glennon. Miss Glennon was assigned to me by the Clinic after my retirement, a unique favor since all other emeritus doctors share three secretaries in the Emeritus Room. I have been profoundly grateful ever since. She helps to route my friends through the maze of Clinic appointments, juggles all my enterprises with elan and good humor and keeps track of the ebb and flow of my money. When Alice was ill we agreed that Zita Glennon should have power of attorney and it was she who steered us all through the numb time of the funeral, with that combination of compassion and common sense that are priceless in a tragedy. She's even become a focus for my large and untidy family and keeps an eye on their interests too.

Next to us Clark Nelson, the Clinic's archivist, collects and sorts a century of history related to the Mayo Clinic and my family. He even squirrels away everything he can find in my handwriting, which gives me a strange feeling. You wonder what generations to come are going to make of notes to the milkman or memos to remind myself to visit someone in the hospital.

I sit behind my desk, which almost fills the tiny office my father modestly allotted himself, and work on *Postgraduate Medicine*, or write columns for the insurance company's journal, or handle the problems of the University of Minnesota's Board of Regents. I've grown accustomed to the bric-a-brac in my quarters, which always fascinates newcomers: the picture of the Plummer Building, taken just after it was built, and the one of my old schoolhouse, and some amateur snaps taken of my father in surgery by visiting doctors, and my honorable discharge from the Army.

I look up at my diploma from the University of Pennsylvania School of Medicine and sometimes wonder how I ever managed to get it. Next to it is a little honorary thing I got from Chile; I don't know why they gave it, but maybe they had a warm spot in their hearts for me. And one from Cuba in 1931, which was when Alice and I took that trip in the Caribbean. Next to it is a Physician's Prayer, which I like:

"Dear Lord, Thou Great Physician, I kneel before Thee, Since every good and perfect gift must come from Thee, I pray: Give skill to my hand, clear vision to my mind, Kindness and Sympathy to my heart. Give me singleness of Purpose, Strength to lift at least a part of the burden of my suffering fellow men, and a True Realization of the privilege that is mine. Take from my heart all Guile and Worldliness, that with the simple faith of a child I may rely on Thee. Amen."

I sometimes go to church and I repeat the prayers that people in my church always say, but I don't believe much of what I am saying. But the Physician's Prayer touches me, and I keep it handy.

There's something from the king of Italy near the Physician's Prayer, signed by Vittorio Emanuele III, but I don't know why he gave it to me. Beside it is the certificate from Robert Packer Hospital in Sayre, attesting that I was resident house surgeon there for a year. I still marvel that I finished there. And my American Board of Surgery certification, something that says I'm an honorary fellow of the Philadelphia Proctologic Society, and my M.S. from the University of Minnesota, and then one of Grandfather's prescriptions, signed "W. W. Mayo" and giving his address as the "Office over Poole's Drug Store."

They aren't in any order. Next is a photograph of my mother with my older sister and me leaning against her; I am the one sucking the thumb, wearing ruffles. Then Jack Dempsey posed with my father, and Sir Herbert Mayo of Adelaide, and something that says I'm an Honorary Fellow of the International College of Dentists, and some vintage

330

pictures of the Mayo Board Room, and a Rochester street, and St. Marys Hospital in its early days.

The confronting wall, as you come into my office, has an oil painting of my father's face. His expression is quiet, reflective and proud, and it draws attention despite the clutter all around it. Some of the pictures I treasure are valuable historically, like the one of a covered wagon on Broadway Street in Rochester in 1864. I also have photographs of most of the buildings razed to make way for the Clinic, and the Episcopal Church the family attends, and a haughty picture of my grandfather, looking something like a stagecoach robber. And one of my grandmother, holding an infant Uncle Will on her ample lap, and the house that Grandfather built just outside of town. And Father's first car, bought in 1904, and more family pictures, among them a photograph, taken at Christmas one year, of Alice and me and the eight growing children grouped around our grand piano, grinning.

And more pictures of our boats, the *Oronoco*, the *Minnesota* and the lovely *North Star*. And a study of Mother and Father, their heads touching and a soft, romantic look on their faces. And some aerial pictures of Nadzab and Finschaffen, and my brother Joe's M.D. from Iowa and my Princeton diploma, and a few valued mottoes, like "The hurrier I go the behinder I get" and "Protest the rising tide of conformity."

Then there is something which declares that I am Chief Admiral of the Great Navy of the State of Nebraska, and another which documents my membership in the Dunrovin Institute of Piscatorial Arts and Sciences, and one which makes me a Commodore of the Oklahoma Navy. Those organizations haven't had too much impact on world history, but they have had plenty on me.

There are pictures of friends, like Johnny Popovic from Yugoslavia, and J. Edgar Hoover and Dr. Morris Fishbein. President Dwight Eisenhower inscribed his picture, "To Charles W. Mayo, with admiration and warm regards from his friend," and General Jimmy Doolittle wrote on his, "To Charles W. Mayo, with whom it was a distinct pleasure to collaborate and 'operate.'" President Harry Truman wrote, "Kindest regards and best wishes to Dr. Charles W. Mayo, a great doctor," and Hubert Humphrey put "To Chuck and Alice" on his picture and President Lyndon Johnson signed his "With affection and appreciation." He also sent me a little note I value: "Dear Doctor Mayo: Any counsel and advice you give me is always respectfully and thoughtfully considered. Lady Bird and I send you our warm best wishes."

There's a small bookcase in my office where I keep some of the medical books my friends write and the five bound volumes of my own papers. I have a small bust of John Kennedy on top of it, presented me by the International League of Garment Workers Union in 1965, and an ash tray with "PRINCETON '21" on it, and a beer stein given me by the University of Minnesota in 1964, and a knife and fork that I bought in India, and a surgical tool of Grandfather's, and the American Legion Distinguished Service Medal, and a chunk of taconite.

The taconite tells a story. It is a hard rock formation plentiful in Minnesota which was found, after hundreds of millions had been spent on research, to be capable of producing high-grade iron ore. It is costly, because it takes three tons of rock to get one ton of iron ore, but the state began to run out of mines that could produce the ore cheaply and wanted to attract outside investors to establish taconite mines and factories. To do this, tax relief would have to be offered and this would require an amendment to the state constitution, backed by two-thirds of the voters.

The state governor then, Karl Rolvaag, and attorney general, Walter Mondale, came to see me in Rochester asking that I head up a citizens committee to get support for the amendment. I could see its worth, since mining is a big industry in my state and the depletion of the existing mines threatened the jobs of thousands of people, so I agreed. We worked for about a year before the referendum vote was taken, and it was backed by 84 per cent of the voters. Alice and I were in Australia at the time, but we arranged for proxy votes before we left. Taconite has been great for Minnesota ever since, bringing in millions of dollars.

The taconite sample therefore has good associations for me, and so does the stand on my window sill that bears miniature silk flags of the United Nations. The room is crowded with benign reminders of almost everything that happened to me in my life, and in the life of my father, Uncle Will, Grandfather and the Mayo Clinic. It is no decorator's dream but it's cozy, and I like it that way.

FIFTEEN

The spring after my retirement, May of 1964, the Mayo Clinic became one hundred years old. Rochester held a Mayo Recognition Day, with symphonic music, choral singing and film clips in the Mayo Civic Auditorium. Some fifty medical and scientific groups scheduled their meetings and seminars in Rochester throughout the year, including an international symposium that included General Lauris Norstad, retired NATO commander, and Dr. Edward Teller, the nuclear scientist and author. The U.S. Post Office issued a five-cent stamp with Father and Uncle Will on it, posed in bronze, and Rochester installed tablets on Mayo homesites.

The Rochester *Post-Bulletin* put out a special supplement with plenty of pictures and history. There again were Grandfather, glowering into the sun beside his horse and buggy, and Grandmother's sorrowing steady gaze, and the sign proclaiming the varied office hours of the Drs. William W. Mayo, William J. Mayo, Charles H. Mayo, A. W. Stinchfield, and Christopher Graham. One or another of them was available six days a week, from eight in the morning until eight at night, and Uncle Kit had office hours on Sunday from eleven to one.

The newspaper plucked some quotes from the thousands of speeches and articles that Father and Uncle Will wrote. I liked the one from Father, "Many of us nowadays are eating not wisely but too well . . . too many of us are putting four dollar meals into these 98 cent bodies," and Uncle Will's unexpectedly hedonistic-sounding, "Anything which gives us pleasure and does no harm physically is a good thing."

Uncle Will had words for these restless times: ". . . with all its advantages, our democracy is often hampered by the appeal of the demagogue to the emotions and prejudices of a public interested in its own affairs and not fully informed as to the merits of the proposition under discussion. . . ."

And: "Democracy is safe only so long as culture is in the ascendency, only so long as all citizens are interested in maintaining a just government, only so long as the fundamental conception of democracy is recognized as resting on the moral obligation, the conscience of the people, rather than on legal enactments."

The Clinic observed its centennial year with about four hundred doctors on staff, all of them in private practice, and six hundred doctors in some stage of advanced training. Mayo doctors quip, "We grow our own staff." The Clinic trains 2 per cent of all the residents in the United States and a few stay on staff; most of the others become medical missionaries all over the world for the Mayo style of clinic.

About one in every fifty people in Rochester is a doctor—some children never meet a man who is called "mister," and a rise of fine homes populated mostly by doctors and their families is known as "Pill Hill." Because of the heavy concentration of bright people, Rochester has advantages unusual in small cities of fifty thousand: bookstores, symphony concerts, plays and recitals are well patronized. It also is a good city for the infirm: all curbs in the downtown area have slopes for wheelchairs and all Clinic buildings and the Methodist Hospital are connected by large, airy underground passageways.

The reputation of the Mayo Clinic was founded on surgery, but its real contribution to the world is the example it sets in efficient and effective group practice. Doctors on the Mayo staff are salaried quite handsomely and have no overhead costs: no office space to rent, no secretarial help to pay, no files to keep. The Clinic takes care of all these details, as well as the multitude of forms that exasperate and exhaust doctors in solitary private practice. Doctors at the Clinic have nothing to do but practice medicine, and they are goaded and guided to exceed themselves by the good doctors they see constantly.

The trend in medicine today is strongly toward what is being called team practice. It has alluring appeal to doctors for many good reasons, one of which is the securing of normal working hours. A panel of medical educators, meeting in Washington in 1966, predicted that the typical practice of the mid-seventies would consist of expert medical groups working with advanced technology in complex medical centers and that, to avoid duplication of costly equipment and to efficiently utilize scarce technical manpower, medical centers will be affiliated and interrelated in their responsibilities to patients. That was the view of Dr. John Parks, who is Dean of Medicine at George Washington University, and it's a good description of what the Mayo Clinic has been offering for more than a hundred years.

Patients today have mobility to travel to medical centers. In the end, it will save them time because at Mayo we schedule tests and examinations over a three-day period that would take a month or more in scattered facilities. Some doctors worry that group practice may mean a loss of autonomy for them, but I have found that the opposite is true. Doctors are free to attend medical conventions and make clinical trips, knowing their salaries will continue to be paid; the Clinic even keeps up all salaries of those doctors who serve in war.

Further, doctors in our group practice never hesitate to advise tests or hospitalization from a fear that the patient cannot meet the costs—that's the problem of the business office, which grades fees.

Group practice has some benefits to offer in solving the problems we are facing in medical education, which now is so long and costly that it is almost a profession for the privileged only. I have wondered if young doctors could specialize earlier than they now do if they practiced within a group of mature doctors who could supervise and counsel. It is worth considering.

Medicine is undergoing a revolutionary period in the 1960's. For one example of this, there is the change in research emphasis. We are getting away from the old attitude that a doctor's reputation depends on how much research he produces, and embarking on a period where basic research, such as that which developed insulin and cortisone, will be done by universities. Clinical research, dealing with improved treatment and surgery techniques, will be carried on by practicing doctors, with speeded-up dissemination of their ideas through closed-circuit television and films. Medicine is already computerized in some hospitals, with machines reminding nurses to give medications, and case histories easily retrieved from mechanical memories.

But two huge areas are scarcely touched: the problem of having the right kind of people enter medical schools and receive the right kind of training; and the serious gap between the specialist and the patient, not always well filled by the general practitioner.

The general practitioner is a much improved professional in recent years, since certification was established and regular upgrading seminars arranged, but he is still working too hard to be abreast of all medical developments and he may be dangerously isolated. The Mayo Clinic started offering familiarization sessions to general practitioners some years ago and they were immediately so successful that they had to be tripled in size. The doctor attending the course gets a credit; it is an example of continuing education.

I've always felt that medical schools should offer post-graduate training in the science of general practice. I envision it being a two-year course, with a degree, the first year spent interning and the second in graduate study. I would call the course Family Care and it should be regarded as equal to specializing; certainly, its graduates will have as arduous and gratifying career as any specialist.

Group medicine seems to me to offer a solution to the plight of family doctors stranded in limbo in solitary offices, unable to absorb the contents of all the medical journals they receive because they desperately lack the time. A group practice, properly coalesced around the major specialties, should also include general practitioners in the smaller centers, and enter into close liaison with the general practitioners over a wide area when they are in larger communities.

The doctor who makes house calls is becoming an antique, to the despair of patients all over the country. It is true that diagnosis in a patient's bedroom is hampered by the absence of the tools found in doctors' offices and hospitals, but the presence of the doctor brought immeasurable comfort to the sick person and the family. They say now that this is an inefficient waste of the doctor's time, and perhaps it is, but I wonder if we couldn't train people to make house calls. They could be known as doctor's aides and given perhaps a three-year course in recognizing symptoms, taking histories, making examinations and changing dressings. They would be supervised by the fully-fledged doctor to whom they would report, consulting with him by telephone if the situation seemed to be an emergency. I can envision that this sort of paraprofessional would be useful in making visits to the chronically ill, who could be returned to the emotional warmth of their own homes rather than taking precious space in hospitals urgently required for active cases.

I have no kind word for those who say we should screen applicants to medical schools on the basis of those who show unselfish motives and a burning desire to serve mankind. It would be an invasion of the individual's rights if society set up such a standard and it would not produce better doctors. Monetary greed or longing for prestige are as compelling motives for a doctor to do his best as any humanitarian intention. One either goes into medicine for the rewards or for the love of it, and either way the result can be a very good doctor.

There does seem to be sound reasoning in the move by some medical schools to base their admissions on humanities, more so than the sciences like chemistry, mathematics and physics that aren't really needed much by practicing doctors. I would also like to see premedical school shortened—the demand for a degree before entering medical school cruelly and unnecessarily prolongs medical training. I would have two years, most of it humanities, and then four years in a medical school. And I would eliminate internship as part of the residency program, giving us a total of three years pruned from medical training and making it possible for a doctor to begin practicing well before his middle years.

The country isn't getting enough doctors—when I retired, it was something like eight thousand a year, well below the need. We must enlarge medical schools everywhere and build more of them, and I don't think it means we must lower our standards of admission an iota; there are plenty of talented people in this country. Our high-school students have never before in history been so well educated, and I'm all in favor of university students being given more responsibility. They are adults and should be treated as such, if they are to learn to take the weight of being conscientious citizens.

338

During the desperate months in 1967 when the Board of Regents of the University of Minnesota was seeking a new president, the Students' Council requested representation on the committees that were considering candidates. As chairman of the board, I thought this was a sensible and useful request, and I agreed to it. Three students were appointed, juniors or seniors as we stipulated, and they sat with the alumni committee. It worked fine: they were a big help and, curiously, their preferences didn't differ from those of the older members. About the same time I approved a trial at Carleton College, where students wanted permission to have liquor and female visitors in their rooms. Carleton is an Episcopalian college and there was plenty of opposition, but I believed that the students deserved an opportunity to demonstrate that they were ready to handle that responsibility.

Responsibility is one word that I stress when I am talking about good qualities in a doctor, but the secret of the great professional is that he gives service above self. Only paths of high principles and policies can lead to success, in my opinion; no other route can build lasting happiness. I used to tell audiences of graduates that service isn't a watchword to be used today, misplaced tomorrow, found the next day and then lost again. Rather, it is so vital to the good life that it should be padlocked to the personality, and slept on, and guarded most jealously.

There are no inferior jobs in any organization. No matter what the assigned task, if it is done well and with dignity it contributes to the function of everything around it and should be valued accordingly by all.

This talk of quality, and the quality professional, brings me to mention my son, Charles Horace Mayo II, who possesses all the components that I consider important in a surgeon. He finished his fellowship in 1964 and was advised that he was not wanted on the staff of the Mayo Clinic. The decision was made by the eleven men on the Board of Governors, nine

339

of them doctors, and they never revealed their reasons. A lot of people came to me and said they couldn't understand it, and I received their shocked sympathy with a show of good humor that I was far from feeling. Charlie was stunned, but quickly concealed what he was feeling too.

Perhaps the Board didn't think Charlie was good enough to be a Mayo staff surgeon, but I knew his work intimately and I find it impossible to accept that as a reason. It comes down to the name: so many people, particularly in Rochester, have glorified the name Mayo that quite a few people at the Clinic have a hostile reaction to it. But an equal, or even leading cause for rejecting Charlie is a matter of personality. He is a nonconformist, as I am, and I think the Board wanted to avoid having another strongly independent voice in the Clinic.

Father and Uncle Will had arranged that I would serve on the Clinic's governing body for life; they made no stipulation about succeeding generations of Mayos, nor should they have. But the Mayo graves must have been unquiet the summer that Charlie left Rochester and looked elsewhere to put down his roots.

For a while, I couldn't figure out what he was up to. He seemed to be taking a lot of further education that mystified me, like the time I met someone who told me casually that he was in Charlie's Norwegian class. *Norwegian class!* Eventually he bought a beautiful, sprawling home so like ours that we all call it Mayowood North, on the outskirts of Minneapolis, and he is an assistant professor at the University of Minnesota and is involved in research as well. We never talk about the Clinic. He is also Medical Director of the St. Paul Hospital and Casualty Company, owned by Mutual of Omaha.

Charlie has children who come to Mayowood a good deal, and Ned's and Maria's children live on the property, so I began to discover in my retirement that I have a number of grandchildren underfoot. I loathe being called Grand-

340

father, so I suggested that they should call me Grandchuck, which they do. Alice then became Grandalice, which has a lovely sound. My relationship with these small people is somewhat uneasy. For instance, I had been teasing Charlie's son, Little Charlie, one day in what I took to be the fatuous manner required by my role. He drew up and looked at me curiously, and then said, in a conclusive tone, "Grandchuck just needs a little more growing up."

One time I was on the balcony outside our bedroom when eight or nine children appeared in the courtyard below on their way to visit Alice. "Who are you?" they called. "God," I informed them. "Kneel." They did so, and I lifted my hands and intoned, "Arise," and they did. There was something heady about it, so I had them kneel and arise again before advising them, "Now, go and have a good time but don't get into any trouble."

Later that day I went to visit my friend Bob Hinckley, recovering from surgery in the hospital. "Hello, God," he greeted me. His wife, who had overheard the dialogue, had informed him, "Do you know who Grandalice is married to? GOD!"

One November day in 1964, I was flying to Pittsburgh to attend a meeting to do with *Postgraduate Medicine*. The plane was unable to land because of bad weather, which didn't help me feel any better. Throughout the entire trip I had been growing more nervous and sick, sweating and shaking and fighting down the conviction that I was dying. The plane landed at Washington and I carried our bags some distance and up some stairs before collapsing in a chair while Alice did the telephoning to find a hotel. As soon as we got into the hotel room, I was violently nauseated and ran for the bathroom, where I threw up blood.

I felt better immediately, but Alice called Bill Howell, who has a Mayo-like Clinic in Washington, and he arrived about midnight and insisted that I should go to the hospital. I protested, but was overruled. It was, of course, that old

341

ulcer that I first discovered in 1929. Throughout the years since, the scar from it showed clearly on all my stomach X rays.

I learned something from it. If you have an ulcer, you should avoid aspirin or its derivatives and Bromo-Seltzer or Alka-Seltzer; about 80 per cent of ulcers that bleed show a history of those substances taken regularly. My downfall was my habit of taking Bromo-Seltzer as a precaution against the morning miseries, or for any stomach upset. I have not taken it since then.

Doctors and nurses make wretched patients, and I was no exception. I turned down the blood transfusion they wanted to give me because sometimes hepatitis is carried in donor blood without its being detected. Instead I agreed to a routine of iron injections in my tail, moaning loyally that I would prefer taconite. They took so many blood samples for tests that I swore that if I didn't already have anemia from the loss of blood, I would certainly get it from their zealousness.

It is a rule that anyone over the age of fifty who bleeds from a stomach ulcer should have surgery and resection of the stomach. As a surgeon, I was appalled when this was suggested to me and refused it flatly. "I'll take the medical treatment instead," I told them. For a while I dined on creamy milk, and no roughage, and my recovery was complete. The Georgetown University Hospital did a fine job, with a great deal of free medical advice from me.

My proclivity for dissent didn't seem to fade now that I was free of my old adversary, the Mayo Board of Governors. I tangled with Dr. Robert Howard, Dean of the Medical School at the University of Minnesota, when he dropped the practical nursing program. I thought it valuable and regretted his decision, to no avail.

And I detested the decision of the Mayo Clinic to go on a five-day-week schedule. Nine days after this was instituted, I was the keynote speaker at a distinguished gathering of

342

Mayo staff and emeritus doctors who were honoring the anniversary of my father's birth. I used the occasion to tell them what I thought of the five-day week: "This Clinic was built upon a seven-day-week service to patients and the hospitals must continue on the seven-day week to give the quality of service expected of them," I stated. "I know of no individual in any job or any organization that reached or maintained a distinguished goal on a five-day week. Quality must suffer simply on the unavailability of qualified people, no matter what measures are taken to make less time count for as much or more."

The Clinic the next day issued a suave statement: "During his long association with this institution, Dr. Mayo has always supported those views which had as their objective the best possible care of the patient. In his remarks concerning the future of the institution, which were appended to his recollections about his father, Dr. Mayo has again demonstrated his deep and continuing interest in the affairs of the Mayo Clinic and in the welfare of its patients.

"Mayo Clinic will continue those policies which will offer to both the sick and the well medical care of the highest standard." The Clinic spokesman said the five-day week had been unavoidable because of the pressure from nonmedical people. I'm surprised that the idea of five-day-week shifts didn't occur to them, with the Clinic continuing to hum.

In the same speech, I got some other complaints off my chest. I spoke against too much basic research at the Clinic, which should be emphasizing clinical research that directly helps patients. "A free enterprise system clinic should limit basic research to relatively few of the most promising lines of investigation and direct others, whose interest centers in this type of research, to tax-supported medical schools where such problems rightfully belong."

It was a thrust that hit home, and raised some choler, as did my hint that clinical trips should be getting greater support so Mayo doctors would have improved knowledge of what was happening all over the world. And I also attacked the proposal I had heard of to establish an undergraduate medical school at the Mayo Clinic. The postgraduate school had proven to be compatible with a private group practice, I felt, but an undergraduate school would not. I deplored the strain on tax dollars for the state to support another medical school, when Minnesota was already educating a surplus of doctors for its own needs. I felt it would mean a further step toward socialism—"and the money would be coming from you and me."

I said my piece, but I don't think it was gratefully received. The Clinic has a tape of my remarks that evening which stops after the jokes and anecdotes I told about my father, which is all I had been expected to say. I don't know what they did with the part of the tape recording my criticisms, but I can imagine.

People who supposed that I was a thoroughgoing liberal because of my defense of the United Nations might have been disappointed when I fought against Medicare as doggedly as I had fought for other causes. I gave a lot of speeches about it, particularly after I retired, and stressed that it wouldn't work, and that it would be bad for medicine. I think our citizens are less and less beguiled by the fallacy that what the government provides is free. No government service is, or ever will be, free. Our forefathers didn't come to this country to live in a socialized state. Rather, they came that they might work and achieve the freedoms we still retain. I just never thought this country needed Medicare, and I still don't.

After my retirement from the Clinic I could begin to accept money for some of the outside things I had been doing for years, like editing *Postgraduate Medicine,* and I was free to take some new posts. One of these was on the board of directors of the First National Bank in Rochester and I managed to make an impression at almost the very first meeting I attended. My friend J. Edgar Hoover had sent me a copy of his new book, facetiously titled *How to Rob a Bank*. I took it along to the monthly meeting of the bank directors and the bank president, grinning, held it up for all to see. The bank's vice-president, sitting next to me, seemed as amused as everyone else. A few minutes later he was asked to leave the meeting and was taken to the courthouse. It turned out that he *had* robbed the bank, of $130,000. I was depressed about that, because I liked the man; and I wished that I hadn't brought the book that day.

My task as chairman of the Board of Regents of the University of Minnesota turned out to be onerous a few years after I was elected, when Dr. O. Meredith Wilson, our brilliant president, resigned to go to the Center for Advanced Study in the Behavioral Sciences at Stanford, an equivalent of the Institute for Advanced Study at Princeton. The most important function of a board of regents is to get a good president and then back him to the hilt and we searched painstakingly for a long time to get the right man. In the spring of 1967 I resigned as chairman. Lester Malkerson became chairman and through his efforts we were rewarded in 1967 when Dr. Malcolm C. Moos took the post. He had been with the Ford Foundation, as director of the Office of Government and Law, and before that he was a speech writer for President Eisenhower. It was a historical occasion when he took office because he is the first graduate of the University to become its president.

The University of Minnesota has said some kind things about me. When I was elected regent for a six-year term in 1959, I was introduced glowingly: "There are relatively few people in the recorded history of mankind whose names are synonymous with excellence. But the man who stands before this assembled audience possesses a four-lettered name, MAYO, that is known the world over, and one which evokes a response of gratitude and admiration."

It is certainly an improvement over the introduction I

345

have heard often: "May I introduce Dr. Charles W. Mayo, son of the Mayo brothers." I always felt it left the audience in some doubt as to which was my mother and which my father.

In September, 1964, the University honored me with the Regents Award and an accompanying scroll:

"Famous bearer of a famous name, he has not inherited, but has won, his place in his profession by exceptional skill and creativity in applying surgery to human ills. Moved by compassion and sympathy to a life of service, he has often observed at first hand the tragic role that pain plays in human life; yet, in pain's despite, he searches out and conveys to all around him an appreciation of life's warm humor, enlivening and enriching whatever gathering he enters.

"Exuberant servant of his community, his state and his nation, he has brought the mellow light of understanding and the sharp ray of indignation to international problems."

There's a lot of malarkey in that, but I have the scroll in a leather folder and I keep it nearby.

Though my income improved after I left the Clinic, the cost of running Mayowood continued to be beyond my means. I had sold almost two-thirds of the land that Father left, reducing the property to about 1700 acres. Ned's efforts at scientific farming were certain to produce good results but they required an initial outlay of many thousands of dollars. Alice and I discussed the matter for a long time and then informed the children that we were thinking of giving the house to the Olmsted County Historical Society. If they wanted it to stay in the family, they had only to say so.

They thought it over and we gave them plenty of time, nearly three years. They all realized that none of them had the resources to keep the house going, not even if they pooled what they could. We therefore gave the house and ten acres of gardens around it to the Society in 1966, with the proviso that we would continue to live in it during our lifetimes. Alice and I centered our occupancy in the graceful living room she had created, with its adjoining copper and pine kitchen and a sunny office for me. Upstairs we had a bedroom wing, reached by a private hall. We had no need for the massive dining room any more, but ate in a small one beside a window looking out on the statuary and lanterns in an enclosed courtyard garden.

The Society conducts tourists through the other main rooms a few times a week, bringing them out by bus. I never seemed to get tour days straight for the first while and I was always wandering into a staring mass of inquisitive faces, but eventually we became adept at skulking around out of sight while a hundred people or more moved through the house.

I think the tours help Ned's business. The tour buses drive right past the greenhouse where he shows his antiques and the passengers cannot miss seeing his elegant green and gold sign, which proclaims: WE FEATURE GOOD LOOKING THINGS. Most of his expensive pieces are sold by sending photographs to collectors, but quite a bit is picked up by some of the thousand patients a day who stream through the Clinic, or by their families.

My retirement gives me time to spend with our children who, to some extent, are almost friendly strangers to me. Ned suggests that this is the price a father who puts his heart into his career must pay, and there is truth in that. Alice presided over small family dinners, gracious and animated in the candlelight as she exchanged chatter and opinions and good debate on all subjects, while I mostly listened and counted my blessings. Ned and Rita came often, and Maria, since they lived nearby; Charlie and Cari visited from the Twin Cities from time to time, Alex and Joe more rarely; once a year, Muff arrived for a long summer visit from Mexico and put zest in the house. And also panic, because I don't think she ever came without having to go to the Clinic at least once for stitches, usually from falling off a horse. She

347

has a flair for the unexpected, like the time she enhanced a birthday party of mine by renting a live lion cub and setting it in a cage among the hors d'oeuvres; my zodiac sign is Leo, which is what inspired her.

Every now and then someone I value comes to Rochester for the first time and I endeavor to show him through all the Clinic buildings and the hospitals. I always complain that I don't know what the hell everyone is doing, but in fact I have kept abreast of most of the developments. Whenever I encounter a colleague who seems to be idle, I urge him to get busy, "because I don't want my pension to drop," and I appreciate the genuine-seeming warmth with which employees call hello to me. "How are you?" they ask, and I always reply, "Just perfect."

At least my conscience is clear. I know that I must have done some things wrong while I was in practice, but I was too dumb to know what they were. If I had my life to do over again, I would still come to the Mayo Clinic and do just about everything I did all over again.

I never shirked anything, and I worked hard. I think it is fair to say that. Some part of the fame that came to me was because of my name: I have always known that, but I tried to give value in full measure. The Mayo name is on the Clinic, on the origin of group medicine, on a number of surgical instruments, curved clamps and dissecting scissors, invented by my father and me, on a type of bedside tray that is seen everywhere, on a universally used operative procedure in gynecological surgery that is called the Mayo operation, on a tiny vessel Father discovered that marks the division between the stomach and the duodenum and is known as the vein of Mayo; and, of course, on the ubiquitous Mayo diet.

Small wonder that *Medical World News* magazine in 1965 included me as one of the twenty most famous retired doctors in the world. A lot of it is the name, but I hope not all.

348

I wrote a poem while in New Guinea that expresses some of the strain I have felt all my life:

> God grant that I may be
> More than a nonentity.
> A little bad, a little good,
> Makes but mediocrity.
> In daily problems, daily deeds,
> Solutions, actions, roses, weeds,
> Give me guidance, give me strength
> To grow my garden with thy seeds.

It's a bit pious, but I meant it. My regrets are for the future: I wish that Charlie could have been in the Mayo Clinic. His son Little Charlie came to watch us operate together once or twice and I was deeply moved to look up and see the avid fascination with which he followed what we were doing. So my father watched his father operate, and I watched my father, and Charlie watched me; and now Little Charlie, the fifth generation, sat in the gallery and watched his father at work. I would have liked the Mayos to go on for generations more in that tradition in the Clinic.

This book was undertaken because Alice wanted it. She was fiercely, protectively proud of me and insisted that I should write about my life. Shortly after it was launched, we returned from a trip to visit Muff in Mexico and Alice went to the Clinic for some tests to determine the cause of sudden nosebleeds, and other minor but troublesome symptoms. It was diagnosed as myeloma, an incurable form of cancer.

After that she lived for a year and a half with pain and fear, but gallantly. On her worst days, she would say, "There must be a purpose to all this. I can't believe that it is *meaningless*." Mrs. Tony nursed her with tenderness and deep love, bringing her pills in delicate fluted silver dishes. "If you have to do something unpleasant," Alice would grin, washing them down with ice water from a crystal glass, "you might as well do it in style."

She was totally feminine and fretted that she looked unwell, which wasn't true. Her vivid blue eyes were bright and gay in her small face and, when the pain let her, she was as vibrant and luminous as a happy child. I never left the city as we waited together for the inevitable end, but I know my despair made me remote. The happiest day of my life was the day I married her, and the worst was November 9, 1967, the day she died.

I wrote her a letter that she seemed to think highly of, dated October 28, 1944, from New Guinea. I will close with it:

Dearest—

Just before bed last night, I knocked off this little ditty for you:

> She
> Is away.
> Far, far away.
> I think of her, as
> I hope she thinks of
> Me.
>
> Thought
> Of here
> Or there is
> Born of wishful dreams;
> Recompense for happiness that's
> Sought.

Hope
And plans
For after war
And a successful peace
With present problems urge us to
Cope.

Grieve?
Not I
And neither she.
The cause is just
And surely in reunion is
Reprieve.

B
Mayo
Mayo
Mayo; the story of my family
and my career